Lecture Notes in Computer Science 8785

Commenced Publication in 1973
Founding and Former Series Editors:
Gerhard Goos, Juris Hartmanis, and Jan van Leeuwen

T0225990

István Majzik   Marco Vieira (Eds.)

Software Engineering for Resilient Systems

6th International Workshop, SERENE 2014
Budapest, Hungary, October 15-16, 2014
Proceedings

 Springer

Volume Editors

István Majzik
Budapest University of Technology and Economics
Magyar tudósok krt.2
1117 Budapest, Hungary
E-mail: majzik@mit.bme.hu

Marco Vieira
University of Coimbra
CISUC, Department of Informatics Engineering
Pólo II, Pinhal de Marrocos
3030-290 Coimbra, Portugal
E-mail: mvieira@dei.uc.pt

ISSN 0302-9743   e-ISSN 1611-3349
ISBN 978-3-319-12240-3   e-ISBN 978-3-319-12241-0
DOI 10.1007/978-3-319-12241-0
Springer Cham Heidelberg New York Dordrecht London

Library of Congress Control Number: 2014950396

LNCS Sublibrary: SL 2 – Programming and Software Engineering

© Springer International Publishing Switzerland 2014

Typesetting: Camera-ready by author, data conversion by Scientific Publishing Services, Chennai, India

Printed on acid-free paper

Springer is part of Springer Science+Business Media (www.springer.com)

Preface

Welcome to the proceedings of the 6th Workshop on Software Engineering for Resilient Systems (SERENE 2014). The workshop took place in Budapest (Hungary) during October 15-16, 2014.

The SERENE workshop series is supported by the ERCIM (European Research Consortium in Informatics and Mathematics) Working Group on Software Engineering for Resilient Systems. The previous workshops were held in Newcastle upon Tyne (2008), London (2010), Geneva (2011), Pisa (2012), and Kiev (2013). The aim of the workshop series is to bring together researchers and practitioners working on developing and applying advanced software engineering techniques to ensure resilience – an ability of a system to persistently deliver its services in a dependable way even when facing changes, unforeseen failures, and intrusions. Ensuring software resilience is motivated by the increasingly pervasive use of software in evolvable and critical systems like transportation, health care, manufacturing, and IT infrastructure management.

The SERENE 2014 workshop provided a forum to disseminate research results and exchange ideas on advances in all areas of software engineering for resilient systems, including, but not limited to:

Design of resilient systems

- Requirements engineering and re-engineering for resilience
- Frameworks, patterns and software architectures for resilience
- Engineering of self-healing autonomic systems
- Design of trustworthy and intrusion-safe systems
- Resilience at run-time (mechanisms, reasoning and adaptation)

Verification, validation and evaluation of resilience

- Modelling and model-based analysis of resilience properties
- Formal and semi-formal techniques for verification and validation
- Experimental evaluations of resilient systems
- Quantitative approaches to ensuring resilience
- Resilience prediction

Case studies and applications

- Empirical studies in the domain of resilient systems
- Cloud computing and resilient service provisioning
- Resilient cyber-physical systems and infrastructures
- Global aspects of resilience engineering: education, training and cooperation

The workshop received 22 submissions including technical papers describing original theoretical or practical work, experience/industry papers describing practitioner experience or field studies addressing an application domain, and project papers describing goals and results of ongoing projects related to the SERENE topics.

After a rigorous review process by the Program Committee members and external reviewers, 12 papers were selected for presentation. These included 11 technical papers and one project paper. We were pleased with the quality of the submissions, and we believe that the accepted papers will foster innovative practical solutions as well as future research.

In addition to the paper sessions, the workshop program also included a keynote by a prominent researcher working on resilience engineering, Vincenzo de Florio from the University of Antwerp. The volume also includes the invited paper describing the research presented by the keynote speaker.

The workshop program was the result of the hard work of many individuals. First of all, we want to thank all authors who submitted their research work. We are grateful to the Program Committee members and the external reviewers for their efforts. We would like to thank the members of the SERENE Steering Committee and SERENE Working Group for their help in publicizing the event and contributing to the technical program. Last but not least, we would like to acknowledge the contribution of the staff at the Budapest University of Technology and Economics for local arrangements (Web, publicity, finance, administration, and local organization).

August 2014

István Majzik
Marco Vieira
András Pataricza

Organization

General Chair

András Pataricza   Budapest University of Technology and Economics, Hungary

Steering Committee

Didier Buchs   University of Geneva, Switzerland
Henry Muccini   University of L'Aquila, Italy
Patrizio Pelliccione   Chalmers University of Technology and University of Gothenburg, Sweden
Alexander Romanovsky   Newcastle University, UK
Elena Troubitsyna   Åbo Akademi University, Finland

Program Chairs

István Majzik   Budapest University of Technology and Economics, Hungary
Marco Vieira   University of Coimbra, Portugal

Program Committee

Paris Avgeriou   University of Groningen, The Netherlands
Didier Buchs   University of Geneva, Switzerland
Andrea Ceccarelli   University of Florence, Italy
Vincenzo De Florio   University of Antwerp, The Netherlands
Nikolaos Georgantas   Inria, France
Felicita Di Giandomenico   CNR-ISTI, Italy
Giovanna Di Marzo Serugendo   University of Geneva, Switzerland
Holger Giese   University of Potsdam, Germany
Nicolas Guelfi   University of Luxembourg, Luxembourg
Kaustubh Joshi   AT&T, USA
Mohamed Kaaniche   LAAS-CNRS, France
Vyacheslav Kharchenko   National Aerospace University, Ukraine
Zsolt Kocsis   IBM, Hungary
Nuno Laranjeiro   University of Coimbra, Portugal
Paolo Masci   Queen Mary University, UK
Henry Muccini   University of L'Aquila, Italy
Sadaf Mustafiz   McGill University, Canada
Patrizio Pelliccione   Chalmers University of Technology and University of Gothenburg, Sweden

Alexander Romanovsky   Newcastle University, UK
Juan Carlos Ruiz   Technical University of Valencia, Spain
Stefano Russo   University of Naples Federico II, Italy
Peter Schneider-Kamp   University of Southern Denmark, Denmark
Elena Troubitsyna   Åbo Akademi University, Finland
Katinka Wolter   Freie University Berlin, Germany
Apostolos Zarras   University of Ioannina, Greece

External Reviewers

Rui André Oliveira   University of Coimbra, Portugal
Johannes Dyck   University of Postdam, Germany
Zoltán Szatmári   Budapest University of Technology and
                              Economics, Hungary
Sebastian Wätzoldt   University of Postdam, Germany
Roberto Nardone   University of Naples Federico II, Italy
David Lawrence   University of Geneva, Switzerland
András Vörös   Budapest University of Technology
                              and Economics, Hungary
Christian Manteuffel   University of Groningen, The Netherlands

Table of Contents

Monitoring

Community Resilience Engineering:
Reflections and Preliminary Contributions

Vincenzo De Florio[1], Hong Sun[2], and Chris Blondia[1]

[1] MOSAIC/University of Antwerp and MOSAIC/iMinds Research Institute
Middelheimlaan 1, 2020 Antwerp, Belgium
{vincenzo.deflorio,chris.blondia}@uantwerpen.be
[2] AGFA Healthcare, 100 Moutstraat, Ghent, Belgium
hong.sun@agfa.com

Abstract. An important challenge for human societies is that of mastering the complexity of Community Resilience, namely "the sustained ability of a community to utilize available resources to respond to, withstand, and recover from adverse situations". The above concise definition puts the accent on an important requirement: a community's ability to make use in an intelligent way of the available resources, both institutional and spontaneous, in order to match the complex evolution of the "significant multi-hazard threats characterizing a crisis". Failing to address such requirement exposes a community to extensive failures that are known to exacerbate the consequences of natural and human-induced crises. As a consequence, we experience today an urgent need to respond to the challenges of community resilience engineering. This problem, some reflections, and preliminary prototypical contributions constitute the topics of the present article.

1 Introduction

A well-known article by Garrett Hardin states how no exclusively technological solution exists to several significant societal problems [1]. The problem of the optimal response to a crisis both natural and human-induced is likely to be one such problem. Direct experience accrued during, e.g., the Katrina hurricane crisis, showed that effective solutions to disastrous events and highly turbulent conditions call for the involvement of society as a complex and very dense "collective agent" [2]. The emerging attribute advocated by the Authors of the cited paper is so-called *Community Resilience* (CR). While the need for CR has been identified and justified, to the best of our knowledge no organizational solution has been so far proposed such that the "grand potential" of CR—including, e.g., collective intelligence, advance autonomic behaviors, and the ability to tap into the "wells" of social energy—may be harnessed into methods; architectures; and solutions, to be deployed in preparation, during, and following critical events.

Our paper is structured as follows: first, in Sect. 2 we introduce CR. In Sect. 3 we enumerate those that we consider as the major requirements of any effective community-resilient approach. After this we describe in Sect. 4 an organization matching the above attributes—the fractal social organizations—and its

I. Majzik and M. Vieira (Eds.): SERENE 2014, LNCS 8785, pp. 1–8, 2014.
© Springer International Publishing Switzerland 2014

building block, the service-oriented community. Section 5 briefly introduces a few elements of a fractally-organized middleware component currently in use in Flemish project "Little Sister" as well as other ancillary technology that we deem could provide support towards the design of CR engineering solutions. Our conclusions are finally stated in Sect. 6.

2 Community Resilience: Definition and Lessons Learned

According to RAND [3], Community Resilience (CR) is defined as

> "A measure of the sustained ability of a community to utilize available resources to respond to, withstand, and recover from adverse situations. [...] Resilient communities withstand and recover from disasters. They also learn from past disasters to strengthen future recovery efforts."

A second important asset towards understanding Community Resilience is paper [2] in which the Authors provide an insightful discussion of several important factors that resulted in the resilience behaviors that manifested during the Hurricane Katrina events. Their definition of resilience is slightly different from RAND's: CR is defined as

> "A community or region's capability to prepare for, respond to, and recover from significant multi-hazard threats with minimum damage to public safety and health, the economy, and national security."

A remarkable fact observed by the authors of the cited paper is that the response to the Katrina disaster was far from ideal:

> "Through extensive media coverage, the world saw remarkably inadequate rescue operations, the failure of complete evacuation, [...] What amazed many worldwide was that these extensive failures, often attributed to conditions in developing countries, occurred in the most powerful and wealthiest country in the world."

This is particularly surprising in that the severity of the situation was well known, as it was also well known how the New Orleans area would have had difficulties in the face of catastrophic events:

> "New Orleans was *a catastrophe waiting to happen* with extensive and repeated warnings from both scientists and the media that the 'big one' would eventually hit the city."

The major lesson that we derived from this case is that an event like Katrina disrupts several concentric "social layers" at the same time, possibly associated to multiple response organizations, and that one of the major problems following the event is one of *coordination*. Multiple concurrent responses are triggered in each of the social layers, including

 – the individual, the family, people sharing the same location, citizens, etc.;
 – pre-existing organizations of the city, the region, the state, the nation;
 – pre-existing organizations for civil protection, defense, order, etc.

A major classification of the above responders distinguishes institutional responders (namely the social layers corresponding to the above pre-existing organizations) from informal responders (non-institutional responders, originating in "households, friends and family, neighborhoods, non-governmental and voluntary organizations, businesses, and industry" and corresponding to what is known in the domain of ambient assisted living as "informal care-givers" [4].)

We observe how coordination failures during the Katrina crisis derived from a number of reasons, the most important of which are—we deem—the following ones:

 – Conflicting goals and conflicting actions among the triggered responders. Multiple uncoordinated efforts often resulted in wasting resources and in some cases they masked each other out.
 – As a simplistic way to avoid or recover from this kind of failures, institutional responders tended to refuse or did not blend their action with that of informal responders.
 – Resources owned by institutional responders were not shared promptly and dynamically according to the experienced needs.

Report [2] provides us with rich and valuable knowledge, which helps understand how relevant the above reasons were in determining the quality of resilience and the speed of the recovery after Katrina. It also provides us with a major challenge, which the authors enunciate as follows:

> "[Responders] would have been able to do more if the tri-level system (city, state, federal) of emergency response was able to *effectively use, collaborate with, and coordinate the combined public and private efforts.* How to do so, in advance of hazard events, is a central task of enhancing community resilience."

This paper focuses on community resilience engineering, which we define here as the design and the development of an engineering practice towards the definition of methods, tools, theories, and applications, such that community-resilient responses to crises may be orchestrated and conducted. This paper in particular addresses the following questions: Is it possible to find a satisfactory answer to the above challenge? Which tools, which form of organizations may serve as an effective foundation on top of which community resilience may be built? In order to answer the above questions we first introduce those that we deem to be the major requirements of community-resilient organizations.

3   Community Resilience: Requirements

When considering the Katrina response and its failures, our major lessons learned are that engineering solutions towards CR should ideally be characterized by the following requirements:

- Scalability: The building blocks of the response organization should be applicable at all social layers, ranging from micro scale (individual or small groups) up to macro level (national or world-wide institutions).
- Fractal organization: The building blocks of the response organizations should be free from the hard restrictions of pure hierarchical organizations. The action and role of each social layer should not be restricted by its hierarchical level into that of a controller or that of a controlled, but rather dynamically defined.
- Context-orientation: The above mentioned action and role should be defined through an assessment of the context and situations at hand, possibly involving multiple collaborating entities and layers.
- Self-servicing: Forms of mutualistic collaboration should be identified so that common requirements may become mutually satisfactory and enable the exploitation of the self-serve potential of our societies.
- Service-orientation: Services and assets should be easily and quickly localizable, shareable, and accountable.
- Semantically described: Services, requests, and assets across the social layers should be semantically described in a uniform way allowing for machine processing (for instance, to construct a global view of the state of the community, or for matching services among the members).
- Collaborativeness: Collaboration among entities in different social layers should be easy to settle and result in the spontaneous emergence of new temporary inter-layered "social responders". Said *social overlay networks* would combine responders of different scale and different originating social layers and exist until some originating purpose is being reached.
- Modularity: Self-similar collaborative "patterns", or modules, should be reusable at different scales. A dynamic ranking mechanism should allow the performance of modules in a given context to be tracked.

4 Service-Oriented Communities and Fractal Social Organizations

In previous sections we have discussed the challenges of Community Resilience, and especially those pertaining to response / recovery / reduction [2]. As mentioned already, through the cited report we learned how one of the major problems following the Katrina disasters was one of coordination. Coordination among institutional responders was difficult and inefficient, and even more so it was between institutional and informal responders. We learned how a major challenge of Community Resilience is that of being able to solve those coordination problems. A possible way to reformulate that challenge is that of being able to conquer the complexity and engineer practical methods to dynamically create a coherent and effective organization-of-organizations (OoO) as a "smart" response to disasters. The major goal of such an OoO would be that of enabling mutualistic relationships between all the involved social layers and produce mutually satisfactory, self-serving, controllable "social behaviors" [5] enhancing the efficiency and the speed of intervention. Fractal Social Organizations (FSO) are one such possible OoO. In a nutshell, they are an organization-of-organizations whose building blocks are custom socio-technical systems called Service-oriented Communities (SoC). In what follows we describe in more detail SoC and FSO.

4.1   Service-Oriented Communities

A SoC [6] is a service-oriented architecture that creates a community of peer-level entities—for instance human beings, cyber-physical things, and organizations thereof. These entities are called *members*. No predefined classification exists among members. No specific role is defined; for instance there are no predefined clients or servers, service requesters or service providers, care-givers or care-takers. Depending on the situation at hand a member may be on the receiving end or at the providing end of a service. Members (may) react to changes. If something occurs in a SoC, some of its members may become active. Being active means being willing to play some role. Service availabilities and service requests, together with events, are semantically annotated and published into a service registry. The service registry reacts to publications by checking whether the active members may play roles that enable some action.

This check is done semantically, by discovering whether the published services are compatible with the sought roles. Costs may be associated with a member being enrolled. Enrolments may be done in several ways, each aiming at some preferred goal—for instance speed of response, safety, or cost-effectiveness. Furthermore, the optimization goals may focus on the individual member, or have a social dimension, or take both aspects into account.

A noteworthy aspect of the SoC and the above assumptions is that they enable *mutualistic relationships.* In [7] we suggested that two elderly persons requiring assistance could find an adequate and satisfactory response by helping each other—thus without the intervention of carers.

We are currently experimenting with mutualistic relationship with more than two members and with different roles—for instance mutualistic relationships between two service providers (say, e.g., an institutional responder and a shadow responder in the response phases of some crisis). (Obviously this would call for agreeing on collaboration protocols, establishing common ontologies to reason on possible triggering events, discussing policies and modes of intervention, and several other aspects; we consider this to be outside the scope of the present contribution).

As mentioned before, no predefined role exists in a SoC, though the creation of a new SoC calls for appointing a member with the special role of service coordinator. It is such member that hosts the service registry and performs the semantic processing. The coordinator may be elected and there could be hot backups also maintaining copies of the service registry. A SoC may be specialized for different purposes—for instance crisis management or ambient assistance of the elderly and the impaired. More information on a SoC devoted to the latter and called "Mutual Assistance Community" may be found, e.g., in [7].

A major aspect of the SoC is given by the assumption of a *flat* society: a cloud of social resources are organized and orchestrated under the control of a central "hub"—the service coordinator. Of course this flat organization introduces several shortcomings; for instance, if the size of the community becomes "too big" the coordinator may be slowed down (scalability failure); and in the presence of a single and non-redundant coordinator a single failure may bring the whole community to a halt (resilience failure).

4.2   Fractal Social Organizations

The Fractal Social Organization was created to solve the just highlighted shortcomings. Its definition is as follows: "A Fractal Social Organization is a fractal organization of Service-oriented Communities." As can be easily understood, a Service-oriented Community is a trivial case of a Fractal Social Organization consisting of a single node. In practice, if a SoC is allowed to include other SoC as their members, we end up with a distributed hierarchy of SoC, one nested into the other. This is a little like nested directories in a file system or "matryoshka dolls" (but such that each doll may contain more than a single smaller doll.)

Society provides many examples of such *fractal organizations*; "the tri-level system (city, state, federal) of emergency response" mentioned in [2] is one such case. The added value of the FSO is that it implements a sort of *cybernetic sociocracy*. Sociocracy teaches us that it is possible to lay a secondary organizational structure over an existing one. The idea is that the elements of a layer (in sociocracy, a "circle") may decide that a certain matter deserves system-wide attention; if so, they appoint a member as representative of the whole circle. Then the appointed member becomes (temporarily) part of an upper circle and can discuss the matter with the members of that circle (e.g., propose an alternative way to organize a process or deal with a threat). This allows information to flow beyond the boundaries of strict hierarchies; real-life experimentation proved that this enhances considerably an organization's resilience. Through the sociocratic rules, an organization may tap on the "well" of its social energy and create collective forms of intelligence as those discussed in [8]. FSO propose a similar concept. Whenever a condition calls for roles, the coordinator looks for roles by semantically matching the services in its registry. If all roles can be found within the community, the corresponding activity is launched. When certain roles are missing, the coordinator raises an exception to the next upper layer—the next matryoshka doll up above, we could say. The role shortage event is thus propagated to the next level upward in the hierarchy. This goes on until the first suitable candidate member for playing the required role is found or until some threshold is met. The resulting responding team is what we called a social overlay network: a network of collaborating members that are not restricted to a single layer but can span dynamically across multiple layers of the FSO. Such new responding team is in fact a new ad hoc Service-oriented Community whose objective and lifespan are determined by the originating event.

5 Towards Community Resilience Solutions

A prototypical and limited implementation of an FSO is given by the software architecture and in particular the middleware of project Little Sister[1]. As already mentioned, Little Sister addresses telemonitoring for home care through a connectionist approach in which the collective action of an interconnected network of simple units (currently low-fidelity cameras and RFIDs) replaces the adoption of more powerful, expensive, and power-hungry devices. The Little Sister software architecture may be described as a multi-tier distributed system in which the above mentioned simple units are wrapped and exposed as manageable web services. In Little Sister a **tri-level system** consisting of the individual rooms in a house; the houses in a building; and the building itself; is fractally organized by having the system maintain dedicated, manageable service groups representing the members of each level. Members exchange information by a standard publish-and-subscribe mechanism. Events are triggered by the units in each level. If actuation logic is available in the originating level, the event is managed and sinked. Whenever the event calls for resources unavailable in the current level, it is propagated to the next upper level, if any; otherwise, an alarm is triggered. This translates into a simple, statically predefined, and statically structured FSO architecture. A prototypical implementation of a semantic framework for FSO is also reported in [10]. SPARQL endpoints are set up with Fuseki for each SoC at the bottom layer. SoCs located at upper layers are composed by aggregating those at lower layers. Such an aggregation is realized by issuing federated SPARQL queries: a query to a SoC located at upper layers are dispatched to those bottom SoCs under the queried upper layer SoC. With such an approach, data only resides in SPARQL endpoints at bottom layers. SoCs at upper layer exist virtually thus do not need to hold data, and they can be ad-hoc organized. By distributing the data to SPARQL endpoints at bottom layer, this approach also avoids a central point of failure. Future work will include removing the current limitations, restructuring the system for CR, and embedding "intelligence" into the architecture by making use of adaptive software frameworks such as ACCADA [11] and Transformer [12], whose major added value in the context of CR would be their ability to trade-off dynamically multiple adaptation plans concurrently proposed by organizations participating in the crisis management.

6 Conclusions

Our vision about Community Resilience Engineering has been briefly presented. Obviously much is yet to be done. The FSO protocols have not been formalized and only a partial and static version of the system is currently available. Among the

---

[1] Little Sister is a Flemish project funded by iMinds as well as by the Flemish Government Agency for Innovation by Science and Technology (IWT). Little Sister is to design a low-cost autonomous technology to provide protection and assistance to the elderly population [9, 10].

many issues still missing we highlight here the following major ones: defining interfaces to reflect the state of an organization as well as the knowledge it has accrued during a crisis event; expose such knowledge; define crisis management ontologies; describe organizational services semantically; enable inter-organizational mutualistic cooperation; prepare for crises through co-evolutive strategies [13]; instruct the communities on how to become a "living component" of a hosting organization; log the evolution of social overlay networks emerging during a crisis in function of the evolution of the critical events; create tools for the analysis of the logs so as to enable the identification of reiterating responses (which could be reused as CR templates possibly re-occurring at different scales); simulating the operation of FSO-compliant organizations during a crisis; and of course experimenting our approach in real-life situations. Despite so dense a research agenda we observe how the specific traits of the FSO and its building block closely match requirements such as the one in Sect. 3. This correspondence leads us to conjecture that mature designs of the FSO and SoC may provide us with an answer to the questions drawn in the introduction and designers with an effective practical "tool" for the engineering of community-resilient socio-technical responses to crises.

References

1. Hardin, G.: The tragedy of the commons. Science 162(3859), 1243–1248 (1968)
2. Colten, C.E., Kates, R.W., Laska, S.B.: Community resilience: Lessons from New Orleans and hurricane Katrina. Technical Report 3, CARRI (2008)
3. RAND: Community resilience (2014),
   http://www.rand.org/topics/community-resilience.html
4. Sun, H., et al.: The missing ones: Key ingredients towards effective ambient assisted living systems. J. Ambient Intell. Smart Environ. 2(2) (2010)
5. De Florio, V.: Behavior, organization, substance: Three gestalts of general systems theory. In: Proc. of the 2014 Conf. on N. Wiener in the 21st Century. IEEE (2014)
6. De Florio, V., et al.: Models and concepts for socio-technical complex systems: Towards fractal social organizations. Sys. Res. and Behav. Sci. 30(6) (2013)
7. Sun, H., De Florio, V., Gui, N., Blondia, C.: Participant: A new concept for optimally assisting the elder people. In: Proc. of the 20th IEEE Int.l Symp. on Computer-Based Medical Systems (CBMS 2007), Maribor, Slovenia (2007)
8. Pór, G.: Nurturing systemic wisdom through knowledge ecology. The System Thinker 11(8), 1–5 (2000)
9. Anonymous: LittleSister: Low-cost monitoring for care and retail (2013),
   http://www.iminds.be/en/research/overview-projects/
   p/detail/littlesister
10. De Florio, V., Sun, H., Buys, J., Blondia, C.: On the impact of fractal organization on the performance of socio-technical systems. In: Proc. of the 2013 Int.l Workshop on Intelligent Techniques for Ubiq. Systems (ITUS 2013), Vietri, Italy (2013)
11. Gui, N., De Florio, V., Sun, H., Blondia, C.: ACCADA: A framework for continuous context-aware deployment and adaptation. In: Guerraoui, R., Petit, F. (eds.) SSS 2009. LNCS, vol. 5873, pp. 325–340. Springer, Heidelberg (2009)
12. Gui, N., et al.: Transformer: an adaptation framework with contextual adaptation behavior composition support. Software: Practice & Experience (2012)
13. Adner, R., Kapoor, R.: Value creation in innovation ecosystems. Strategic Management Journal 31, 306–333 (2010)

Enhancing Architecture Design Decisions Evolution with Group Decision Making Principles

Ivano Malavolta[1], Henry Muccini[2], and Smrithi Rekha V.[3]

[1] Gran Sasso Science Institute, L'Aquila, Italy
[2] Department of Information Engineering, Computer Science and Mathematics,
University of L'Aquila, Italy
[3] Amrita School of Business, Amrita Vishwa Vidyapeetham, India
ivano.malavolta@gssi.infn.it, henry.muccini@univaq.it,
v_smrithirekha@cb.amrita.edu

Abstract. In order to build resilient systems, robust architectures are needed. The software architecture community clearly recognizes that robust architectures come from a robust decision-making process. The community also acknowledges that software architecture decision making is not an individual activity but a group process where architectural design decisions are made by groups of heterogeneous and dispersed stakeholders. The decision-making process is not just data driven, but also *people driven*, and group decision making methodologies have been studied from multiple perspectives (e.g., psychology, organizational behavior, economics) with the clear understanding that a poor-quality decision making process is more likely than a high-quality process leading to undesirable outcomes (including disastrous fiascoes).

In this work, we propose to explicitly include group decision making strategies into an architecting phase, so to clearly document not only the architectural decisions that may lead to the success or failure of a system, but also group decision making factors driving the way architecture design decisions are made. In this regard, this work defines a group design decision metamodel (for representing group design decisions and their relationships), together with ways to trace group design decisions towards other system life-cycle artifacts, and a change impact analysis engine for supporting evolving design decisions.

1 Introduction

Dependability and resilience in software engineering have been analyzed since a long time from a (purely) technical perspective, by proposing architectures and processes for realizing dependable[1] and resilient systems[1,2], by modeling and analysing properties of resilience [3,4], by monitoring the system state at run-time [5], and so on.

More recently, human and social aspects are being considered as an important factor when developing quality systems. The role of the human beings in automated software testing has been the topic of a Dagstuhl seminar [6]. The role of socio-technical coordination has been remarked by James Herbsleb in his keynote at ICSE 2014 (the 36th

---

[1] Architecting Dependable Systems series of workshop: http://www.cs.kent.ac.uk/people/staff/rdl/ADSFuture/resources.htm

I. Majzik and M. Vieira (Eds.): SERENE 2014, LNCS 8785, pp. 9–23, 2014.

International Conference on Software Engineering) and through his publications. The *Social Software Engineering* workshop is at its sixth edition, this year being co-located with the Foundations of Software Engineering (FSE 2014) conference. The way people work together impacts their productivity and the quality of the outcome and hence group decision making processes and methods have been carefully analyzed in a number of areas [7,8].

Along these lines, we have been recently analyzing *group decision making* principles in the *architecture design decision* process. Architecture design decisions (ADDs) are considered first class entities when architecting software systems [9,10,11]. They capture potential alternative solutions, and the rationale for deciding among competing solutions. It has been recognised that ADDs have to be explicitly documented and kept synchronized with (potentially evolving) requirements and the selected architectural solution. Group decision making (GDM), instead, consists of a set of methods and principles driving the way groups make collaborative decisions. In recent work, we have been analyzing how group decision making principles and methods have been implemented in state-of-the-art ADD approaches. More specifically, in [12] we have interviewed a number of architects working in (or collaborating with) industry to identify how architectural decisions are taken. As expected, most of the architectural decisions are made in groups, distributed or co-located, decisions involving a number of different stakeholders.

This work, by building upon our previous work presented at SERENE 2011 [13] (where an approach to support ADD evolution has been discussed) and by explicitly taking into account the group decision making principles we had highlighted in our recent papers [14,12], proposes an approach to incorporate GDM strategies explicitly into evolving architecture design decisions. It proposes a reference metamodel for group decision making, that describes the minimal reasoning elements necessary to suitably realize a group decision making approach as part of an architecture design decision process. The contribution of this work is mainly in the following lines: a) it provides a metamodel to include GDM principles explicitly into architecture design decisions (therefore, enabling the extension of current ADD methods to take into consideration GDM principles and methods); b) it describes how the relationships among ADDs can be explicitly represented using the defined metamodel, and c) it defines bidirectional traceability links between ADDs, requirements and architectural elements which will help in analyzing the impact of evolution on those artifacts.

In this paper we have extensively extended the ADD metamodel presented [13] in order to include a number of missing GDM factors. The traceability and change propagation engines had to be highly revised in order to incorporate the new needs dictated by GDM. We expect this work to provide the baseline to build new approaches and tools for group-based architecture design decisions.

The main components of this paper are five sections, organized as follows. Section 2 provides background information on architecture design decisions and group decision making. Section 3 presents the main contribution of this work, in terms of a metamodel for group decision making in software architecture. Section 4 introduces some examples to show how this proposal can be used in practical terms. Related works are presented in Section 5, while conclusions and future work are discussed in Section 6.

2   Background

The SA research community is currently looking at SA as a decision making process involving a group of stakeholders [12]. This needs a revision of the metamodels to accommodate group decisions which will in turn impact the SA decision methods and tools. Group Decision Making enjoys a significant position in management research. Research points out that decisions made by groups are often perceived to be more reliable than those by individuals. Groups are considered to be means of aggregating individual view points as well as combining multiple perspectives to make high quality decisions [15]. Groups are better than individuals because: a) Groups have access to bigger pool of information b) Groups bring in diverse perspectives c) More alternatives may be uncovered d) More reliable as multiple people are involved before a decision is made

Researchers also recognize that there may be some issues with GDM. It may take more time to arrive at consensus when more people are involved, conflicts may arise when multiple perspectives are presented and could also result in Groupthink which is caused by the group members' desire for conformity without considering all the critical viewpoints [8]. Hence focusing on the GDM process helps to resolve these issues. Several well tested GDM methods exist which are used by organizations. GDM methods are broadly categorized as semi-formal methods like brainstorming, ranking based methods like voting or nominal group technique and structured methods like Analytics Hierarchy Processing [7]. There are numerous GDM methods and we discuss a few here.

Brainstorming: This is a semi-formal method were participants discuss the issues and brainstorm solutions. The discussions are moderated by a leader.

Voting: Participants indicate their preferences on a pre-determined set of alternatives through votes.

Nominal Group Technique (NGT): This technique involves allotting time to individual participants to think and present their viewpoints (preempting the others from speaking) and then discussing as a group.

Delphi Technique: This is an iterative process involving several rounds of discussions with each round involving feedback from previous iterations.

Analytic Hierarchy Processing (AHP): This is a structured technique that involves pairwise comparison of alternatives and criteria and weighing the alternatives based on the criteria before making a decision.

Given this significant role played by GDM methods in enhancing the outcome of the decision making process, it is important the SA community recognizes the need to integrate GDM into current SA decision methods. This is especially valuable in the context of rapidly evolving software. Software evolution also includes the evolution of the underlying architecture, the decisions and the rationale. When multiple stakeholders are involved, it may be important to factor in their preference of criteria and alternative solutions before making changes to the decisions and thereby the resulting architecture. Hence we need to explicitly model multiple stakeholder viewpoints in the SA decision making process. Current metamodels, though they recognize the involvement of multiple stakeholders, do not have explicit integration of GDM. This calls for a modification of the existing metamodels of SA decision making to include various aspects of GDM.

3   Architectural Evolution and Group Decision Making

Given a generic architecture design decision approach, a group decision making (GDM) process and method builds on top of it to regulate how multiple stakeholders make decisions when working together. In this light, the proposed extension (to our SERENE 2011 work in [13]) aims at the straightforward integration of existing group decision making (GDM) methods into architecture design decision approaches. The proposed approach is designed keeping in mind the *everything-is-a-model* principle of Model-Driven Engineering [16] and hence each artifact that has to be considered during the evolution change analysis is represented as a distinct model.

Figure 1 gives an overview of the approach for architectural group design decisions evolution. The approach foresees three main components: the *GDM model*, *traceability links* between software artifacts, and *a change impact analysis* approach.

The **GDM model** includes the GDM principles, and all the design decisions resulting from the collaboration of groups of stakeholders during the design process. The GDM model also classifies design decisions depending on their type and their status, and keeps track of the various relationships between them. Design decisions can be linked to any kind of modeling artifact produced throughout the system development life-cycle like requirements or SA descriptions. In this specific work we primarily focus on group design decisions and their evolution, so it basically treats other modeling artifacts as black boxes.

Traceability is realized as a set of tracing links from each modeling artifact to the GDM model (see the arrows in Figure 1). *Tracing links* are contained into special models (e.g., wm_{SA}, wm_{re}, and wm_{ot} in Figure 1) called *weaving models*. A unique aspect of our approach is that tracing links are represented as models; also this aspect is perfectly in line with the everything-is-a-model MDE principle [16], and represents an interesting added value for our approach.

In particular, the use of weaving models allows designers to keep the models of the artifacts *free from any traceability metadata*. This makes the proposed approach *independent from the used modeling languages*, allowing stakeholders to use their preferred notation to describe the system according to their specific concerns. Moreover, the use of weaving models opens up for an **accurate evolution impact analysis** since they provide traceability information both at the model-level and at the model-element level. Intuitively, a designer not only can specify that a design decision dd_x pertains to an entire architectural model am, but also that dd_x pertains only to components c_1 and c_2 in am. Further details on the importance of weaving models can be obtained from our previous work [13]. The weaving models wm_{SA}, wm_{re}, and wm_{ot} extend those presented in [13] by defining new traceability links between the new (colored in Figure 2) GDM metaclasses and the other related artefacts.

Arranging architecture-related artifacts using models and weaving models enables us to reformulate the design decisions evolution[2] impact analysis into the activities of:

---

[2] In this work we consider *evolution* to be a set of incremental changes of a model in response to changing external factors [17], as it is considered in the model management research area; these external factors can include changes to requirements, issues, technology availability, and so on.

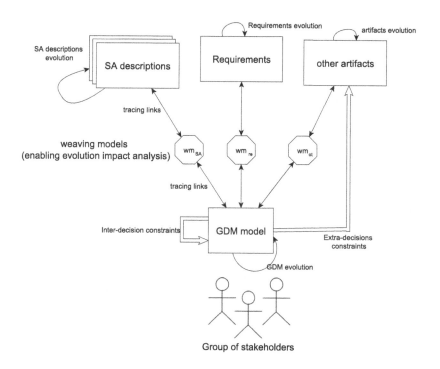

Fig. 1. Overview of the approach components

identifying and checking which design decisions and which parts of other architecture-related artifacts are not aligned with the evolved GDM model. Changes in an GDM model element can have an impact either on elements (e.g., design decisions conflicting with a rejected decision become valid alternatives), or also to external related artifacts (e.g., a component realizing a rejected decision must be checked and probably modified).

In the next sections we describe the GDM-enhanced design decision metamodel (Section 3.1), our proposal to trace design decisions towards other system life-cycle artifacts (Section 3.1), our extension of the change impact analysis engine for supporting GDM (Section 3.1) and the high-level software architecture of the tool realizing the whole approach (Section 3.2).

3.1   Extended Metamodel to Support GDM

In MDE a model always conforms to a metamodel, so we propose the GDM metamodel for representing group design decisions and their relationships. In the proposed approach design decisions are represented within a GDM model. A GDM model represents: *group of stakeholders, GDM sessions, design decisions and their relationships, stakeholder preferences and design reasoning history*. In line with [13], for the sake of generic applicability, the GDM metamodel is notation- and tool-independent so that it is able to represent design decisions and their evolution in a generic manner.

The GDM metamodel has been defined by analyzing the current state of the art in GDM (see [14]) and design decisions representation and reasoning (e.g., [9], [18], [19]). We designed GDM so that it (i) presents the most common aspects and relationships of design decisions, and (ii) contains concepts to define the evolution of an ADD (like its state, history and scope).

Figure 2 graphically shows the metamodel for group design decisions models. As already said, it is an extension of the generic metamodel presented in [13]. In Figure 2 the colored metaclasses are the extensions we made, whereas yellow metaclasses are part of the base metamodel being extended.

In the **base part of the metamodel**, DesignDecision is its main concept. It contains attributes like *description*, *state* that represents the current state of the decision (e.g., idea, tentative, decided, rejected, etc.), *timestamp* that specifies when the design decision has been created, *history* that keeps track of the evolution history of the decision (mainly, author, timestamp and status of each past version of the decision, and so on). The *evolved* attribute is used as a marker to identify which design decisions have been subject to an evolution. This will be used during the evolution impact analysis, which is in charge of managing traceability between the various versions of evolving architectural design decisions models (see [13] for further details on the GDM model evolution management).

Each design decision can be related to some other design decisions by means of typed relationships, e.g., *constrains*, *enables*, *conflictsWith*, and so on (please refer to [9] for a comprehensive description of all the types of relationships). The *comprises* relationship exists when a high-level decision is composed of a set of more specific decisions; differently from all the other relationships (which are represented as simple reference), it is represented as a composition reference because the lifetime of comprised decisions must correspond to the lifetime of the comprising decision [13].

The GDM metamodel distinguishes between internal and external group design decisions (where *internal* refers to group design decisions that have a direct impact only on other design decisions and are not related to any design artifact outside the GDM model, while *external* refers to decisions who have a direct impact to elements in other related artifacts).

This distinction is useful during evolution impact analysis since it allows the tool to tune the scope of the evolution change analysis depending on which design decisions have been evolved.

Designers must associate a Rationale to each design decision in order to keep track of the reasons behind the decision. In order to keep design decisions cognitively manageable and well scoped, they can be organized into categories. Stakeholders are the member of a group, which will be described later in this section.

The **extension of the metamodel** takes into consideration the aspects related to group decision making in the context of architecture description. In the following we describe the elements of our extension.

A Group represents a collection of stakeholders (e.g., software architects, developers, designers, testers, users, etc.) who have regular contact and mutual influence when working together to achieve a common set of goals. The *memberships* relationship

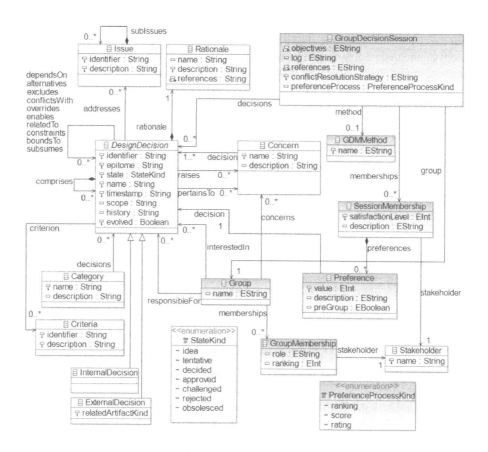

Fig. 2. Generic metamodel for supporting software architecture decision making

represents the participation of each stakeholder in the group. Each group member can have also a set of *concerns* identifying the key design problems related to or raised by a specific design decision. A group or group member can be either *responsible for* or *interested in* a set of design decisions.

GroupMemberships connects the *stakeholder* with a particular group. As suggested in [14], it would be useful to account for hierarchy or expertise differences among stakeholder, i.e., a *ranking*. Indeed, it would be useful to prioritize stakeholders based on some criteria like seniority or expertise to make the process more robust[7]. However, since some organizations may have flat structures where all stakeholders enjoy equal priority, the ranking attribute is optional. Also, each member of a group can optionally have a *role* within the group she belongs to; this attribute can be used by a reasoning engine so that it can prioritize decision makers, senior architects, and so on. This attribute is kept optional so to limit the amount of mandatory information. Each stakeholder can belong to multiple groups.

A GroupDecisionSession represents a single continuous meeting, or a series of meetings of a *group* of stakeholders. Each group decision session has a set of *objectives* because in any decision making exercise, every member needs to be clear about the objectives before the start of the process. In addition to the set of established objectives, the main outcome of a group decision session is the set of design *decisions* identified, modified or, more in general, related to it. Also, each group decision session has an history *log* and a set of *references* in order to allow session members to carefully record all the activities performed.

Conflicts are inherent to GDM: appropriate conflict resolution strategy could be applied to the used SA decision making method [14]. In this context, the *conflictResolutionStrategy* attribute uniquely identifies the conflict resolution strategy applied in the group decision session. The most popular strategy is the collaborative style of conflict resolution [12].

Stakeholders participating in GDM shall be enabled to indicate preferences [14]. For example, in [20] the alternative scenarios are scored and the stakeholders vote the alternatives and the voting method has been chosen to enable the groups to arrive at consensus in a timely manner. According to this, each group decision session has a *preferenceProcess* attribute describing the process used for recording the preferences of each stakeholder. Preference processes can be based either on a *ranking*, *scoring*, or a *rating* system.

The `GDMMethod` is referenced by a group decision session and it represents the specific architecture design decision method used for evaluating the various design decisions considered during the session. Some popular GDM methods are: brainstorming, voting, Nominal Group Technique (NGT), Delphi technique, Analytic Hierarchy Processing (AHP), etc. GDM methods can be shared across different group decision sessions within the whole organization/project.

Each stakeholder participating in a group decision session is linked to the session itself via a `SessionMembership` element. This intermediate element keeps track of the *satisfaction level* that the stakeholder achieved during the session. Indeed, literature points that satisfaction of group members is a key factor [14] since it is an important indicator of the success of the GDM process. Moreover, a *description* of the experience of the stakeholder while participating to the group decision session is recorded, together with an indication of their *preferred choices*.

`Preference` refers to the preferred choice of alternative/decision for a stakeholder. A `Preference` is composed of its cardinal value (so that it can be easily compared with respect to the preferences of other stakeholders within the group) and its description. Also, stakeholders often come with certain preferential biases before the GDM process [21] and during the discussion as more and more information is exchanged, stakeholders tend to revisit their preferences; along this line, the *preGroup* boolean attribute is *true* when the preference has been expressed before the group decision session.

Providing a concrete syntax for GDM models is out of the scope of this work, so we build on and reuse the simplified graph-based representation presented in [13].

Tracing Group Design Decisions to Other Modeling Artifacts. The need for tracing design decisions to/from other system life-cycle artifacts is well understood, especially when those artifacts are requirements specifications or architecture descriptions. As introduced in the beginning of this section, in our approach tracing links are contained into special models (technically called weaving models). A weaving model can be seen as a means for setting fine-grained relationships between models and executing operations on them. The types of relations that can be expressed in our weaving models has been described in detail in [13]. Basically, each weaving model has a reference to the GDM model, a reference to the modeling artifact being woven, and a set of links. Each link represents a fine-grained, many-to-many, traceability link between one or more group design decisions and one or more elements of the linked modeling artifact. For example, a weaving model may allow designers to associate many architectural components to a single design decision, to assign many design decisions to a single component, or to assign a single design decision to a single component. Each link can be either a *tracing* link if the linked artifact elements trace to/from the linked design decisions, or a *conflict* link if the linked artifact elements are not compliant with the linked design decisions [13].

The use of weaving models to store links between decisions and other artifacts allows us to keep design decisions sharply separated from other artifacts. Furthermore, designers now can focus on GDM models when they need to reason on ADD-specific issues, and on other modeling artifacts when they wants to focus on other aspects of the system under construction. We believe that this distinction helps in keeping all the artifacts well organized and in simplifying the effort to perform the various architecting activities.

Group Decisions Impact Analysis. In our approach design decisions validation is performed by executing a set of constraints ruling the involved elements to be checked [13]. Since the proposed approach heavily relies on MDE, and since we want designers to specify constraints with an high-level language, these constraints are defined in the Object Constraint Language (OCL[3]), an OMG standard language used to describe expressions on models.

In this specific context, we can distinguish between **Inter-decisions constraints**, and **Extra-decisions constraints**: the first kind of constraints is executed on GDM models and aims at checking the internal consistency of GDM models, whereas the second one is executed on weaving models and aims at checking and identifying which elements in other modeling artifacts are impacted by the evolved GDM model.

```
1  context  GroupDecisionSession
2      inv  allMembersPreferenceDefined  :
3          not  self.memberships ->exists(e  |  e = e.preferences ->
               notEmpty())
```

Listing 1.1. Example of OCL contraint validating Design Decisions

In the extended version of the approach, we added a set of OCL constraints with the aim to check the extended GDM model with respect to both inter-decisions and extra-decisions consistency. For example, the listing above shows an inter-decision constraint that checks every instance of GroupDecisionSession within the GDM model, and checks if all its members have expressed at least a preference with respect to a design decision.

---

[3] Object Constraint Language specification: http://www.omg.org/spec/OCL. Verified in July 2014.

The results of this validation gives stakeholders insights and accurate information about which element (being it an architectural element, a requirement, or any other modeling artifact) is not aligned with the evolved design decisions. It is up to the designer now to analyze the information provided by the analysis step and to start a reasoning process with the goal of reaching a certain level of stability among the involved artifacts and the evolved GDM model. Within this process, the OCL-based validation engine helps stakeholders to be reasonably confident about the validity of the system being architected even when design decisions are evolving because any conflicting decision is immediately flagged.

Finally, it is important to note that the set of constraints is an *open set*: designers may add their own constraints depending on the specific project they are working on, or also depending on company-specific internal regulations. The validation engine will automatically consider newly added constraints. This choice allows designers to reuse their knowledge about OCL, without forcing them neither to use languages at a lower level of abstraction nor to learn a new ad-hoc language to specify DD validation procedures.

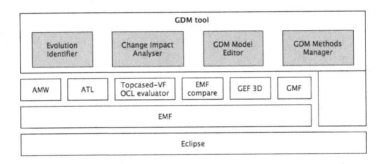

Fig. 3. Tool support

3.2   Tool Support

Figure 3 shows an overview of the main components of the prototype tool we are implementing for supporting the approach presented in this paper. More specifically, the current version of the prototype has been implemented as a set of Eclipse[4] plugins. Eclipse is an open-source development platform comprised of extensible frameworks and tools. We chose Eclipse as base platform as (i) it is based on a plug-in architecture, thus enabling us to easily extend it for our purposes and to distribute our tool in a straightforward manner, and (ii) it allows us to reuse many off-the-shelf components for our purposes, especially when considering MDE engines. Indeed, metamodels can be defined using the Eclipse modeling Framework (EMF)[5], a Java framework and code generation facility for MDE-based tools. Moreover, many architectural languages support the EMF modelling framework [22]. Other reused off-the-shelf components will be described later.

---

[4] http://eclipse.org. Verified in July 2014.

[5] http://www.eclipse.org/modeling/emf. Verified in July 2014.

The GDM tool prototype is composed of four main components, each of them devoted to manage a specific aspect of our approach. More specifically, the **Evolution Identifier** component has the goal of identifying the portions of GDM model that are involved in an evolution round, and to make them distinguishable by the other components within the tool. The *Evolution Identifier* component is implemented as a combination of model-to-model transformations, a model comparison technology. The identification of the evolved GDM elements is a two-steps process: comparison of the GDM model with its latest stable version and evolved design decisions identification. The comparison step is based on EMF Compare[6], an Eclipse plug-in including a generic comparison engine and a facility for creating the corresponding delta model; this delta may itself be represented as a model. As described in [13], evolved design decisions within a GDM model are identified by their *evolved* attribute set to *true*. So, we implemented a model-to-model transformation that takes as input the GDM model and the delta model, selects those design decisions that are related to relevant evolved GDM elements, and updates the GDM model by setting to *true* the *evolved* attribute of all evolved decisions. This transformation is specified using the Atlas Transformation Language (ATL) [23], an hybrid model transformation language.

The **Change Impact Analyser** component is in charge of extending the set of evolved design decisions in the GDM model with respect to all the modeling artifacts used throughout the system development life-cycle. Also this component is based on the ATL model transformation language The identification of the element impacted by a design decision evolution is performed by means of a set of transformations similar to the one realizing the *Evolution Manager* component. The only difference is that in this case the model transformation marks weaving links, instead of GDM model elements. As explained in Section 3.1, weaving links are stored in weaving model. The technology we use for managing weaving models is the Atlas Model Weaver (AMW) [23]. The OCL constraints execution is based on the Topcased-VF OCL evaluator[7].

The **GDM Model Editor** component exposes all the modeling capabilities to stakeholders, so that they can graphically define GDM models in a straighforward manner. This component is based on the well-known Eclipse Graphical Modeling Framework (GMF[8]), a dedicated framework providing generative components and runtime infrastructures for developing graphical editors based on EMF. The GDM model editor presents a graph-based graphical editor to stakeholders, and provides facilities like elements creation, management of their properties, copy-and-paste, export to an image file, etc.

Finally, the **GDM Methods Manager** component aims at providing a certain degree of automation to the GDM process. More specifically, it allows stakeholders to automatically compute the rankings of all the design decisions involved in a group decision session, depending on the specified GDM method. So, for example if the group decision session has AHP as GDM method, then the GDM Methods Manager executes the pairwise comparison and ranking of alternatives, and mathematically computes the best solution at run-time. Clearly, this facility helps in both boosting the group decision sessions, and in always having a correct design decision ranking. This component

---

[6] http://www.eclipse.org/emf/compare. Verified in July 2014.
[7] http://gforge.enseeiht.fr/projects/topcased-vf. Verified in July 2014.
[8] http://www.eclipse.org/modeling/gmp. Verified in July 2014.

is implemented as a set of dedicated Java classes, each of them implementing a specific GDM method, and a set of generic Java classes for updating the GDM model at run-time, i.e., in parallel with stakeholders using the GDM model editor.

The prototype tool is still in its infancy, and our plan is to have the tool ready by the beginning of the year 2015.

4   Benefits of GDM for Resilience

In this section we discuss how including GDM in SA decision making metamodel is beneficial to manage evolving systems. As mentioned in earlier sections, while managing the evolution of sofware systems, we need to manage the evolution of the architecture together with the design decisions and design rationale. In addition to this, since these decisions are made by a group of people, all their viewpoints need to be considered before making changes. In the state-of-the-art metamodels, since GDM is not visibily modeled, changes to decisions is assumed to be a straightforward process which concerns only modification of either the requirements or decisions or the architectural elements. Hence SA knowledge was captured only about these aspects. This has a direct bearing on the tools created based on the metamodels and hence very few of them support GDM. Integrating GDM into our previous SA evolution metamodel may be beneficial in several scenarios some of which are:

a. In a multi-stakeholder system, each stakeholder proposes different set of alternatives, criteria and preferences about solutions. When changes are proposed to a system, not only do the requirements and artifacts evolve, but also the decisions made by these group members. Hence it may require a revisiting of the alternatives proposed by all stakeholders before choosing the next best alternative which necessitates an explicit modeling of GDM simplifies this process.

b. When decisions or criteria need modifications, it may not only result in conflicting decisions but may demand modifications in preferences indicated by stakeholders. This may need an iterative GDM process which allows the revisiting of preferences to support evolution.

c. Software Architects prefer making timely decisions. When the architecture evolves, it may be necessary to make time-bound decisions to quickly accommodate the changes. When tools are built based on the extended metamodel, they would assist quick decision-making using one of the listed GDM methods.

d. Evolution is often an expensive process. When multiple stakeholders are involved, they have more information to decide from and hence may suggest modifications to only those aspects of the system that are absolutely necessary thereby moderating the cost of evolution.

e. Fundamentally GDM assumes diverse objectives. While architectures evolve, they may have a direct impact on these varied objectives of multiple stakeholders. Hence a robust metamodel with GDM may be required to balance conflicting objectives.

5   Related Work

In our previous work on GDM [20], we had presented our study of 29 practitioners and researchers involved with architecting of Software Systems. The study was mainly to understand the state-of-the-art GDM practices in the SA community, how far it matches with methods discussed in literature and what challenges the community faces. This study has greatly helped us in understanding actual needs of the industry. As per our findings, GDM in Software Architecture is a combination of formal and informal methods where a group of stakeholders with diverse expertise make decisions. The community acknowledges that the current tools are not sufficient to assist in GDM and hence valuable knowledge about the process is lost. They also face several challenges and often find themselves entering into conflicts but have limited expertise to enhance their process to handle these issues. We further extended our study in [14] to evaluate current SA decision making methods discussed in literature to see if they can support GDM. We found that with the exception of a few methods, most of them are not yet suitable to accommodate group decisions.

Tofan et al, in [24], have done an extensive and systematic study of state of research in SA decisions. They have analyzed about 144 papers that discuss SA decisions and categorized them based on six research questions. They found that only 22 of them broadly discuss group decision-making and hence there is lot of scope for improvement in the fundamental SA decision making methods to include groups.Several Architectural Knowledge (AK) management tools have been compared in [25]. The authors have used ten criteria to compare the tools. They mention that the current version of most of the tools, which are based on the IEEE 42010 as well as on SA decision making metamodels, lack proper support for collaborative sharing of knowledge and hence do not facilitate GDM.

6   Conclusions and Future Work

Robust architectures come from a robust decision-making process. Two important factors (among others) impact the robustness of the decision making process: collaborating people shall work following explicitly defined GDM principles and processes in order to reach a consensus; decisions (as well as other artifacts) may evolve over time and need to be kept in sync. The continuous synchronization between evolving decisions and architectural and related artefacts, would help to produce systems more resilient to changing decisions. In this context, this work has presented an extension of the evolving architecture design decision framework presented in [13]. Such an enhancement has demanded the extension of the metamodel with new meta-elements and meta-relationships, to extend the traceability and tracing links previously proposed with new weaving models, and to extend and revise the impact analysis approach. A sketch of the tool architecture has been presented as well.

As future work, we are working towards the design and implementation of a collaborative working environment, where architects and decision makers who are geographically dispersed can participate in the collaborative architectural design of a software system. Such a framework will enable the architects to document the GDM practices in use, to store alternative and selected decisions, to report on changes and how they may impact other software artifacts. More than this, the framework will include the possibility to create new plugins, each one implementing a specific GDM method.

References

1. Cirani, S., Fedotova, N., Veltri, L.: A resilient architecture for dht-based distributed collaborative environments. In: Proceedings of the 2008 RISE/EFTS Joint International Workshop on Software Engineering for Resilient Systems, SERENE 2008, pp. 1–8. ACM, New York (2008)
2. Stoicescu, M., Fabre, J.-C., Roy, M.: Architecting resilient computing systems: Overall approach and open issues. In: Troubitsyna, E.A. (ed.) SERENE 2011. LNCS, vol. 6968, pp. 48–62. Springer, Heidelberg (2011)
3. Rodríguez, R.J., Merseguer, J., Bernardi, S.: Modelling and analysing resilience as a security issue within uml. In: Proceedings of the 2nd International Workshop on Software Engineering for Resilient Systems, SERENE 2010, pp. 42–51. ACM, New York (2010)
4. Prokhorova, Y., Troubitsyna, E.: Linking modelling in event-B with safety cases. In: Avgeriou, P. (ed.) SERENE 2012. LNCS, vol. 7527, pp. 47–62. Springer, Heidelberg (2012)
5. Ben Hamida, A., Bertolino, A., Calabrò, A., De Angelis, G., Lago, N., Lesbegueries, J.: Monitoring service choreographies from multiple sources. In: Avgeriou, P. (ed.) SERENE 2012. LNCS, vol. 7527, pp. 134–149. Springer, Heidelberg (2012)
6. Harman, M., Muccini, H., Schulte, W., Xie, T.: 10111 executive summary – practical software testing: Tool automation and human factors. In: Harman, M., Muccini, H., Schulte, W., Xie, T. (eds.) Practical Software Testing: Tool Automation and Human Factors, Dagstuhl. Dagstuhl Seminar Proceedings, vol. 10111. Schloss Dagstuhl - Leibniz-Zentrum fuer Informatik, Germany (2010)
7. Saaty, T.L., Vargas, L.G.: Decision making with the analytic network process. Springer (2006)
8. Aldag, R.J., Fuller, S.R.: Beyond fiasco: A reappraisal of the groupthink phenomenon and a new model of group decision processes. Psychological Bulletin 113(3), 533 (1993)
9. Kruchten, P.: An Ontology of Architectural Design Decisions in Software Intensive Systems. In: 2nd Groningen Workshop Software Variability, pp. 54–61 (October 2004)
10. Jansen, A., Bosch, J.: Software architecture as a set of architectural design decisions. In: WICSA 2005 (2005)
11. Potts, C., Bruns, G.: Recording the reasons for design decisions. In: 10th International Conference on Software Engineering, ICSE 1988, pp. 418–427 (1988)
12. Rekha, V., Muccini, H.: A study on group decision-making in software architecture. In: 2014 IEEE/IFIP Conference on Software Architecture (WICSA), pp. 185–194 (April 2014)
13. Malavolta, I., Muccini, H., Smrithi Rekha, V.: Supporting architectural design decisions evolution through model driven engineering. In: Troubitsyna, E.A. (ed.) SERENE 2011. LNCS, vol. 6968, pp. 63–77. Springer, Heidelberg (2011)
14. Smrithi Rekha, V., Muccini, H.: Suitability of software architecture decision making methods for group decisions. In: Avgeriou, P., Zdun, U. (eds.) ECSA 2014. LNCS, vol. 8627, pp. 17–32. Springer, Heidelberg (2014)
15. Brodbeck, F.C., Kerschreiter, R., Mojzisch, A., Schulz-Hardt, S.: Group decision making under conditions of distributed knowledge: The information asymmetries model. Academy of Management Review 32(2), 459–479 (2007)
16. Schmidt, D.C.: Guest Editor's Introduction: Model-Driven Engineering. Computer 39(2), 25–31 (2006)

17. Levendovszky, T., Rumpe, B., Schätz, B., Sprinkle, J.: Model evolution and management. In: Giese, H., Karsai, G., Lee, E., Rumpe, B., Schätz, B. (eds.) MBEERTS. LNCS, vol. 6100, pp. 241–270. Springer, Heidelberg (2010)
18. Eklund, U., Arts, T.: A classification of value for software architecture decisions. In: Babar, M.A., Gorton, I. (eds.) ECSA 2010. LNCS, vol. 6285, pp. 368–375. Springer, Heidelberg (2010)
19. ISO: Final committee draft of Systems and Software Engineering – Architectural Description (ISO/IECFCD 42010). Working doc.: ISO/IEC JTC 1/SC 7 N 000, IEEE (2009)
20. Moore, M., Kaman, R., Klein, M., Asundi, J.: Quantifying the value of architecture design decisions: lessons from the field. In: Proceedings of the 25th International Conference on Software Engineering, pp. 557–562 (May 2003)
21. Stasser, G., Titus, W.: Pooling of Unshared Information in Group Decision Making: Biased Information Sampling During Discussion. Journal of Personality and Social Psychology 48(6), 1467–1478 (1985)
22. Lago, P., Malavolta, I., Muccini, H., Pelliccione, P., Tang, A.: The road ahead for architectural languages. IEEE Software 99(PrePrints), 1 (2014)
23. Jouault, F., Kurtev, I.: Transforming Models with ATL. In: Bruel, J.-M. (ed.) MoDELS 2005. LNCS, vol. 3844, pp. 128–138. Springer, Heidelberg (2006)
24. Tofan, D., Galster, M., Avgeriou, P., Schuitema, W.: Past and future of software architectural decisions – a systematic mapping study. Information and Software Technology 56(8), 850–872 (2014)
25. Tang, A., Avgeriou, P., Jansen, A., Capilla, R., Ali Babar, M.: A comparative study of architecture knowledge management tools. Journal of Systems and Software 83(3), 352–370 (2010)

The Role of Parts in the System Behaviour

Davide Di Ruscio[1], Ivano Malavolta[2], and Patrizio Pelliccione[3]

[1] University of L'Aquila,
Department of Information Engineering, Computer Science and Mathematics, Italy
[2] Gran Sasso Science Institute, L'Aquila, Italy
[3] Chalmers University of Technology — University of Gothenburg,
Department of Computer Science and Engineering, Sweden
`davide.diruscio@univaq.it, ivano.malavolta@gssi.infn.it,`
`patrizio.pelliccione@gu.se`

Abstract. In today's world, we are surrounded by software-based systems that control so many critical activities. Every few years we experiment dramatic software failures and this asks for software that gives evidence of resilience and continuity. Moreover, we are observing an unavoidable shift from stand-alone systems to systems of systems, to ecosystems, to cyber-physical systems and in general to systems that are composed of various independent parts that collaborate and cooperate to realise the desired goal.

Our thesis is that the resilience of such systems should be constructed compositionally and incrementally out of the resilience of system parts. Understanding the role of parts in the system behaviour will (i) promote a "divide-and-conquer strategy" on the verification of systems, (ii) enable the verification of systems that continuously evolve during their life-time, (iii) allow the detection and isolation of faults, and (iv) facilitate the definition of suitable reaction strategies. In this paper we propose a methodology that integrates needs of flexibility and agility with needs of resilience. We instantiate the methodology in the domain of a swarm of autonomous quadrotors that cooperate in order to achieve a given goal.

1 Introduction

Increasingly, we are surrounded by software-based systems that provide services that are increasingly becoming ineluctable elements of everyday life. Examples of served domains are transportation, telecommunication, and health-care. According to Marc Andreessen[1] *"Software is eating the world"*[2]: for instance, the major music companies are software companies: Apple's iTunes, Spotify and Pandora. As another example, the today world's largest bookseller is a software company i.e., Amazon.

Software controls so many critical activities, and thus, at societal level, software is required to provide evidence of resilience and continuity. Every few years we experiment

---

[1] Mr. Andreessen is co-founder and general partner of the venture capital firm Andreessen-Horowitz, which has invested in Facebook, Groupon, Skype, Twitter, Zynga, and Foursquare, among others. He is also an investor in LinkedIn and co-founded Netscape, one of the first browser companies.

[2] `http://goo.gl/FCGord`

I. Majzik and M. Vieira (Eds.): SERENE 2014, LNCS 8785, pp. 24–39, 2014.

dramatic software failures, e.g.: (i) the Knight Capital Group announced on August 2, 2012 that it lost $440 million when it sold all the stocks it accidentally bought the day before due to a software bug; (ii) in 10 years, about 10,000,000 cars have been recalled due to software-related problems by Ford, Cadillac, General Motors, Jaguar, Nissan, Pontiac, Volvo, Chrysler Group, Honda, Lexus, Toyota and others.

This motivates a growing interest, both industrial and academic, in techniques that can provide evidence about the software resilience. Modern systems are no more stand-alone; they are composed of several sub-systems, often independent each other but that collaborate to realize the system goal. Examples of these systems are systems of systems, ecosystems, and cyber-physical systems characterized by high dynamicity that might affect each subsystem, the way they are interconnected and the environment in which they live. Our thesis is that the resilience of systems that are composed of various independent parts that collaborate and cooperate to realise the desired goal should be constructed compositionally out of the resilience of system parts. Indeed, complex interacting collective systems often expose emerging properties that represent unexpected behaviours that stem from interactions between the system parts and with the system's environment [1]. Emergent properties might be beneficial, but they can be also harmful, e.g., if they compromise the system safety. While considering critical systems it might be dangerous to accept and permit uncontrolled behaviours. Therefore, our idea is to exploit the system specification at run-time in order to force the system to only expose desired behaviours. In other words, each single part of the system should understand under which conditions it can ensure a correct behaviour and be robust to failures and to malicious attacks.

In this paper we propose a methodology that builds on lessons learned in integrating flexible and agile development processes with the need of resilience. The methodology starts from the dichotomy that exists between building systems and expressing system specifications. On one hand, systems are built out of existing components; they are suitably composed and integrated so to realize a system goal [2]. On the other hand, the specification of systems is often defined only at system level without providing details about the expected behaviour of each single part composing the system [3, 4]. A fundamental aspect is to decompose the system goal in a set of sub-system specifications that describe the role of the system parts in the system behaviour: this enables incremental and compositional verification and permits to maintain the desired degree of resilience despite the evolution and the adaptation of systems to continuous environment changes. These concepts are better explained by focusing on the domain of a swarm of autonomous quadrotors that collaborate to realize a common goal. In this example each quadrotor is an autonomous node that behaves independently by each other; however, each node realises specific tasks that concur to the realization of the mission, which is the system's goal.

The remainder of the paper is structured as follows: Section 2 describes development processes that integrate agility and flexibility with the need of resilience. Section 3 discusses the importance of understanding the contribution of single parts for ensuring the resilience of the entire system. Section 4 illustrates the development process in the context of a swarm of autonomous quadrotors. Related works are discussed in Section 5, whereas Section 6 concludes the paper and outlines some perspective work.

2 Agility and Resilience

Modern software systems are composed of several different parts that are independent but that collaborate to realize the goal of the sysyem. Such systems are inherently dynamic since they need to operate in a continuously changing environment and must be able to evolve and quickly adapt to different types of changes, even unanticipated, while guaranteeing the resilience today's users expect [2]. As highlighted in [5–7], uncertainty is becoming a first-class concern of today's software systems. Uncertainty calls for strategies able to determine under what conditions desired goals will be achieved and behavioral invariance will be preserved [5–7].

The development of safety-critical systems is traditionally associated to waterfall and V-lifecycles that involve huge effort in planning, specification, and documentation. These development processes are typically rigorous and enable software certification. However, the adoption of these processes makes it difficult to manage requirements volatility and the introduction of new technologies. Moreover, such processes can lead to substantial costs in producing and maintaining documentation.

Agile methods are very attractive to software companies since they promise flexibility and speed by focusing more on continuous process management and code-level quality than classic software engineering process models [8]. Recent works [9] demonstrate that agile methods are not inherently at odds with the requirements of safety critical development even though they cannot be directly applied as they are. In particular, agile methodologies might define as necessary some activities that are enablers of resilience for safety-critical systems [8]. Examples of such activities are the following:

Up-front design and incremental development of safety arguments [9]: the rationale of the up-front design is to enable hazard analysis, safety analysis, and certification. Moreover, iterative and incremental development should construct not only software, but also arguments that the software is acceptably safe.

Safety-by-Design [8]: strongly typed interfaces that accept request events and returns request responses where a state machine internal to the component determines whether the request can be satisfied in the component's current state [8]. This supports the notion of intrinsic safety [10], i.e., no component can be in an unexpected state. This would enable also simulation and verification activities able to check if the composition of all the considered components work properly.

Lightweight traceability of requirements at development time [8]: requirements management in lockstep with code management. Developers write potential requirements in a wiki. A collaborative review process analyses, refines, and decides which requirements are rejected (stored for potential revision in the future), and which requirements are accepted. Accepted requirements are introduced into the product backlog; the team selects the requirements suitable for implementation in the current sprint. Synchronization between requirements management and code management is ensured.

Identify high-risk system properties that need special handling [11]: integration of formal specification into agile methods for high-risk system properties, before they are implemented in the next sprint. Less critical parts of the system are implemented in parallel without any formality.

3 Understanding the Role of Parts to Ensure Resilience

A key point for ensuring resilience is having a precise description of the system speci-fication. As said by Leslie Lamport: "*A specification is a written description of what a system is supposed to do. Specifying a system helps us understand it. It's a good idea to understand a system before building it, so it's a good idea to write a specification of a system before implementing it.*" [12]. A specification is an abstraction of the system aimed at describing some aspects and at ignoring others. Specifications describe state-ments of intents whose satisfaction requires the cooperation of parts of the system [13]; unfortunately, often specifications do not state explicitly the role of the system's parts. The importance of having a precise specification of system's parts is well recognized and it is still an open research challenge [14, 15]. These sub-specifications represent the technical requirements on the system sub-parts and assumptions on their environment. According to [4] we call these sub-specifications *operational requirements*.

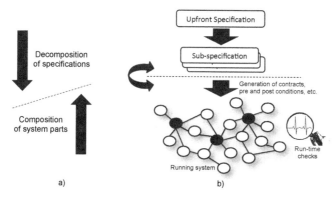

Fig. 1. a) Decomposition and Composition; b) Agility and Resilience

Figure 1.a highlights the importance of decomposing the system specification in a set of sub-specifications. The figure is completed by observing that the way of produc-ing software is changing: it is increasingly produced according to a certain goal and by integrating existing software through the use of integrator means (e.g., architectures, connectors, integration patterns) that ease the collaboration and integration of existing services in a resilient way [2]. As shown in Figure 1.b, the proposed methodology con-sists of a number of tasks and artefacts as described below.

Upfront Specification: As suggested by the work presented in [9], an important aspect to ensure resilience is having an upfront design that represents the specification of the high-level goal of the system. Having a full upfront design of a complex system is of-ten difficult and impractical due to the high degree of uncertainty and to the overhead related the management of the design during the whole system lifetime. Thus, the up-front specification can be incrementally refined as new information is available or new requirements are considered.

Sub-Specification: The next step is to refine and map the high-level goals into precise specifications of software behaviour [16], called sub-specification in Figure 1.b. Such a specification consists of operational requirements, contracts or pre- and post- conditions so to enable proofs at run-time. Depending on the system and on the considered development process, pre- and post- conditions or contracts might be chosen. Pre- and post-conditions can be interpreted as the assumptions that the component/sub-system makes on its environment in order to guarantee its properties [17]. According to the design-by-contract paradigm [14], contracts instead encode operational requirements in target programming languages, i.e., pre-, post-conditions and invariants are written by using the syntax of the used programming language, thus they are specified at a lower level of abstraction. It is important to remark that generating sub-specifications from the upfront one is a complex task that cannot be always automated. In the domain of choreographed systems we managed to automate the generation of sub-specifications [18], even though this is not always the case since it depends on the considered application domain and on the complexity of the modeled software systems.

Generation of Contracts, pre- and post- Conditions: As discussed in [8], contracts and pre- and post- conditions might assume the form of state machines to be used for performing verification at run-time and to regulate the behaviour of the system during its execution according to the specification. In particular, the idea is to associate a state machine encoding the (sub-)specification to its corresponding component/sub-system.

Run-Time Checks: According to the performed actions and to the sent and received messages, the obtained state machine is animated and the computational state of the real system is thus explicitly represented. Thus, once a message that differs from what expected is received, the message is blocked and suitable recovery strategies might be adopted. This promotes the intrinsic safety notion [10] that aims at protecting each system part from strange behaviours. This will permit to isolate potential problems, or prevent from malicious attacks. A similar approach has been proposed in [19] where the encoded state machine was used to ensure that the final code behave according to a checked and verified software architecture behavioural model. Moreover, each system part should explicitly deal with exceptional situations, for instance by implementing the idealized component model [20, 21]. According to this model, when the *normal behavior* of a component raises an exception, called local exception, its exception handling part is automatically invoked. If the exception is successfully handled, the component resumes its normal behaviour, otherwise an *external exception* is signalled to the enclosing context. Two are the possible types of exceptions caused by external invocations: *failure exceptions* due to a failure in processing a valid request, and *interface exceptions* due to an invalid service request.

It is important to remark that *running system* and *specifications* in Fig, 1 need to be kept aligned. This is of crucial importance since as previously explained the specification becomes part of the implementation; therefore coherence and consistency between specification and running system must be ensured. It is important to note also that here we are not promoting to have the system code aligned with models as typically done in the case of code generation and round-trip engineering. Here we are proposing to have requirements and system properties properly identified, made explicit, and encoded in the running system. The encoded properties should be considered as an implementation of a monitor, which is executed in parallel with the system, and which controls both the (sub-)system behaviour and its interactions with the environment. The property, encoded as a state machine, should be defined at a proper abstraction level to do not compromise the performance of the system, and its usability with unnecessary details.

4   Ensuring Resilience in a Swarm of Autonomous Quadrotors

In this section we discuss the application of the methodology shown in Fig. 1 in the domain of civilian missions executed by swarms of autonomous quadrotors. In particular, Section 4.1 introduces the domain of interest and outline the different kinds of resilience that it is possible to have when using swarms of autonomous quadrotors. Section 4.2 introduces the FLYAQ [22] software platform consisting of languages and tools that have been conceived to manage resilient quadrocopters according to the methodology shown in Fig. 1. Section 4.3 discusses a concrete application of FLYAQ.

4.1   Overview and Resilience

A quadrotor is a multicopter that is lifted and propelled by four rotors. Quadrotors are classified in the family of UAV (Unmanned Aerial Vehicle), e.g., drones without a human pilot on board that can be either controlled autonomously by computers in the vehicle, or under the remote control of a pilot on the ground or in another vehicle. Quadrotors are programmed with a very low level language or providing very basic primitives; this issue introduces an "error-prone" process even for experienced users and asks developers strong expertise about the dynamics and the technical characteristics of the used quadrotor. It also makes the specification of missions unaffordable for a non-technical user, which has typically a very poor (if any) experience in software programming. Therefore, the specification of a mission is already difficult when considering a single quadrotor and it becomes even more complex when dealing with missions involving a swarm of quadrotors. In this paper we refer to the FLYAQ platform [22] that has been conceived to eliminate this technological barrier. FLYAQ allows non-technical operators to straightforwardly define civilian missions of flying drones swarms at a high level of abstraction, thus hiding the complexity of the low-level and flight dynamics-related information of the drones.

The overall system is composed of a swarm of independent quadrotors, a ground station that is the hub to perform reconfigurations and that receives information from the run-time execution, and laptops or tablet that are used by the end-user to define and monitor the mission. Currently the ground station is controlling everything, then the mission is centrally coordinated by the ground station that sends instructions to the quadrotors composing the swarm. However, in this paper we move towards a decentralization of the mission with the idea of distributing the computation to quadrotors; in this way resilience is distributed on each quadrotor, thus we are not relying on the communication channels anymore, rather the resilience of the entire system is built on top of the resilience of single parts.

Before discussing strategies adopted to ensure resilience, we further analyse and describe resilience in the domain of a swarm of quadrotors. Specifically, we distinguish between resilience of a single quadrotor, and resilience of the entire system.

Resilience of a Single Quadrotor: A quadrotor should be resilient and tolerant to both software and hardware faults. Quadrotors will be more and more required to adhere to standards, rules, and regulations just like an aircraft. Certification affects software, hardware, as well as those platforms that are used to produce, test, or devices and sensors to be installed on quadrotors.

Hardware: this involves (i) redundancy of engines, rotors, transmission and communication system, (ii) emergency system able to execute a safe emergency landing in case of malfunctioning quadrotors, and (iii) using parachutes.

Software: this involves strategies to make the quadrotor resilient to (i) errors in the code, such as wrong mission design (impossible to realize the mission with the available resources), or wrong code, (ii) inaccurate or unpredictable context - automatic obstacles avoidance or reaction to strong wind, (iii) attacks from malicious entities, e.g., spoofing attack - a program might masquerade as another by falsifying data and thereby trying to gain an illegitimate advantage in terms of communication.

Resilience of the Entire System: The overall system has the objective of realizing the mission even when facing changes and unforeseen failures at run-time. Static checks can be made at design time, once the mission has been designed (e.g., to check the feasibility of the mission according to the available drones, weather conditions, quadrotors equipments, etc.). However, the challenge here is to construct a reconfiguration engine which is able to react to changes and problems at run-time, and then maintaining a desired degree of resilience at run-time. More details about the resilience of the entire system might be found in [22]. In the following we focus on the resilience of a single quadrotor from the software perspective, while we rely on the hardware resilience provided by the constructor of drones.

4.2   Building a Resilient Quadrocopter: Software Perspective

By starting from an upfront specification, which is the goal of the mission, FLYAQ generates the sub-specifications for each actor of the system. In FLYAQ, the upfront specification is provided by means of the Monitoring Mission Language (MML) and the Context Language (CL) [23]. MML is a domain-specific language for representing a monitoring mission as an ordered sequence of tasks to be performed by the swarm. Basically, an MML task is a predefined sub-mission which can be executed by a set of drones, it can be performed until completion or it can be interrupted by an event. Examples of tasks provided by MML include: covering a specific area by acquiring images on a grid with a given graphic resolution, looking for some visual marker within a specific area, keeping a certain position on a given geographical point, coming back to a geographical point defined as the home of the mission, etc. CL models contain the specification of contextual information of the mission. For example, in FLYAQ context models contain information about obstacles, no fly zones, emergency places where to land in case of emergency. Moreover, the FLYAQ platform uses an intermediate language called Quadrotor Behaviour Language (QBL). Such a language represents detailed instructions for each single quadrotor of the swarm, and it is used at run-time for instructing each single quadrotor. From an high-level point of view, the beahaviour of each drone is composed of a set of movements (e.g., take off, land, go to a specific geographical point), each of them having a set of pre- and post-actions, which are executed by the drone before (or after) the movement. Examples of actions include: taking a picture, starting or stopping a video streaming session, sending a message to the ground station, and sending a message to another drone.

Sub-specifications are instead described as state machines, in which each state represents an internal computational state of the quadrotor, while a transition from one state to another can represent either (i) a message that is sent or received by the quadrotor, or (ii) an operation that is internal to the quadrotor, such as moving to a precise geographical point, hovering for two seconds, taking a picture, etc. A formal definition of sub-specification is given in Definition. 1.

Definition 1 (Sub-specification). *Let Msg be a finite set of messages that a quadrotor can exchange, let Act be a finite set of internal actions that a quadrotor can perform, like take off, landing, movements, taking pictures, etc. A sub-specification is a tuple $Spec=(N,S,s_0,A,T)$ where:*

- *N is the state machine name.*
- *S is a finite set of states.*
- *$s_0 \in S$ is the initial state.*
- *A is a finite set of transition labels.*
- *T is a finite set of transitions. A transition $t \in T$ is a tuple $t=(s_s,s_t,label,type)$ where:*
  - *$s_s \in S$ is the source state;*
  - *$s_t \in S$ is the target state;*
  - *$label \in A$ is the transition label;*
  - *$type=\{!m_1;?m_2;\tau\}$ is the transition type: send, receive, or internal, respectively, where $m_1,m_2 \in Msg$, $\tau \in Act$;*

The (sub-)specification is contained in the software component that resides in each quadrotor. As shown in Figure 2 the software component is composed of four main

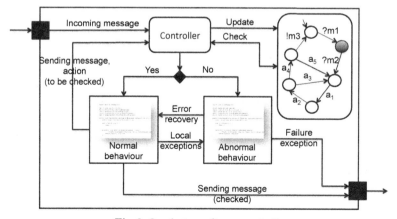

Fig. 2. Quadrotor software controller

parts: *Controller*, *(Sub-)Specification*, *Normal behaviour*, and *Exceptional behaviour*. To explain how these components will exploit the specification at run-time we distinguish between four different situations:

Received Message: when a message is received from the context (which can be the ground station or another quadrotor), before interpreting the message the controller checks the specification to check if the message is expected. If the message is allowed in the current computational state, then the message is forwarded to the normal part of the component, otherwise the message is forwarded to the exceptional part.

Sent Message: before authorizing the sending of a message the controller checks the conformity of the behaviour with the specification.

Performing an Action: before performing an internal action, the controller checks the status of the specification to see if the action is allowed in the actual computational state. In the case of positive answer the specification is updated by changing the current state to the target state of the executed transition, whereas in the case of negative answer the exception part of the node is called into action.

Performed Action: when an action is performed a transition is fired in the specification and a target state is reached. Then the configuration of the quadrotors is analysed to identify possible failures and to check whether actual status of sensors and devices (like battery consumption) diverge from what expected. In case of problems the exceptional part of the node has to manage and possibly solve the problem.

4.3 Example

In this section we put in practice the proposed approach discussed in the previous section on a concrete example. It describes a mission for monitoring a large public event for security reasons. The event (http://www.laquila2015.it/) is the 88th national gathering of the Alpini, an elite mountain warfare military corps of the Italian Army. The event will take place in L'Aquila (Italy) on 15-17 May 2015. A crowd of more than 70,000 participants took part of the past edition of the Alpini's national gathering, and the same number of participants is expected to come to the city of L'Aquila in 2015. Clearly, having such a large number of participants in a three-days event poses many challenges to the organizers, mainly about security and safety issues. In this context, FLYAQ will play a relevant role since it will enable organizers to have a swarm of autonomous quadrotors that continuously monitor the city center during the event. In the following sections we describe the upfront specification of the monitoring mission that will be executed every hour, and its corresponding sub-specifications.

Upfront Specification: Figure 3 shows the *MML mission model* for monitoring the annual Alpini gathering event. More specifically, Figure 3(a) shows the tasks of the mission as a UML activity diagram, and Figure 3(b) shows the same tasks of the UML activity diagram as an overlay to a geographical map of the city. The mission is composed of two tasks that will be performed in parallel, namely:

-- *Photo grid task (PG1):* this task is performed above the main square of the city (see the blue rectangle in Figure 3(b)), where there will be the main talks from the institutions, musical concerts, etc. The photo grid task identifies a virtual grid within the area, each cell of the grid having a size of ten meters. The drones executing the task will fly over each cell of the grid at an altitude of 25 meters, and then will take a picture of the area directly below them; thus, the result of the photo grid task is a set of high-definition pictures fully covering the main square of the city. The photo grid task can be assigned to multiple drones.

– *Road task (R1)*: this task refers to a polyline corresponding to the main streets in the central area of the city (see the blue polyline in Figure 3(b)). This task can be assigned to a single drone, that will (i) fly along the polyline at an altitude of 25 meters, and (ii) take a picture every 200 meters along the polyline.

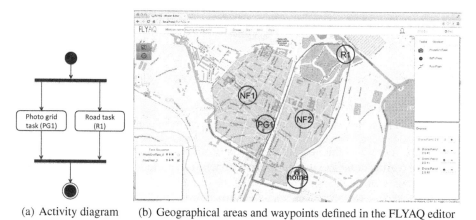

(a) Activity diagram   (b) Geographical areas and waypoints defined in the FLYAQ editor

Fig. 3. The Alpini event monitoring mission

The mission will be realized by three drones that will be positioned in a large parking close to the city center (see the *home* circle in Figure 3(b)): two drones will take care of executing the photo grid task, whereas a single drone will execute the road task independently. As previously explained, the FLYAQ platform allows the user to define contextual information about the mission. In this example, the *CL context model* contains two *no fly* areas called NF1 and NF2. Those areas correspond to the zones within the city center with residential buildings. Each drone performing the mission cannot fly over no-fly areas under any possible conditions. As discussed in Section 4.2, the FLYAQ platform is able to automatically generate a *QBL behavioural model* from the mission model. Figure 4 graphically shows the behavioural model corresponding to the example mission. The behavioural model is composed of three behavioural traces, each of them representing the behaviour of a single drone. A behavioural trace is composed of a set of atomic movements that the drone will perform to complete its portion of mission[3]. In the following we describe the kinds of the used behavioural actions:

– Start: represents the initial setup of the drone;
– Stop: represents the final movement used to end any sequence of movements;

---

[3] Tasks are not part of the behavioural model, we show the mission task representing each sub-behaviour trace in Figure 4 only for the sake of clarity.

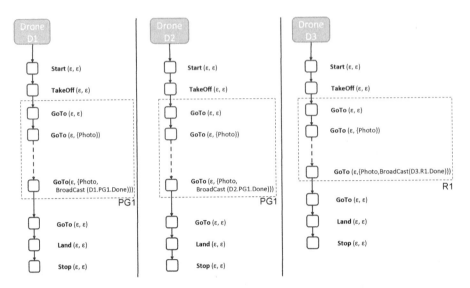

Fig. 4. Behavioural model of the Alpini event monitoring mission

- TakeOff: represents the take off operation of the drone; in the behavioural model each take off is complete when the drone reaches an altitude of two meters;
- Land: represents the landing operation of the drone;
- GoTo: is the movement towards a given target geographical coordinate.

Each drone executes the sequence of all the movements of its assigned behavioural trace. In Figure 4 arrows denote the transition between a movement to the next one. A drone can perform a number of actions before or after the execution of a specific movement. Pre- and post-actions of each movement are enclosed with parenthesis on the right of the movement name. The behavioural model of the modelled mission are:

- Photo: represents the action of taking a high-definition photo below the drone;
- BroadCast: represents the action of sending a message to all the drone within the swarm; in the example the broadcast message represents the notification of the completion of a given task for synchronization purposes.

By looking at Figure 4 it is evident that the behavioural trace of each drone follows a specific pattern, that is: the drone (i) starts and takes off, (ii), moves to the initial geographical point of the first task to be performed, (iii) realizes the mission tasks assigned to it, (iv) notifies to all the other drones of the swarm the completion of the assigned task, (v) comes back to its initial position, (vi) lands, and then stops itself. This execution pattern helps us in efficiently maintaining the transformation engine in charge of creating a behavioural model from the upfront specification.

Sub-specifications: Figure 5 shows the sub-specifications of all the drones used in the mission. Drone D1 and drone D2 are assigned to photo grid task PG1, and drone D3 is assigned to road task R1. The state machines in figure will be automatically generated by the behavioural model of the mission, which is in turn automatically generated from the mission model containing the two high-level tasks.

Drones D1 and D2 have a very similar behaviour since they have been assigned to the same high-level task (i.e., PG1), and the behavioural generator equally splits the duties of the drones into two equal portions. Basically, after the preliminary actions of starting up and taking off, each drone assigned to a photo grid task must travel to the initial geographical point of the task, i.e., (x_{pg1}, y_{pg1}), and then the state machine contains a chain of transitions representing (i) go to movements, i.e., $g(x_{lat}, y_{lon})$ and (ii) photo actions, i.e., $p()$. In the current example, the photo grid task generated a grid containing 40 points, and thus each drone has been assigned to 20 points in which a photo must be taken. When the last point of the grid has been photographed each drone notifies all the other drones within the mission that it just completed its assigned part, comes back to its initial geographical point (i.e., $home$), lands and stops itself. Drone 3 has been assigned to the road task R1; this task has a reference polyline which is 3550 meters long, and the drone must take a picture every 200 meters. This means that Drone 3 must take a total of 17 pictures, then, similarly to all the other drones, it notifies the completion of its part of mission to all the other drones of the swarm, comes back to its initial geographical point, lands, and stops itself.

Notice that each state of the state machines in Figure 5 contains a set of properties that define the operational context and status of the drone when entering it. Examples of properties include: the position of the drone is within a certain range, the battery level is above a certain threshold, the status of its sensors is correct, etc. At run-time, when a drone is entering a specific state, the controller checks if the current operational

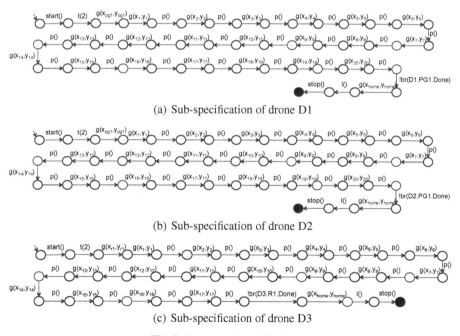

(a) Sub-specification of drone D1

(b) Sub-specification of drone D2

(c) Sub-specification of drone D3

Fig. 5. Drones sub-specifications

context and the status of the drone match the values of the properties defined in the state. As seen in Section 4.2, if those checks are satisfied, then the drone can continue the execution of the remaining state machine, otherwise the controller switches to the logic implementing the abnormal part of the drone, thus trying to recover after the error.

In the following we provide three example scenarios in which the combination of run-time controller and the behavioural state machine may be a good strategy for providing the needed level of resilience to a drone performing a mission on the field. Firstly, assuming that the drone is reaching a certain behavioural state that refers to a specific geographical position (x, y), and suddenly a strong *gust of wind* pushes the drone outside the allowed range with respect to (x, y), then the controller recognizes this unexpected situation and switches its execution to the exceptional behaviour in order to try to bring the drone back to the exact position. Secondly, assuming that an attacker is trying to flood the drone by sending a huge set of messages to it and that the drone is in a state in which there is no outgoing transition with a receive message action, then the controller is able to recognize this dangerous situation and thus it switches its execution to the exceptional behaviour in order to recover from it (e.g., by bringing the drone under attack to its home position). Finally, assuming that an engine of the drone gets broken and that a drone is reaching a certain state with the property $(enginesRPM >= 3000)$, then the controller is able to straightforwardly detect the fault (since the current RPM of the broken engine is equal to zero), and thus it switches its execution to the expectional behaviour in order to, e.g., immediately land the drone in a safe area.

5 Related Work

High-Level Goals Decomposition: Identifying from high-level goals requirements of components, parts of the system or operations is still an open problem. Most of the approaches that use specifications, such as formal methods, assume such operational requirements to be given. However, deriving "correct" operational requirements from high-level goals is challenging and is often delegated to error prone processes.

Letier and Lamwsveerde [4] propose an iterative approach that allows the derivation of operational requirements from high-level goals expressed in real-time linear temporal logic (RT-LTL). The approach is based on operationalisation patterns. Operationalization is a process that maps declarative property specifications to operational specifications satisfying them. The approach produces operational requirements in the form of pre-, post-, and trigger- conditions. The approach is guaranteed to be correct. Informally, here correct means that the conjunction of the operational requirements entails the RT-LTL specification. The approach is limited to a collection of goals and requirement templates provided by the authors. Moreover, the approach necessitates a fully refined, labour-intensive, and error-prone goal model that requires specific expertise.

The tool-supported framework proposed in [3] combines model-checking and Inductive Logic Programming (ILP) to elaborate and refine operational requirements in the form of pre- and trigger- conditions that are correct and complete with respect to a set of system goals. System goals are in the form of LTL formulas. The approach works incrementally by refining an existing partial specification of operational requirements, which is verified with respect to the system goal. The work in [24] focuses on the service-oriented computing paradigm and proposes an interesting approach to automatically generate behavioral interfaces of the partner services, by decomposing the requirements specification of a service composition.

Incremental and Compositional Verification: Authors of [15] present a framework for performing assume-guarantee reasoning in an incremental and fully automatic fashion. Assume-guarantee theory has been originally introduced in the thesis of Cliff Jones [25] and subsequently developed by many others, including Amir Pnueli [26]. In assume guarantee, the environment is represented as a set of properties that it should satisfy to correctly interact with the component. These properties are called assumptions, which means that they are the assumptions that a component makes on its environment. If these assumptions are satisfied by the environment, then the component that behaves in this environment will satisfy other properties, which are called guarantees. By combining the set of assume/guarantee properties in an appropriate way, it is possible to demonstrate the correctness of the entire system without constructing the complete system. The approach presented in [15] automatically generates, via a learning algorithm, assumptions that the environment needs to satisfy for the property to hold. These assumptions are initially approximate, but become gradually more precise by means of counter-examples obtained by model checking the component and its environment. In [27] authors observe that in reality, a component is only required to satisfy properties in certain specific environments. Then, they generate assumptions that exactly characterise those environments in which the component satisfies its required property.

Exception Processing: In Literature a number of approaches have been proposed to deal with the problem of processing exceptions, i.e., the management of abnormal conditions and errors that can occur during software executions. Such situation may include running out of memory, and resource allocation errors. In this context, in [28] the authors propose a layered software architecture that includes a recovery layer specifically conceived to manage faults. Such a layer executes recover meta programs implementing strategies able to automatize as much as possible the management of application faults. In [29] the author proposes the adoption of a recovery language to implement error recovery and reconfiguration procedures. In particular, the recovery language comes into play as soon as an error is detected by an underlying error detection layer, or when some erroneous condition is signalled by the application processes.

6   Conclusions and Future Work

In this paper we discussed how the resilience of critical systems can be constructed compositionally and incrementally out of the resilience of system parts. To this end, a general methodology has been introduced based on upfront specifications of the considered system that are refined into sub-specifications that are in turn amenable to manipulations and run-time monitoring activities. A concrete application of the methodology has been discussed in the domain of civilian monitoring missions that are executed by swarms of quadrotors. By relying on previous experiences of the authors (see [18]), we plan to (i) extend the current version of the FLYAQ platform in order to include the controllers of the drones described in Section 4.2 and the management of normal and abnormal behaviours based on an explicit and abstract representation of the system state, and (ii) to apply the implemented methodology to a real industrial case study.

References

1. Johnson, C.W.: What are emergent properties and how do they affect the engineering of complex systems? Reliability Engineering & System Safety 91(12), 1475–1481 (2006), Complexity in Design and Engineering

2. Inverardi, P., Autili, M., Di Ruscio, D., Pelliccione, P., Tivoli, M.: Producing software by integration: Challenges and research directions (keynote). In: Procs. of ESEC/FSE 2013, pp. 2–12. ACM (2013)

3. Alrajeh, D., Ray, O., Russo, A., Uchitel, S.: Using abduction and induction for operational requirements elaboration. Journal of Applied Logic 7(3), 275–288 (2009)

4. Letier, E., van Lamsweerde, A.: Deriving operational software specifications from system goals. In: Procs. of SIGSOFT 2002/FSE-10, pp. 119–128. ACM (2002)

5. Autili, M., Cortellessa, V., Di Ruscio, D., Inverardi, P., Pelliccione, P., Tivoli, M.: Eagle: Engineering software in the ubiquitous globe by leveraging uncertainty. In: Procs. of ESEC/FSE 2011, pp. 488–491. ACM (2011)

6. Garlan, D.: Software engineering in an uncertain world. In: Procs. of the FSE/SDP Workshop on Future of Software Engineering Research, FoSER 2010, pp. 125–128. ACM (2010)

7. Ghezzi, C.: Evolution, adaptation, and the quest for incrementality. In: Calinescu, R., Garlan, D. (eds.) Monterey Workshop 2012. LNCS, vol. 7539, pp. 369–379. Springer, Heidelberg (2012)

8. Gary, K., Enquobahrie, A., Ibanez, L., Cheng, P., Yaniv, Z., Cleary, K., Kokoori, S., Muffih, B., Heidenreich, J.: Agile methods for open source safety-critical software. Softw. Pract. Exper. 41(9), 945–962 (2011)

9. Ge, X., Paige, R., McDermid, J.: An iterative approach for development of safety-critical software and safety arguments. In: Agile Conf. (AGILE), pp. 35–43 (August 2010)

10. Leveson, N.G.: Software safety: Why, what, and how. ACM Comput. Surv. 18(2), 125–163 (1986)

11. Wolff, S.: Scrum goes formal: Agile methods for safety-critical systems. In: Software Engineering: Rigorous and Agile Approaches (FormSERA), pp. 23–29 (June 2012)

12. Lamport, L.: Specifying Systems: The TLA+ Language and Tools for Hardware and Software Engineers. Addison-Wesley Longman Publishing Co., Inc. (2002)

13. van Lamsweerde, A.: Goal-oriented requirements enginering: A roundtrip from research to practice. In: Procs. of RE 2004, pp. 4–7. IEEE Comp. Soc. (2004)

14. Meyer, B.: Object-oriented Software Construction, 2nd edn. Prentice-Hall, Inc. (1997)

15. Cobleigh, J.M., Giannakopoulou, D., Păsăreanu, C.S.: Learning assumptions for compositional verification. In: Garavel, H., Hatcliff, J. (eds.) TACAS 2003. LNCS, vol. 2619, pp. 331–346. Springer, Heidelberg (2003)

16. van Lamsweerde, A.: Requirements engineering in the year 00: A research perspective. In: Proc. of the 22nd Int. Conf. on Software Engineering, ICSE 2000, pp. 5–19. ACM (2000)

17. Cobleigh, J.M., Giannakopoulou, D., Păsăreanu, C.S.: Learning assumptions for compositional verification. In: Garavel, H., Hatcliff, J. (eds.) TACAS 2003. LNCS, vol. 2619, pp. 331–346. Springer, Heidelberg (2003)

18. Autili, M., Di Ruscio, D., Di Salle, A., Inverardi, P., Tivoli, M.: A model-based synthesis process for choreography realizability enforcement. In: Cortellessa, V., Varró, D. (eds.) FASE 2013. LNCS, vol. 7793, pp. 37–52. Springer, Heidelberg (2013)

19. Bucchiarone, A., Di Ruscio, D., Muccini, H., Pelliccione, P.: From Requirements to Java code: an Architecture-centric Approach for producing quality systems. In: Model-Driven Software Development: Integrating Quality Assurance (2008)
20. Rubira, C.M.F., de Lemos, R., Ferreira, G.R.M., Castor Filho, F.: Exception handling in the development of dependable component-based systems. Softw. Pract. Exper. 35(3), 195–236 (2005)
21. Lee, P.A., Anderson, T.: Fault Tolerance: Principles and Practice, 2nd edn. Springer (1990)
22. Di Ruscio, D., Malavolta, I., Pelliccione, P.: Engineering a platform for mission planning of autonomous and resilient quadrotors. In: Gorbenko, A., Romanovsky, A., Kharchenko, V. (eds.) SERENE 2013. LNCS, vol. 8166, pp. 33–47. Springer, Heidelberg (2013)
23. Di Ruscio, D., Malavolta, I., Pelliccione, P.: A family of domain-specific languages for specifying civilian missions of multi-robot systems. In: First Workshop on Model-Driven Robot Software Engineering - MORSE 2014 (2014)
24. Bianculli, D., Giannakopoulou, D., Păsăreanu, C.S.: Interface decomposition for service compositions. In: Procs. of ICSE 2011, pp. 501–510. ACM (2011)
25. Jones, C.: Development Methods for Computer Programs Including a Notion of Interference. PhD thesis. Oxford University Computing Laboratory, Programming Research Group (1981)
26. Pnueli, A.: Logics and models of concurrent systems, pp. 123–144. Springer (1985)
27. Giannakopoulou, D., Păsăreanu, C.S., Barringer, H.: Component verification with automatically generated assumptions. Automated Software Engg. 12(3), 297–320 (2005)
28. Clematis, A., Dodero, G., Gianuzzi, V.: Designing fault tolerant software with a recovery meta program. In: Proceedings of the Ninth Annual International Phoenix Conference on Computers and Communications, pp. 864–865 (March 1990)
29. Florio, V.D.: A Fault-Tolerance Linguistic Structure for Distributed Applications. PhD thesis, Katholieke Universiteit Leuven, ESAT Department, ACCA Division, 3000 Leuven, Belgium (October 2012)

Automatic Generation of Description Files
for Highly Available Services

Maxime Turenne[1], Ali Kanso[2], Abdelouahed Gherbi[1], and Ronan Barrett[3]

[1] Software and IT Engineering Department, École de Technologie Supérieure,
Montréal, Canada
`maxime.turenne.1@ens.etsmtl.ca, abdelouahed.gherbi@etsmtl.ca`
[2] Ericsson Research, Ericsson, Montréal, Canada
`ali.kanso@ericsson.com`
[3] Ericsson Development, Ericsson, Stockholm, Sweden
`ronan.barrett@ericsson.com`

Abstract. Highly available services are becoming a part of our everyday life; yet building highly available systems remains a challenging task for most system integrators who are expected build reliable systems from none reliable components. The service availability forum (SAForum) defines open standards for building and maintaining HA systems using the SAForum middleware. Nevertheless this task remains tedious and error prone due to the complexity of this middleware configuration. In this paper, we present a solution to automate the generation of description files for HA systems which enables the automated generation of the middleware configuration. In order to achieve this we propose an approach based on a new domain specific language extending the UML component diagrams, along with a corresponding set of model transformations. We also present our prototype implementation and a case study as a proof of concept.

Keywords: High Availability, Model Driven Software Engineering, Unified Modeling Language, UML component diagrams, SAForum standards.

1   Introduction

The Information and Communications Technology (ICT) sector has witnessed a significant change over the last decade, where we see the advent of new service delivery models over broadband access. This means that more revenue generating and critical applications are being delivered using ICT systems. The High Availability (HA) of such systems is an essential non-functional requirement that the service providers aim to achieve. Nonetheless software developers and system integrators still find it challenging to design and implement HA systems. Moreover, the classic HA solutions have suffered from platform dependencies and vendor lock-in. To address this issue, the Service Availability Forum (SAForum)[1] [1] was established by world leading telecom and computing companies in an effort to standardize the way HA systems are

---

[1] The SAForum is a consortium of industry-leading companies including HP, Motorola, Ericsson and others working towards a unified view for achieving carrier-grade service availability.

I. Majzik and M. Vieira (Eds.): SERENE 2014, LNCS 8785, pp. 40–54, 2014.
© Springer International Publishing Switzerland 2014

built, and enable the portability and interoperability of highly available services across any platform compliant with the standards. In fact, the SAForum establishes a set of specifications defining standard Application Programming Interfaces (APIs), and guidelines to develop and deploy highly available systems. These specifications also define the architecture of a middleware (i.e. the SAForum middleware) capable of maintaining a cluster of servers and the services they host highly available. More specifically, the middleware is a distributed application deployed across the cluster's nodes. At runtime, the middleware will monitor the components providing the services, and in case a failure is detected, the middleware will automatically clean up the faulty components, fail over the services provided by the faulty component to a healthy replica, and attempt to repair the faulty component.

The Availability Management Framework (AMF) [2] constitutes the core of the SAForum middleware. It is AMF that maintains the HA in the cluster and reacts to failures. AMF's runtime behavior is mainly based on a configuration file (referred to as the AMF configuration) defined by the system integrator(s) designing the HA solution. The AMF configuration specifies the software components that AMF will instantiate at runtime, and defines the redundancy scheme employed (active/active, active/standby etc.), and the default recovery action for a given component, as well as the escalation policy in case the recovery action fails. In order to define the AMF configuration, the system integrator needs to refer to the types description file[2] [3]. The types description file is provided by software vendors/providers to describe the software that will be managed by the SAForum middleware. This types description file will describe the type of the software in terms of the service types it can provide and in which capacity, as well as its dependencies and deployment limitations. The format of the types description file is defined by a standardized XML schema [3], and the content should comply with a set of informally described constraints in two different SAForum specifications [2], [4]. The manual definition of the types description file is a tedious and error prone task that requires deep knowledge of the specification details that many software developers do not necessarily have. In fact, the developers not only need to understand the structure of the elements of this file, but they should also respect the domain constraints that are spread across hundreds of pages in the specifications. In this paper, we present an alternative and more intuitive approach for the automatic generation of the types description file. Our approach is based on a high-level modeling language that software developers can easily understand, and that abstracts the domain specific details that our approach automatically generates. More specifically, our approach is based on extending the UML component diagrams [5] to enable expressing the requirements of our domain. In addition, we define a sequence of model transformations that eventually yield to the generation of the types description file. Our contribution will: (1) enable the system integrators to automatically generate middleware configurations; (2) enable the software vendors to describe their software in a SAForum compliant manner using an approach that facilitates the creation and validation of types description files.

---

[2] The formal name is the Entity Types File (ETF), for the sake of clarity, we will use the terms types description file and ETF file interchangeably.

This paper is organized as follows: in Section 2 we present the background to our work. Section 3 illustrates our approach, and the methodology we followed. In Section 4 we detail prototype implementation. We survey the related work in Section 5. Finally, we conclude and discuss the future directions in Section 6.

2   Background

2.1   The AMF Configuration

Achieving HA by means of dedicated middleware deployments such as [6,7,8] has been long used in the industry. Using such technologies also requires defining a system configuration describing the various elements to be managed. The AMF configuration, however, demarks itself through two main differentiating elements: (1) the service and the entity providing the service are logically decoupled from a configuration stand point. (2) The AMF configuration supports the hierarchical composition of services. In other terms, it acknowledges the fact that multiple inter-dependent components can collaborate to provide a more comprehensive service.

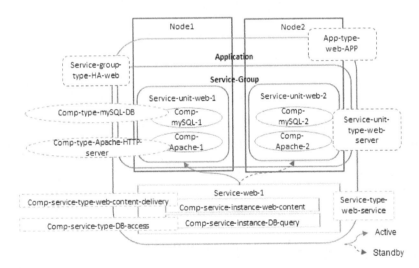

Fig. 1. AMF configuration example

Fig. 1 illustrates a simplified example that shows the main elements of the AMF configuration. This example is made of four components deployed on two nodes. The dashed figures represent the type of the element represented by the figure of the same color. At the bottom we have the elements that represent the abstraction of the service provided by the above components. The hierarchical composition of services is reflected in this example by the fact that providing a web service is rarely made by only one type of component, but with a grouping of components that together provide a higher level of service. This is why this configuration is organised in two service units (web-1 and web-2) providing the service (web-1).

Based on the types description file (henceforth referred to as the Entity Types File: ETF) defined by the software vendor, the system integrator can create a configuration that satisfies his/her service needs. In a previous work [9,10], we defined and implemented an automated approach allowing for this configuration generation. Our approach was based on the assumption that the configuration generator would use an existing ETF file and high level service requirements in order to generate the configuration, as shown in Fig. 2.[3]

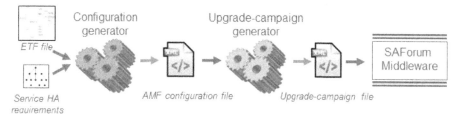

Fig. 2. Previous configuration generation approach

2.2   The Entity Types File

The types used in the AMF configuration and the upgrade campaign description files are directly derived from the types defined in the ETF file. Since the XML schema can only describe the structural aspect of the ETF file, the constraints capturing the semantics of the domain are informally described in the AMF and SMF specifications. As a result, in order to create a valid ETF file, the software developer needs to acquire deep domain knowledge. In a previous work [11], a UML domain model for ETF has been defined. This domain model captures the elements described in the standardized schema along with domain constraints. While this helps in validating instances of this domain model, the complexity of defining such instances is not significantly reduced since this domain model did not abstract the schema details any further. The domain model is essentially a one to one mapping of the ETF schema concepts, and therefore, using this domain model would require the same level of knowledge of the specification as using of the schema. Moreover, since in a given system various software applications each composed of multiple components are used, defining the instance of the domain model for such large applications manually is a complex task. Therefore, the automatic generation of the ETF is needed by the community of practitioners using the SAForum middleware.

---

[3] Note that the configuration can be directly passed to the middleware in case of initial system deployment. In case of upgrade, the new configuration is passed to the upgrade campaign generator that can detect the changes compared to the current one, and generates an upgrade campaign file accordingly.

3   Approach for the Automatic Generation of ETF File

In order to automate the generation of ETF files, we propose a software developer friendly approach. This is achieved by minimizing the exposure of the software developer to the language of the SAForum domain and instead shifting to a language that is more intuitive to software developers. The main idea is to map the functionality and architecture of the actual software into the ETF file, while abstracting the low level details of the ETF domain from the developer. This abstraction is done by: (1) using intuitive UML-based constructs to model the content of ETF; and (2) automating the generation of the information that can be inferred from the basic elements of the ETF concepts. We defined our approach by closely examining the semantic similarities between the ETF file, which is mainly composed of the component types and the component-service-types they provide, and the UML component diagram which specifies the components and their interfaces. The interface is typically associated with a given functionality that the component provides, hence, there is an analogy between the concepts of the component-service-type and the interface. Moreover, the component-type bears a similar meaning to the UML component[4] in terms of providing certain functionalities and requiring others. Therefore, we decided to use the UML component diagram to model the content of the ETF files. However, the UML component diagram expressiveness capability is only limited to basic components providing and requiring basic interfaces. Therefore, we needed to extend the UML components diagram with other constructs that allow us to express the requirements of our domain. We defined a Domain Specific Language (DSL) with the objective of allowing the designer to specify the content of the ETF file using a familiar UML component diagram syntax. Starting from models expressed using this DSL, we automatically generate the ETF XML file through a series of model transformations. During these transformations, we use the domain model defined by [11] as an intermediate model. The domain constraints integrated in our DSL are automatically checked during the design process to ensure that the designer's model is valid. This model gets then transformed to an instance of the ETF domain model. The generated ETF domain model instance then gets transformed to the ETF XML file. Fig. 4 presents the different steps followed to generate the ETF file. We implemented our approach using the following methodology:

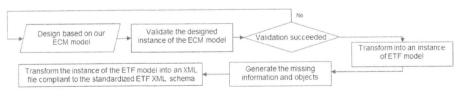

Fig. 3. The ETF generation approach

---

[4] In this section we use the term component type and the UML component interchangeably, since in our DSL, the UML component represents the component type of the software.

1. Extend the UML component diagram with the new domain specific constructs. This consti-tutes the concrete syntax of our DSL.
2. Define the metamodel of our DSL which henceforth is referred to as the ETF Component Model (ECM). This metamodel formally captures the added extensions.
3. Define the OCL constraints reflecting the domain constraints and add them to our DSL metamodel.
4. Define the transformation algorithms to transform an instance of our ECM into an ETF XML file.

3.1   Adding the Domain Specific Constructs to the UML Component Diagram

In Subsection 2.1, we presented the different component categories specified in the SAForum specifications. The ETF schema also allows the specification of the component type's dependency, where the dependent and the sponsor component need to be placed on the same node, and more specifically in the same service-unit. Since the UML component diagram does not consider the notion of a component category nor the "Colocation Dependency", we had to extend it with these constructs to express the specifics of our domain as shown in Fig. 5.

The SAF interface is used to denote that a given component type implements the SAForum APIs. Therefore, when the designer specifies that a component provides the SAF Interface this implies that the component is SA-aware. A component type providing the Proxy Interface implies that this component type is a proxy for another component type that requires this interface. In order to implement the Proxy Interface, the component type must already implement the SAF Interface, since it must be SA-aware to be able to proxy a proxied component type. By requiring the Proxy Interface, the component type automatically becomes a proxied component type, and therefore the constraints of the proxied apply to this component type. We apply the same logic for the container interface, where the component requiring this interface are considered contained. The regular interface notation is used to represent the component-service-type that the component type provides. The Colocation Dependency may exist between the require interface and the provide interface to denote that a given component provides a given interface only if another component provides another interface.

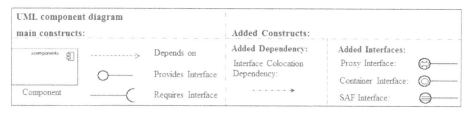

Fig. 4. The main added constructs to the UML component diagram

3.2   Defining the ECM Metamodel

The metamodel of our DSL, the ECM, is mainly composed of two packages, the *Components* and the *Interfaces* as shown in Fig. 6. The *Interfaces* package has the *Interface* class at the top of the hierarchy. Since the *SAFInterface* (i.e. the SAForum APIs) is not associated with a specific workload at runtime, i.e. we do not provide a service through this interface, it specializes the class *Interface* directly without having any attributes. In other words, this interface exists to help categorizing the component rather than the service. On the other hand, the *Proxy, Container*, and *Regular* interfaces are associated with a workload at runtime, and since they describe the service provided by the component, they inherit from the *ServiceInterface* which specializes the Class *Interface*. The *RegularInterface* represents the component-service-type that any component can provide, e.g. the SQL interface provided by a database management system can be modeled as a *RegularInterface* while the Proxy and Container Interfaces are reserved for the specific services of proxying another component or the containment of another component.

The *Components* package revolves around the *Component* class which specifies the attributes that any AMF managed component must have regardless of its category, such attributes include the default recovery on error that the middleware must follow to recover the component from failure and the timeout duration after which the middleware assumes the component is faulty since it failed to respond to a middleware request. The component class is specialized by three other classes that better categorize the component where each class includes the relevant attributes. The *NonProxiedNonSaAwareComponent* denotes the components not providing the *SAFInterface* and not requiring the ProxyInterface. The *ProxiedComponent* denotes the components requiring the *ProxyInterface*. Finally, the *SaAwareComponent* denotes the components implementing the *SAFInterface* and it is further specialized by the *ContainedComponent* and the *IndependentComponent*. Our Component hierarchy is a simplification of the one defined in the ETF domain model, since in our metamodel we can infer certain categorizations based on the interface provided by the component, e.g. we do not need the Proxy component class since it does not have any unique attributes, and we can automatically infer that a component is a proxy if it provides the *ProxyInterface*. In fact, due to the definition of the various types of interfaces, the designer is unaware of the different component classes we define at the back end; hence we can abstract the details of the domain from the designer while staying aligned with SAForum concepts since the designer will only use the generic component element in his/her design as we will illustrate in Subsection 4.2.

We capture the Colocation Dependency by the reflexive association in the *ComponentService* association class between the *Component* and the *ServiceInterface*. Finally, it should be noted that each *component* must belong to a *SoftwareBundle* which provides a placeholder for information about the installation and removal of the software that is needed for the automatic runtime installation and upgrade of the software.

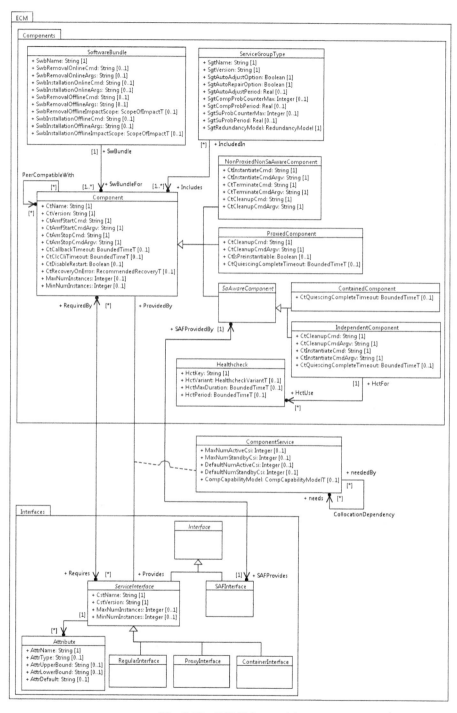

Fig. 5. The ECM Metamodel

3.3   Defining the OCL Constraints

The structural modeling of our ECM model cannot capture all the constraints of the SAForum domain. Therefore, we needed to annotate our model in a formal manner with the domain constraints. We use OCL to express those constraints since OCL is the de facto language to express constraints on UML models. To avoid redefining all the OCL constraints from scratch, we aimed at reusing the constraints defined by [11] on the ETF domain model. Nevertheless, since our model is structurally different and has fewer classes and some different concepts, we had to redefine those OCL constraints for our ECM metamodel. The fact that the constraints are well documented in [11] simplified the process of defining our OCL constraints.

Fig. 7 shows one of our OCL constraints ensuring that the contained and container components do not have colocation dependencies, since according to the specifications they are not allowed to be in the same service-unit.

It is worth noting that not all the domain constraints can be integrated with our ECM metamodel, since some of them are in the context of ETF types that are specified in the ETF model, but not in our ECM. Therefore, we embed such constraints in our transformation methods in order to generate a complete and valid instance of the ETF model by construction as we will explain in the next subsection.

```
context ContainedComponent
invariant C_CT1: self.componentServiceProvides
    ->forAll(cs : ComponentService | cs.needs
        ->forAll(cs2 : ComponentService | cs2.ProvidedBy
            ->forAll(c : Component | c.oclIsTypeOf(ContainedComponent)))));
context ContainedComponent
invariant C_CT2: self.componentServiceProvides
    ->forAll(cs : ComponentService | cs.neededBy
        ->forAll(cs2 : ComponentService | cs2.ProvidedBy
            ->forAll(c : Component | c.oclIsTypeOf(ContainedComponent)))));
```

Fig. 6. The Container/Contained OCL constraints

3.4   Defining the Transformation Algorithm

Our ETF generation process is based on two model-to-model transformations. In the first transformation, we generate an instance of the ETF domain model and in the second one we generate an instance of the ETF schema.

In the first transformation, we start from a validated ECM model. As a first step, we transform the Components, Interfaces, software bundle into component-types, component-service-types, and software bundle that are defined in the ETF domain model. This is a one to one mapping. The second step is to generate the types that we chose not to include in our ECM metamodel since we can automatically infer them. These types include the service-unit types and the service-types. We use the dependencies defined in the ECM model (i.e. an instance of our ECM metamodel) to guide us through this generation. The Colocation Dependency that we created in our ECM metamodel is not only mapped into the component-type dependency that is specified in ETF domain model, but it also indicates that the sponsor and the dependent must be grouped in the same service-unit type. Therefore, we use this information to generate the service-unit-type. After the creation of the service-unit-types, we target the generation of the service-types. For that purpose, we look into the interfaces provided by the components with collocated dependencies, and group their corresponding component-service-types to generate the service-type provided by the service-unit-type. The require dependencies are mapped into the service-type dependency specified at the service-unit-type level in ETF domain model, whereas a service-unit-type can provide a service-type if another service-type is being provided.

In the third step, we generate the service-group-types and the application-types. In the case where the designer specifies in the ECM model a service-group-type with a specific redundancy model grouping the ECM components that should belong to this type, we generate a corresponding ETF service-group-type. This generated service-group-type will group the service-unit-types grouping the corresponding component-types. In the case where the designer does not specify the service-group-type, then the generation of the service-group-types and the application types becomes optional in our approach. This is because the ETF specification does not require the existence of these types. Hence, we leave the decision of setting the preferences of the generation method to the software designer. All the generated types are valid by construction since we embedded the ETF domain model constraints in the transformation methods. Once the instance of the ETF domain model is generated, we define another transformation that maps the elements of this instance into the elements of an instance of the ETF schema. The rationale behind using this multi-step transformation instead of directly generating the ETF file from an ECM model can be summarized as follows: (1) Our ECM metamodel does not include all the ETF types and their corresponding constraints (e.g. the service-unit-types), hence we can benefit from the existing ETF domain model where we can embed the OCL constraints of this domain model in our transformation methods generating the added types and thus ensuring the validity of our created types. (2) The transformation becomes more intuitive since the ECM metamodel and the ETF domain model are both defined in UML. (3) The transformation from an instance of the ETF domain model to an instance ETF schema (i.e. the XML file carrying the ETF file) is rather simple since the two include the same concepts.

4   Prototype Implementation

We tested our work by implementing a fully functional prototype. The prototype fully implements our ECM metamodel and can do a complete transformation between the ECM metamodel and the ETF domain model. The implementation of the ECM includes all the OCL constraints that we defined for our DSL. As a result, the prototype can validate any ECM metamodel instance before the transformation and once validated, all instance of the ECM can be transformed into a valid ETF file. Moreover, we implemented the ETF domain model with all its OCL constraints, and the complete transformation to the ETF schema. The overall process is shown in Fig. 8.

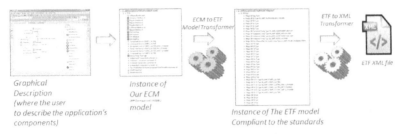

Graphical
Description
(where the user
to describe the application's
components)

Instance of
Our ECM
model

ECM to ETF
Model Transformer

Instance of The ETF model
Compliant to the standards

ETF to XML
Transformer

ETF XML file

Fig. 7. Workflow of our prototype tool

4.1   Technology

We used open source technologies for our prototype. We used the Eclipse Modeling Framework (EMF) [12] as our modeling infrastructure. We implemented our ECM metamodel using Papyrus [13]. Papyrus is an EMF-based Eclipse plug-in which offers advanced support of UML modeling and profiling. Since Papyrus had at the time of the development limited support for the graphical modeling and DSL representation, we used Eclipse Graphical Modeling Framework (GMF) for the graphical design of our ECM concrete syntax. Fig. 8 shows a snapshot of our GMF-based graphical modeling tool. On the right hand side palette, we can see the elements showing the concrete syntax of our DSL, including the various interfaces. On the left hand side, we have the canvas where the designer can draw the ECM model. We used the OCLinEcore Eclipse plugin [14] which allows the integration of our constraints with our Ecore model (derived from the Papyrus UML model) for the ECM metamodel.

4.2   Use Case

As a use case, we defined a software architecture of four components representing a web application. At the front-end we have an HTTP-server component, this component forward user requests to an App-server component that can dynamically create HTML content based on the request. The user data is stored in a database (DB) component by the App-server. Each of the components provides a ServiceInterface reflecting its functionality (respectively HTTP-i, App-i, DB-i). Our HTTP-server is a stateless component that does not need to communicate with the middleware, therefore it is a non-proxied-non-SA-aware component and thus does not implement the SAFInterface, and neither does it require any ProxyInterfce. However, in order to provide its service, the HTTP-server requires the App-server functionality and consequently, it requires the App-i. The App-server is an SA-aware component that implements the SAForum APIs and hence, it provides the SAFInterface. Moreover, it requires a functional DB in order to process requests involving user data, and therefore, it requires the DB-i. For performance purposes, the App-server and the DB must be collocated, and because of that, the Collocation Dependency between the App-i and the DB-i is used. We assume that the DB is a legacy implementation which does not implement the SAFInterface, but can be pre-instantiated, and supports the active/standby operational mode. Therefore, it is a good candidate for being a

ProxiedComponent which requires the ProxyInterface P-i. Our fourth component, the DB-proxy, is defined to proxy the interactions between the DB and the SAForoum middleware. As a result, the DB-proxy implements the SAFInterface as well as the ProxyInterface P-i.

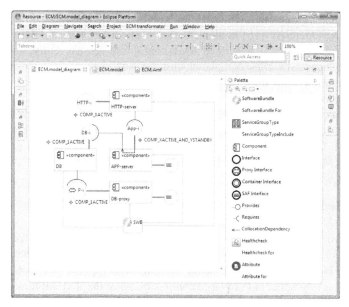

Fig. 8. Snapshot of the tool editor GUI and a use case of the ECM model

Our graphical GMF representation of the model gets automatically transformed into an instance of the Ecore representation of our metamodel. This transformation is done using GMF built-in mechanisms. Our transformation algorithms are then triggered to generate an instance of the ETF domain model, i.e. an Ecore instance of the Ecore representation we defined for the ETF domain model. Thereafter, our second transformation will transform the Ecore instance of the ETF model to an Ecore instance of the ETF XML schema. The latter Ecore instance is then serialized into an ETF XML file.

4.3   Evaluation

Mastering the SAForum domain is not an easy task considering the size and the complexity of the SAForum specifications. Any mistakes made during the design phases of the middleware configuration could lead to the generation of a flawed configuration file or even worst, causing unwanted outage of the service. Therefore, we validated our work by first having the different ECM domain constraints along with the methodology and the transformation steps deeply analyzed by SAForum domain experts. Mainly, the constraints defined for the ECM metamodel have been validated in order to avoid any false assumption about the SAForum domain and similarly, the algorithm of the ECM metamodel to ETF domain model transformation was re-viewed.

Secondly, we performed a practical validation by testing our ETF generation with various use cases where we generated ETF files describing new applications. Furthermore, these ETF files were used as input for the AMF configuration generation tool [10] for generating new AMF configurations and finally, we tested these configurations with the OpenSAF [16] implementation of the SAForum middleware in order to validate the automatically generated AMF configurations. Currently, the ECM tool prototype produces ETF files compliant with the ETF schema and accepted by the AMF configuration generation tool allowing this latter to generate a complete AMF configuration compliant with the OpenSAF middleware.

Finally, since we could not find in the literature any other tools capable of automatically generating ETF files, our tool significantly reduces the time and complexity of designing ETF files within a few minutes compared to the manual error prone definition of such XML file based on the ETF schema.

5   Related Work

In previous works [9,10], we presented an approach for the automatic generation of configurations and upgrade campaign files. In those works, we made the assumption that a valid ETF file already exists, and can be used as input to our tools. However, we realized that in practice: (1) In large companies using the SAForum middleware, a big portion of the software is developed in-house, and therefore the software vendor or provider and the software user or maintainer are the same company. (2) Even software vendors developing SAForum compliant software prefer to shield their developers from having to manually create and validate ETF files. (3) The use case of using a proxy to allow the SAForum middleware to manage legacy software (non-SAForum compliant) is widely spread, and requires the existence of an ETF file to generate the AMF configuration that includes the legacy applications. For all those reasons, we decided to extend the previous tool chain shown in Fig. 2 to include one more step for the automatic generation of the ETF file.

The work presented in [11], that we discussed in Subsection 2.2, was a first step towards capturing the domain constraints in a formal way. Nevertheless, it did not reduce the complexity of defining a new ETF file, since the same domain concepts are reused in a different format being the UML profile instead of the XML schema. Moreover, this work did not target the automation of generating ETF files and it mainly focused in the validation of such files, when described according to the created profile. We believe and consider our work as the logical evolution of the first attempt made in [11], whereby our main objective is the design automation of ETF files. We benefitted from this work by using their ETF domain model in an intermediate step to generate our ETF file.

Existing open source implementations of the SAForum middleware such as [15,16] do not support the automatic generation of ETF files and they only provide limited support for the automatic generation of AMF configurations for domain experts. In the work presented in [18,19] the authors use a model driven approach (MDA) in order to develop software applications that can interface with the SAForum. These works did not target the issue of generating AMF configurations that satisfy HA user requirements, nor do they provide any support for generating ETF files that can be used by software vendors.

Several works target the extension of the UML component diagram for different purposes. In [23], the authors extend the component diagram to include the distribution requirements in the early design phase of the software. In [24], the authors define a component-based UML model to capture the requirements of a real-time system that can later on be transformed into a platform specific model. In [25], the authors present an extension to the UML component diagram allowing the specification and analysis of the stakeholders' requirements. These work relate to our approach from the perspective of extending the UML component diagram to satisfy certain domain requirements, however, none of them target the HA domain, nor the generation of middleware configurations.

6   Conclusion and Future Work

In this paper, we presented an approach for the automated generation of ETF files. This automation is useful for both (1) software vendors required to include an ETF description with their SAForum compliant software. (2) For system integrators since it enables the full automation of the SAForum middleware configuration generation based on high level HA requirements. Our approach is based on extending the UML component diagram with new constructs capturing the concepts of our domain, and thereafter performing a series of model transformation to generate the ETF XML file. As a future work, we intend to apply the same approach in the definition of the service HA requirements, where we allow the use of our extended component model to specify the HA and other non-functional requirements expected from each interface.

Acknowledgments. This work is partially supported by the Natural Sciences and Engineering Research Council of Canada (NSERC) and Ericsson Research.

References

1. Service Availability Forum, Application Interface Specification, http://www.saforum.org
2. Service Availability Forum, Application Interface Specification. Availability Management Framework SAI-AIS-AMF-B.04.01, http://www.saforum.org (accessed: April 2013)
3. Service Availability Forum, Entity Types File Schema SAI-AIS-SMF-ETF-A.01.02.xsd
4. Service Availability Forum, Application Interface Specification. Software Management Framework SAI-AIS-SMF-A.01.01
5. The Unified Modeling Language, http://www.uml.org/

6. Fault-Tolerant CORBA Specifications, `http://www.omg.org/technology/documents/corba_spec_catalog.htm`
7. LinuxHA project, `http://www.linux-ha.org`
8. Pacemaker project, `http://clusterlabs.org/`
9. Kanso, A., Hamou-Lhadj, A., Toeroe, M., Khendek, F.: Generating AMF Configurations from *Software Vendor Constraints and User Requirements*. In: Proc. of the Forth International Conference on Availability, Reliability and Security, Fukuoka, Japan, pp. 454–461 (2009)
10. Gherbi, A., Kanso, A., Khendek, F., Hamou-Lhadj, A., Toeroe, M.: A Tool Suite for the Generation and Validation of Configurations for Software Availability. In: Proc. of 24th IEEE/ACM International Conference on Automated Software Engineering, ASE 2009, November 16-20, pp. 671–673 (2009)
11. Salehi, P.: A Model Based Framework for Service Availability Management. PhD thesis, Concordia University (2012)
12. Steinberg, D., Budinsky, F., Merks, E., Paternostro, M.: EMF: eclipse modeling framework. Pearson Education (2008)
13. Papyrus Eclipse Project, `https://www.eclipse.org/papyrus/`
14. Eclipse OCL in Ecore, `http://wiki.eclipse.org/OCL/OCLinEcore`
15. SAFplus implementation, `http://openclovis.com/products/index.htm`
16. OpenSAF foundation, `http://www.opensaf.org/`
17. Salehi, P., Colombo, P., Hamou-Lhadj, A., Khendek, F.: A Model Driven Approach for AMF Configuration Generation. In: Kraemer, F.A., Herrmann, P. (eds.) SAM 2010. LNCS, vol. 6598, pp. 124–143. Springer, Heidelberg (2011)
18. Kövi, A., Varró, D.: An Eclipse-Based Framework for AIS Service Configurations. In: Malek, M., Reitenspieß, M., van Moorsel, A. (eds.) ISAS 2007. LNCS, vol. 4526, pp. 110–126. Springer, Heidelberg (2007)
19. Szatmári, Z., Kövi, A., Reitenspiess, M.: Applying MDA approach for the SA forum platform. In: Proceedings of the 2nd Workshop on Middleware-application Interaction: Affiliated with the DisCoTec Federated Conferences, Oslo, Norway, June 03 (2008)
20. Sahai, A., Singhal, S., Machiraju, V.: Automated Generation of Resource Configurations through Policies. In: Proceedings of the Fifth IEEE International Workshop on Policies for Distributed Systems and Networks, June 07-09, p. 107 (2004)
21. Felfernig, A., Friedrich, G.E., Jannach, D.: UML as Domain Specific Language for the Construction of Knowledge-Based Configuration Systems. Int. Journal of Soft. Eng. Knowl. Eng. 10, 449 (2000)
22. Guozheng, G., Whitehead, E.J.: Automatic generation of rule-based software configuration management systems. In: Proceedings of the 27th International Conference on Software Engineering, ICSE 2005, May 15-21, p. 659 (2005)
23. Espindola, A.P., Becker, K., Zorzo, A.: An extension to UML components to consider distribution issues in early phases of application development. In: Proceedings of the 37th Annual Hawaii International Conference on System Sciences (2004)
24. Lu, S., Halang, W., Zhang, L.: A component-based UML profile to model embedded real-time systems designed by the MDA approach. In: Proceedings of the 11th IEEE International Conference on Embedded and Real-Time Computing Systems and Applications, August 17-19, pp. 563–566 (2005)
25. Mahmood, S., Lai, R.: RE-UML: An Extension to UML for Specifying Component-Based Software System. In: Proceedings of the Australian Software Engineering Conference, ASWEC 2009, April 14-17, pp. 220–228 (2009)

Modelling Resilience of Data Processing Capabilities of CPS

Linas Laibinis[1], Dmitry Klionskiy[2], Elena Troubitsyna[1], Anatoly Dorokhov[2], Johan Lilius[1], and Mikhail Kupriyanov[2]

[1] Åbo Akademi University, Turku, Finland
[2] Saint Petersburg Electrotechnical University "LETI" (SPbETU),
Saint Petersburg, Russian Federation
{linas.laibinis,elena.troubitsyna,johan.lilius}@abo.fi,
klio2003@list.ru, avdorokhov@yandex.ru, mskupriyanov@mail.ru

Abstract. Modern CPS should process large amount of data with high speed and reliability. To ensure that the system can handle varying volumes of data, the system designers usually rely on the architectures with the dynamically scaling degree of parallelism. However, to guarantee resilience of data processing, we should also ensure system fault tolerance, i.e., integrate the mechanisms for dynamic reconfiguration. In this paper, we present an approach to formal modelling and assessment of reconfigurable dynamically scaling systems that guarantees resilience of data processing. We rely on modelling in Event-B to formally define the dynamic system architecture with the integrated dynamically scaling parallelism and reconfiguration. The formal development allows us to derive a complex system architecture and verify its correctness. To quantitatively assess resilience of data processing architecture, we rely on statistical model checking and evaluate the likelihood of successful data processing under different system parameters. The proposed integrated approach facilitates design space exploration and improves predictability in the development of complex data processing capabilities.

Keywords: Formal modelling, Event-B, statistical model-checking.

1 Introduction

Since large volumes of data are generated from monitoring the system internal state and its external environment, development of Cyber-Physical Systems (CPS) puts an increasing emphasis on designing powerful data processing capabilities [4]. Data are received in batches of varying volumes and often should be pre-processed by a data processing (sub-)system, e.g., to filter out noise and derive a compact data representation. Since processed data are used by a CPS at run-time to decide on its actions, we should guarantee a sufficiently high probability of successful processing of each batch of data by a certain deadline.

To achieve this goal, usually data processing systems rely on dynamically scaling architectures that change the degree of parallelism according to the volume

I. Majzik and M. Vieira (Eds.): SERENE 2014, LNCS 8785, pp. 55–70, 2014.
© Springer International Publishing Switzerland 2014

of received data [5]. However, to guarantee resilience of data processing systems, we should also ensure their fault tolerance, i.e., allow the system to dynamically reconfigure to cope with failures of processing components.

In this paper, we propose an integrated approach to modelling data processing capabilities of CPS and assessing their resilience. We rely on formal modelling in Event-B to derive the dynamic system architecture. Event-B [1] is a state-based approach to correct-by-construction system development. System development starts from an abstract specification that is gradually transformed into a detailed system model. Correctness of each model transformation is verified by proofs. The Rodin platform [6] provides us with a powerful automated support for modelling and verification in Event-B.

Our modelling starts with a high-level specification that abstractly represents the main steps of data processing and their properties. In a number of refinement steps, we introduce the detailed representation of the control flow as well as define the mechanisms for scaling the degree of parallelism and reconfiguration. The resultant Event-B model ensures the essential logical properties of the data processing system – correctness of the implementation of the data flow, dynamic scaling and fault tolerance. Rigorous development by refinement allows us to efficiently handle complexity of the data processing architecture and formally reason about the interplay of parallelism and fault tolerance.

To analyse whether the derived architecture satisfies the resilience requirements, we also need to assess the likelihood of successful completion of data processing under given probabilities of component failures. To achieve this, we project the obtained Event-B model into the statistical UPPAAL [7] (UPPAAL-SMC) and experiment with different parameters. Such a quantitative analysis helps us to choose the architecture with the desirable resilience characteristics. We believe that the proposed approach facilitates design space exploration and improves predictability in developing data processing capabilities of CPS.

The paper is structured as follows. In Section 2 we give a brief overview of Event-B. In Sections 3 and 4 we demonstrate how to derive a dynamically scaling reconfigurable architecture of a data processing system. In Section 5, we present the system model in UPPAAL-SMC and demonstrate its use for assessing resilience of various system configurations. Finally, in Section 6 we overview the related work and discuss the proposed approach.

2   Event-B: Background Overview

Event-B [1] is a state-based formal approach that promotes the correct-by-construction development paradigm and formal verification by theorem proving. In Event-B, a system model (*abstract state machine*) encapsulates the model state, represented as a collection of variables, and defines operations on the state, i.e., it describes the dynamic behaviour of a modelled system. The variables are strongly typed by the constraining predicates that together with other important properties of the systems are defined in the model *invariants*. Usually, a machine has an accompanying component, called *context*, which includes user-defined sets, constants and their properties given as a list of model axioms.

The dynamic behaviour of the system is defined by a set of atomic *events*. Generally, an event has the following form:

$$e \mathrel{\widehat{=}} \textbf{any } a \textbf{ where } G_e \textbf{ then } R_e \textbf{ end},$$

where e is the event's name, a is the list of local variables, the *guard* G_e is a predicate over both local and global system variables. The body of an event is defined by a *multiple* (possibly nondeterministic) assignment over the system variables. In Event-B, an assignment represents a corresponding next-state relation R_e. The guard defines the conditions under which the event is *enabled*, i.e., its body can be executed. If several events are enabled at the same time, any of them can be chosen for execution nondeterministically.

Event-B employs a top-down refinement-based approach to system development. Development starts from an abstract specification that nondeterministically models the most essential functional requirements. In a sequence of refinement steps we gradually reduce nondeterminism and introduce detailed design decisions. In particular, we can add new events, split events as well as replace abstract variables by their concrete counterparts, i.e., perform *data refinement*.

The consistency of Event-B models, i.e., verification of well-formedness and invariant preservation as well as correctness of refinement steps, is demonstrated by discharging the relevant proof obligations. The Rodin platform [6] provides an automated support for modelling and verifying. In particular, it automatically generates the required proof obligations and attempts to discharge them.

Event-B adopts an event-based modelling style that facilitate a correct-by-construction development of parallel and distributed systems. Since a data processing system is an example of such systems, Event-B is a natural choice for its formal modelling and verification. In the next section, we present our approach to modelling data processing in Event-B.

3   Abstract Modelling of a Data Processing System

Data Processing Capabilities. Data processing (sub)-system[1] is an important part of a wide class of CPS [4]. Though specific characteristics of data processing may vary, the general purpose is common for the majority of applications. It includes receiving batches of data, pre-processing them (e.g., to filter our noise), and producing a compact data representation to be used as an input for the control functions of CPS.

To guarantee timeliness, each data batch should be processed by a certain deadline. Typically the steps of data processing are computationally-intensive and the system relies on parallel execution to meet the required deadlines. Since the volume of data to be processed varies, the system dynamically adjusts the degree of parallelism to ensure timely output of the results. Due to failures or temporal unavailability of computational resources, sometimes data processing might fail. Yet, the system should ensure a sufficiently low probability of failure – the goal achievable with integration of fault tolerance mechanisms.

---

[1] Since modelling of data processing is our focus, further we refer to it as *the data processing system*.

In this paper, we generalise on our experience in modelling and assessment of a multi-channel data processing of acoustic data – a sub-system of a complex floating oil refinery. The data processing is based on the wavelet-based approach for decomposition of telemetric signals [3]. Different modes of system operation result in significantly varying data volumes to be processed. The system relies on the dynamic scaling of parallelism to ensure the required performance. The pressing demand to improve resilience of the system has motivated our work on augmenting data processing with fault tolerance. The resulting dynamic behaviour of the system is complex, with a tangled control flow and intricate interplay between the dynamic parallelism and reconfiguration. To ensure correctness of such a complex system, we relied on formal modelling and refinement to derive the system architecture in a systematic way and verify its correctness.

In this paper, we omit the details specific to a particular data processing system (e.g., noise filtering methods, data compression algorithms) and present a generic development approach that can be applied to design an architecture of resilient data processing. The aim of our formal development is to derive the dynamically-scaling system architecture augmented with fault tolerance capabilities. We focus on modelling and verifying the following main aspects of the data processing systems:

- ensuring the required data flow between the computational steps of data processing;
- associating specific computational steps with the corresponding processing components;
- orchestrating dynamic parallel execution of the data transformation steps to achieve the adequate degree of parallelisation;
- modelling fault tolerance and reconfiguration strategies that take into account component failures and availability of the computational resources.

Abstract Model. We start by specifying (in an abstract way) the overall system behaviour. The data processing system is cyclic. In our initial specification, we abstract away from modelling the actual steps required for data processing and assume that the received data are processed in one atomic step, ensuring, however, that all the required data transformations are executed (in the required order) according to the defined algorithm. Our goal is to model the required data flow and (in subsequent refinement steps) associate it with the involved computational components. We model the individual data transformation steps as abstract functions that take data of one abstract type and return the transformed data belonging to another type. The concrete types and transformations of the algorithm become specific instances of such abstract data structures.

Therefore, we start our modelling by specifying the required abstract data types and functions. Their definitions are given in the context component of an Event-B model. For instance, the type of the data that are received by the system is introduced as an abstract set *Input_Data*. Moreover, *FP_Data* and *LF_Data* are abstract data types for the results of the first two data transformations.

The data transformation steps are modelled as the abstract functions *Step1 – Step6*. Their actual definitions (types and various constraints) are listed under the **AXIOMS** clause. In our generic model, we demonstrate how to represent the computational steps that include only sequential execution (Steps 1,2 and 5,6) as well as parallel one (Steps 3,4). For example, the following axiom

$$Step2 \in FP\_Data \nrightarrow LF\_Data$$

states that $Step2$ is a partial function that takes the results of the first transformation and transforms them consequently. Moreover, the next axiom

$$dom(Step2) = ran(Step1)$$

states that the domain of this partial function is all the data that can be produced by the previous data transformation, modelled by $Step1$. Similar constraints are defined for all the step functions to ensure the specific required data flow.

The steps that involve parallel computations (modelled by $Step3$ and $Step4$) are modelled in a slightly different way. We exemplify it by the axiom for $Step3$:

$$Step3 \in LF\_Data \nrightarrow (\mathbb{N} \nrightarrow W\_Data)$$

Note that the result of $Step3$ is an array of W_Data elements. In other words, the resulting data are partitioned and can be further processed separately.

The steps with parallelism can produce or accept the data that are partitioned and can be assigned to distinct components for processing. The maximal number of such parallel executions is fully determined by the volume of the received input data. This is formalised by introducing the function M on input data and restricting the allowed data partitioning in the definitions of $Step3$ and $Step4$ as defined by the axioms below:

$$\forall idata, lfdata \cdot idata \in Input\_Data \setminus \{NO\_DATA\} \wedge$$
$$lfdata = Step2(Step1(idata)) \Rightarrow$$
$$dom(Step3(lfdata)) = 1 \mathrel{..} M(idata)$$
$$Max\_M \in \mathbb{N}_1$$
$$\forall idata \cdot idata \in Input\_Data \Rightarrow M(idata) \le Max\_M$$
$$\forall f, x \cdot f \in dom(Step4) \wedge x \in dom(Step4(f)) \Rightarrow$$
$$(\forall x0 \cdot (x \mapsto x0) \in Step4(f) \Leftrightarrow Step4(f)(x) = x0)$$

Here we also introduce the constants NO_DATA and Max_M to indicate correspondingly the situations when no data are received and to define the upper bound for possible parallel execution within the steps 3 and 4.

Let us now consider the dynamic part of the initial system model, described in the machine m0, excerpts from which are given below. The machine m0 relies on the definitions given in its context. It describes a very abstract cyclic system, where the input data $idata$ are received (modelled by the event $receive\_data$), the output $output$ is calculated ($calculate\_output$), and the system gets ready to perform its computational service again ($ready\_to\_receive$). Completion of the data processing is indicated by the value $TRUE$ of the variable $done$. Let us note that all the necessary data transformations are performed atomically within the event $calculate\_output$. However, the required intermediate data transformations (specified within the event) are governed by the abstract functions $Step1 - Step6$ defined in the context, while the intermediate results of these transformations are stored within the local event variables $step1 - step5$.

The essential property of this simple system is formulated as the invariant inv5. It states that the produced output is determined by a functional composition of the functions $Step1 - Step6$, applied to the given input data $idata$.

MACHINE m0
SEES Data0
VARIABLES
    idata output done
INVARIANTS
      ... inv5 : $done = TRUE \Rightarrow$
           $output = (Step1; Step2; Step3; Step4; Step5; Step6)(idata)$

Event *receive_data* $\widehat{=}$

Event *calculate_output* $\widehat{=}$
    any
        step1 step2 step3 step4 step5
    where
        grd1 : $idata \neq NO\_DATA$
        grd2 : $step1 \in FP\_Data$
        grd3 : $step1 = Step1(idata)$
        grd4 : $step2 \in LF\_Data$
        grd5 : $step2 = Step2(step1)$
        grd6 : $step3 \in \mathbb{N} \nrightarrow W\_Data$
        grd7 : $step3 = Step3(step2)$
        grd8 : $step4 \in \mathbb{N} \nrightarrow RW\_Data$
        grd9 : $step4 = Step4(step3)$
        grd10 : $step5 \in RLF\_Data$
        grd11 : $step5 = Step5(step4)$
    then
        act1 : $output := Step6(step5)$
        act2 : $done := TRUE$
    end

Event *ready_to_receive* $\widehat{=}$

4 Deriving Resilient Architecture by Refinement

4.1 Modelling Dynamically Scaling Parallelism

In the following refinement steps, we will gradually elaborate on the structure and behaviour of the abstract system m0, thus unfolding its architecture in the stepwise manner. We assume that there is a master process responsible for the overall execution of the required data transformations. However, this process may delegate particular computational tasks to other processes (software components). The computational tasks – steps – may be performed sequentially or in parallel, depending on the design of the particular system.

In the abstract models, all the system execution steps can be considered as belonging to the master process. During refinement (decomposition) of the system behaviour, new system variables and events will be introduced, modelling both execution steps of the master process and involved components.

First Refinement. In the first refinement step, we focus on refining the steps that do not involve parallel computations, i.e., Steps 1 and 2 in our generic model. We introduce the new events *step1* and *step2* modelling these data transformations as well the new variables *outputStep1* and *outputStep2* storing the results of these computations. Essentially, as a result of this refinement, the event *calculate_output* is decomposed into three events *outputStep1*, *outputStep2*, and *calculate_the_rest*.

The boolean variables *fstep1* and *fstep2* control the required order of data transformations. The following invariants

$$fstep1 = TRUE \Rightarrow outputStep1 = Step1(idata)$$
$$fstep2 = TRUE \Rightarrow outputStep2 = Step2(outputStep1)$$

state that the intermediate results produced after these steps comply with the defined abstract functions *Step1* and *Step2*.

The events modelling the first two computational steps are fairly simple, since they do not involve parallel computations. In the next refinement step, we will consider how such parallel executions can be modelled within Event-B.

Second Refinement. The second refinement concentrates on modelling the data transformation steps that involve parallelism. The maximum number of possible parallel computations depends on the received input data. This principle is formalised by an application of the abstract function $M : Input\_Data \to \mathbb{N}_1$, where $\mathbb{N}_1$ represents positive natural numbers, to the received input data *idata*.

The refined model introduces the new variable *outputStep3* to model the produced results of the parallel execution of the third step. The type of this variable $\mathbb{N} \nrightarrow W\_Data$ indicates that parallel results may be produced in parallel. The domain of this function is $1..M(idata)$.

The new events *step3_partial* and *step3* (given below) model the execution of this step. Note that *step3_partial* is a parameterised event, where the parameter *idx* indicates a specific partition of the output being produced. The final result of this data transformation is produced not atomically, but by a repeated execution (sequential or parallel) of *step3_partial*. The role of the event *step3* is just to monitor the progress and terminate the stage when all the results are calculated.

Event   step3_partial $\cong$
Status convergent
    any
        idx
    where
        grd1 : $fstep2 = TRUE$
        grd2 : $fstep3 = FALSE$
        grd3 : $idx \in 1..M(idata)$
        grd4 : $idx \notin dom(outputStep3)$
    then
        act1 : $outputStep3(idx) := Step3(outputStep2)(idx)$
    end
Event   step3 $\cong$
    when
        grd1 : $fstep2 = TRUE$
        grd2 : $fstep3 = FALSE$
        grd3 : $dom(outputStep3) = 1..M(idata)$
    then
        act1 : $fstep3 := TRUE$
    end
END

An introduction of parallelism splits an atomicity of the abstract event and might accidentally introduce non-termination. To guard against it, we define the following variant expression:

$$1..M(idata) \setminus dom(outputStep3)$$

to prove that the execution of *step3_partial* eventually terminates. The given set expression is proven to be decreased in size (cardinality) after each iteration of *step3_partial*. Since it is a finite set, it cannot be decreased in size forever.

Similarly as before, the boolean variable *fset3* is introduced to control the required execution order, while the event *calculate_the_rest* is further truncated, covering now only the data transformation steps *Step4 – Step6*.

4.2   Introducing Fault Tolerance

In the previous refinement steps, we have focussed on gradual decomposition of the system behaviour by modelling the individual data transformation steps. We abstracted away from associating these steps with the actual computational components. Our next goal is to introduce a representation of the components, model their faults and define reconfiguration mechanisms.

Third Refinement. In the next refinement step, we will explicitly define the link between the computation and the available components. We also introduce a notion of a master process – an orchestrator of the computations that assigns computing tasks to these components. At the same time, we enable modelling of fault tolerance by reconfiguration. In our next specification, the components change their availability status nondeterministically. We assume that a component becomes unavailable when it is either failed or does not have the computational capacity to carry on the required computations. The goal of the master process is to detect component unavailability and reconfigure the data processing control flow, i.e., to reassign the failed tasks to the available components.

To represent this behaviour, we introduce additional data structures into our model context. To represent all possible computational components, we introduce the new abstract type (set) *COMPONENTS*. In addition, we define the constant *Initially_available*, which is a subset of *COMPONENTS* that are immediately available once the system is initialised. Finally, we introduce the enumerated set *STATUS* modelling the availability status of a component.

In the dynamic part of the specification, we introduce the new variable *comp_status* that records the dynamic availability status of the system components. Its initial value is determined by the constant *Initially_available*. Moreover, the two new events, *become_available* and *become_unavailable*, allow the components to change their availability status at any moment[2]. Though we abstract away from representing the actual causes of component failures, we model their effect on the data processing system. This approach allows us to specify reconfiguration without overloading the model.

We focus on modelling the relationships between the reconfiguration and parallelism. The parallel computations of the step 3 now can be carried out by separate components. To allow this behaviour, we introduce the new function variable *assigned3*, $assigned3 \in COMPONENT \rightarrowtail 1 .. M(idata)$, which contains those components that are assigned some computational tasks of the step 3. The function is injective, i.e., no component can execute two tasks at the same time.

---

[2] This behaviour will be restricted by giving some probabilistic values in the quantitative assessment.

The event *step3_assign* given below models assignment by the master process of some step 3 task to an available component. The task should be not yet accomplished, and the component should not already have an assigned task.

Event   *step3_assign* $\widehat{=}$
    any
          comp idx
    where
          grd1 : $comp \in COMPONENT$
          grd2 : $idx \in 1 .. M(idata)$
          grd3 : $fstep2 = TRUE$
          grd4 : $fstep3 = FALSE$
          grd5 : $idx \notin dom(outputStep3)$
          grd6 : $comp\_status(comp) = Available$
          grd7 : $comp \notin dom(assigned3)$
          grd8 : $idx \notin ran(assigned3)$
    then
          act1 : $assigned3(comp) := idx$
    end

The event *step3_partial* can now be modified to require that this partial computation is carried out by a software component that was previously assigned to execute this task.

Event   *step3_partial* $\widehat{=}$
extends *step3_partial*
    any
          comp idx
    where
          grd1 : $fstep2 = TRUE$
          grd2 : $fstep3 = FALSE$
          grd3 : $idx \in 1 .. M(idata)$
          grd4 : $idx \notin dom(outputStep3)$
          grd5 : $comp \in COMPONENT$
          grd6 : $comp\_status(comp) = Available$
          grd8 : $comp \in dom(assigned3)$
          grd7 : $assigned3(comp) = idx$
    then
          act1 : $outputStep3(idx) := Step3(outputStep2)(idx)$
          act2 : $assigned3 := \{comp\} \lhd assigned3$
    end

After the produced results are stored, the component is released from the current assignment and thus can be given a new one. The following invariant captures this property by stating that the sets of accomplished and assigned tasks are always mutually exclusive:

$$dom(outputStep3) \cap ran(assigned3) = \emptyset$$

Since a component for various reasons can become unavailable at any moment, the assigned task does not necessarily lead to its completion. The additional event *step3_reassign* is needed to model the situations when the master process notices that a component with an assigned task has become unavailable and, therefore, the task should be reassigned to another available component.

The events modelling execution of the steps 1 and 2 are also modified to require that there should an available component to perform these computations.

Event $step3\_reassign \;\widehat{=}$
    any
        $comp\ idx\ prev$
    where
        grd1 : $comp \in COMPONENT$
        grd2 : $idx \in 1\,..\,M(idata)$
        grd3 : $fstep2 = TRUE$
        grd4 : $fstep3 = FALSE$
        grd5 : $idx \notin dom(outputStep3)$
        grd6 : $comp\_status(comp) = Available$
        grd7 : $comp \notin dom(assigned3)$
        grd8 : $prev \in COMPONENT$
        grd11 : $prev \in dom(assigned3)$
        grd9 : $assigned3(prev) = idx$
        grd10 : $comp\_status(prev) = Unavailable$
    then
        act1 : $assigned3 := (\{prev\} \vartriangleleft assigned3) \cup \{(comp \mapsto idx)\}$
    end

Fourth Refinement. Similarly to the previous steps, further refinement steps are undertaken to model all computational steps that are performed in parallel. Step4 is one of such steps and hence we need to introduce the new variable *outputStep4* to store all the produced partial results of this step. Also, the new events *step4_partial* and *step4_partial* are added to model partial (sequential or parallel) data transformation and the completion of the step 4 respectively. Similarly to the previous refinements, the variant expression is introduced into the model to facilitate proving of termination of the step 4.

Fifth Refinement. In this refinement step we associate parallel execution of the step 4 computational tasks with particular available software components. In the same way as it was done for the step 3, we introduce the mechanism used by the master process to assign particular computational tasks to available components, keep track of their progress, and reassign the tasks if the components responsible for them have become unavailable. Namely, the new variable *assigned4* as well the new events *step4_assign* and *step4_reassign* are introduced, while the task completion is associated with the specific component responsible for it.

Sixth Refinement. Finally, in the last refinement step, we introduce the last two data transformation steps (the steps 5 and 6) described in the given algorithm. The refinement follows the approach presented for the sequential computational steps. In addition, the events modelling these computational stages are immediately associated with available components responsible for them. The event *calculate_the_rest* now becomes a monitoring event of the master process that simply returns the results of the last step (i.e., step 6) once they are ready.

4.3   Discussion of Formal Development

As a result of the presented chain of formal model refinement steps, we have arrived at the model of a resilient data processing system, i.e., the system that dynamically scales the degree of parallelism according to the volume of the input data and reconfigures the execution flow to cope with failures of computing components. We can now easily decompose the system into the parts representing the master and worker components. After adding concrete communication mechanisms, the master part becomes sufficiently detailed to directly generate software code out of it. The worker part can be further refined to implement specific data processing algorithms, e.g., for noise reduction, data compression, etc. The Rodin platform supports code generation into C++/Ada/Java languages. There are also the installed preprocessing mechanisms that allow the user to specify parallel tasks/threads of execution for the resulting code.

Next, the developed Event-B models will be used as the basis of quantitative system assessment within a statistical model checker. We augment the model with the component performance estimates and the probabilities of failures to evaluate resilience characteristics of the systems with different parameters.

5   Quantitative Assessment in Uppaal

In this section, we will use the model checker Uppaal [7] (and its recent statistical extension Uppaal-SMC, which allows us to combine temporal and stochastical reasoning) to quantitatively assess the software architecture model developed in Event-B. We transform the obtained formal models following the approach proposed in [2] to obtain the input to Uppaal-SMC.

We are interested in evaluating the probability of successful data processing under the given estimates of performance of the individual computational components and their probabilities of failure. Essentially, we are interested in analysing the impact of the dynamic scaling and reconfiguration on resilience. Therefore, in our Uppaal model we focus on representing those calculational steps that involve parallel execution.

We model step 3 as a composition of the master process responsible for orchestrating the whole algorithm (based on data decomposition using wavelets [3]) and a number of worker processes that can be assigned parallel tasks by the master. The main system parameters directly affecting its execution time are

- the size of the received data set, *size*, which, according to the algorithm, directly determines the maximal number of parallel tasks M: $M = log2(size)$,
- the number of system worker components (parallel processes) N.

In our evaluation we will consider different combinations of these parameters as well as other parameters that may affect the system execution time, e.g., the probabilities of worker failures, the time used by the master to monitor the workers, the delay in communication between the master and the workers, etc.

The overall system consists of the Master process and N worker components. The dynamics of both master and worker components are defined as two timed automata given below.

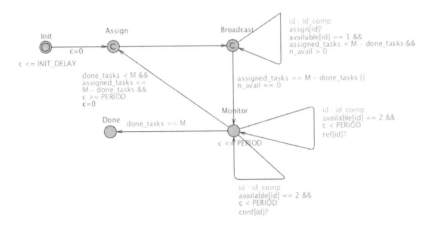

Fig. 1. Timed automata diagram of a master component

The first timed automata (Fig.1) describes the cyclic behaviour of the master, consisting of assigning (by broadcasting) not yet completed tasks to the workers, monitoring their status, and then reassigning the remaining tasks, if necessary. The channels *assign* (for communicating task assignment), *ref* (for communicating component refusal/failure), and *conf* (for communicating successful task completion by a component) are used to synchronise activities between the involved components. The clock invariants, like $c <= PERIOD$, model possible time passage while being in a particular component state.

The second automata (Fig.2) describes the behaviour of a worker component. The given probabilistic weights, e.g., *pw_aa* or *pw_ref*, model probabilities of component staying or becoming (un)available, as well as completing the given task or refusing it. Implicitly we assume that task refusal occurs due to the component failure. Note how, for the state Done, the clock invariant

$$c \leq PERIOD + TASK\_TIME$$

together with the outgoing guard expression $c >= TASK\_TIME$ guarantees that the completed task is executed for at least $TASK\_TIME$ time units, which is the given time estimate for task calculation.

For the created Uppaal models, we have verified a number of time reachability properties, considering different value combinations for system parameters. All the verified properties are of the form

$$\mathsf{Pr}[\leq time\_bound](<> \mathsf{Master.Done})$$

The result is the probability that the Master component eventually reaches the state Master.Done (i.e., the state where all the parallel task calculations are successfully completed) within the given time bound. Moreover, the obtained results can be graphically plotted to show probability distribution or cumulative probability distribution for different values of the clock.

To perform the quantitative assessment of resilience characteristics of the derived architecture, we have to instantiate its abstract parameters. We can experiment by substituting different values for the input data volume, the number

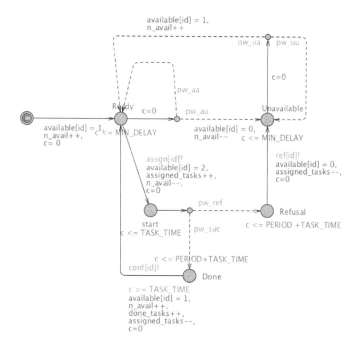

Fig. 2. Timed automata diagram of a node (worker) component

of worker components, etc. and analyse the obtained quantitative evaluations of the modelled system in terms of the execution time and probabilities.

For instance, for the data volume 20000, the degree of parallelism should be set to $M = log2(size)$, which can be approximated in this case to be 14. Let $TASK\_TIME$ be 11. We now can consider different numbers of the worker components in our system.

Let us consider now different numbers of the worker components in our system. For each sample size, we start by considering this number to be $N = 10$.

The plots for probabilistic distribution and cumulative probability distribution for this configuration are displayed in Fig.3 and Fig.4 respectively.

The numbers worth paying close attention to are

- the average time of task execution;
- the execution time that is not exceeded by significantly high number of system runs (given by some cumulative probabilistic threshold).

We also can evaluate how good the selected configuration is by analysing the produced probabilistic distribution in terms of the number and locations of probabilistic peaks for specific execution times. In general, it is considered preferable (from the point of view of system predictability and stability) to have all such peaks occurring before or very close after the average execution time (marked by the green vertical line on the diagrams). Such a good distribution means that, in the cumulative probability diagram, the probabilistic value reaches plateau quickly after the green line indicating the average time.

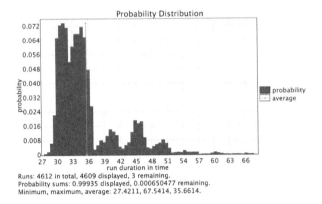

Fig. 3. Probability distribution for the case (sample 20000, N = 10)

In this particular case, the average time to complete the step 3 for this configuration is around 3.5s, while in 90% of system runs the execution time will not exceed 4.6s. Since a fully sequential implementation of this step will take at least $14 * 1.1$ seconds to complete, this is a significant improvement. The probabilistic distribution is quite good as well.

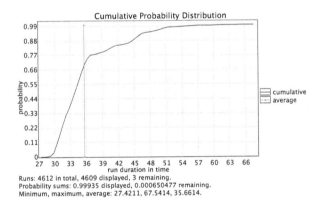

Fig. 4. Cumulative Probability distribution (sample 20000, N = 10)

By analysing different values of the parameters, we can identify the most optimal with respect to the desired resilience characteristics configuration. A detailed example of such an analysis can be found in [3].

6   Discussion

Related Work. The problem of designing and assessing data processing capabilities of CPS is receiving an increasing attention. However, majority of works are originating from the sensor networks field and focus on the resilience of the underlying sensor infrastructure rather than data processing capabilities as such. Among the approaches that close to ours, is the work by Lu Su [8]. The work proposes a set of graph-based analysis techniques for assessing the quality of information/resource consumption ratio in CPS. Similarly to our work, the author proposes a hierarchical architecture for data processing and aggregation and evaluate the resource consumption alternatives. This approach can be seen as a complementary to ours. Our approach better suits the early development stages, while the work of Lu Su provides the designers with the technique to evaluate a particular implementation.

The work presented in this paper also builds on our previous results in integrating formal modelling with quantitative assessment of resilience [9,10]. The main novelty of this work is in using Uppaal-SMT rather than PRISM that has offered a significantly better scalability – the property which is essential when analysing complex reconfigurable parallel architectures.

Conclusions. In this paper, we have proposed an integrated approach to modelling the data processing capabilities of CPS and assessing their resilience. We demonstrated how to formally derive a dynamically scaling reconfigurable system architecture by refinement in Event-B [6]. Refinement process allowed us to systematically introduce the reconfiguration mechanisms that improve system fault tolerance and resilience against stress load and faults, while integration with the statistical model checking helped us to evaluate the likelihood of successful completion of data processing by different deadlines and under different failure probabilities. We believe that the proposed approach enables an efficient design space exploration by allowing the designers to predict resilience of different architectural alternatives. As a future work, we are planning to experiment with a wider range of techniques and tools for quantitative analysis, including continuous time modelling and simulation, and compare the obtained results.

Acknowledgements. This work is supported by the grant of the Russian Foundation for Basic Research N⸋ 14-07-31250/14 and Contract N⸋ 02.G25.31.0058 dated 12.02.2013 (Board of Education of Russia).

References

1. Abrial, J.R.: Modelling in Event-B. Cambridge University Press (2010)
2. Iliasov, A., Laibinis, L., Troubitsyna, E., Romanovsky, A., Latvala, T.: Augmenting Event-B Modelling with Real-Time Verification. In: Proceedings of Workshop on Formal Methods in Software Engineering: Rigorous and Agile Approaches, FormSERA 2012 (2012)
3. Laibinis, L., Klionskiy, D., Troubitsyna, E., Dorokhov, A., Lilius, J., Kupriyanov, M.: The Final Report on the Development Project "Development of Information Preprocessing Algorithms". LETI Reports. Saint Petersburg, Russian Federation (2013)
4. Lee, E.A.: Cyber Physical Systems: Design Challenges. In: 1st IEEE International Symposium on Object Oriented Real-Time Distributed Computing (ISORC), pp. 363–369. IEEE (2008)

5. Naidu, P.: Modern spectrum analysis of time series. CRC Press, New York (1996)
6. Rodin platform: Automated tool environment for Event-B,
   http://rodin-b-sharp.sourceforge.net/
7. Statistical UPPAAL: SMC extension of UPPAAL,
   http://www.cs.aau.dk/~adavid/smc
8. Su, L.: Resource efficient information integration in cyber-physical systems. PhD
   Thesis. Univ. of Urbana Champain, USA (2014)
9. Tarasyuk, A., Troubitsyna, E., Laibinis, L.: Towards Probabilistic Modelling in
   Event-B. In: Méry, D., Merz, S. (eds.) IFM 2010. LNCS, vol. 6396, pp. 275–289.
   Springer, Heidelberg (2010)
10. Tarasyuk, A., Troubitsyna, E., Laibinis, L.: Formal Modelling and Verification
    of Service-Oriented Systems in Probabilistic Event-B. In: Derrick, J., Gnesi, S.,
    Latella, D., Treharne, H. (eds.) IFM 2012. LNCS, vol. 7321, pp. 237–252. Springer,
    Heidelberg (2012)

Formal Fault Tolerance Analysis of Algorithms for Redundant Systems in Early Design Stages

Andrea Höller, Nermin Kajtazovic,
Christopher Preschern, and Christian Kreiner

Institute of Technical Informatics, Graz University of Technology, Austria
{andrea.hoeller,nermin.kajtazovic,christopher.preschern,
christian.kreiner}@tugraz.at

Abstract. Redundant techniques, that use voting principles, are often used to increase the reliability of systems by ensuring fault tolerance. In order to increase the efficiency of these redundancy strategies we propose to exploit the inherent fault masking properties of software-algorithms at application-level. An important step in early development stages is to choose from a class of algorithms that achieve the same goal in different ways, one or more that should be executed redundantly. In order to evaluate the resilience of the algorithm variants, there is a great need for a quantitative reasoning about the algorithms fault tolerance in early design stages.

Here, we propose an approach of analyzing the vulnerability of given algorithm variants to hardware faults in redundant designs by applying a model checker and fault injection modelling. The method is capable of automatically identifying all input and fault combinations that remain undetected by a voting system. This leads to a better understanding of algorithm-specific resilience characteristics.

Keywords: fault tolerance, redundancy, MooN systems, model checker, fault injection, fault masking.

1 Introduction

There is an ongoing trend for using commercial off-the-shelf hardware that is manufactured with ever shrinking feature sizes. Nano-scale CMOS structures cause an increasing number of operational hardware faults caused by soft errors, ageing, device variability, etc. [6]. Thus, it is becoming increasingly important to mitigate the impact of these hardware faults. That is particularly relevant for safety-critical embedded systems, whose failures could result in loss of life, significant property damage, or damage to the environment. For this reason, these systems have to maintain a safe operation even in the presence of faults. Therefore, safety standards, such as the IEC 61508 [10] (general) or the ISO 26262 [11] (automotive), prescribe to guarantee a high level of fault tolerance.

Hardware redundancy is a well-proven concept for designing reliable systems by increasing the reliability of the hardware. This is especially important, if

I. Majzik and M. Vieira (Eds.): SERENE 2014, LNCS 8785, pp. 71–85, 2014.

the reliability of the single hardware components is not sufficiently high for the desired application [15]. In accordance with hardware redundancy, multiple programs implementing the same logical function are executed in multiple hardware channels. A typical redundant system features independently installed sensor inputs and processors (see Fig.1). The software implementations can be the same or diverse. A voter is used to check whether the outputs from the channels match. This achieves a high data integrity meaning that the system either produces correct outputs or detects the presence of a fault.

In order to increase the efficiency of redundancy strategies we propose to exploit the inherent masking properties of hardware faults of algorithms at the application-layer. Typically, there are multiple ways to design an algorithm implementing the same calculation. However, different algorithms have different properties regarding the masking of hardware faults. During the development of reliable systems, the question arises, which of the algorithm candidates provides the best option regarding software-based hardware fault tolerance? When designing redundant systems, it also has to be decided whether to execute the same algorithm variant redundantly or to combine different algorithm variants to achieve a diverse system. However, there is a lack of tools that allow the comparison of the fault tolerance of different algorithms in early design stages.

In this paper, we present a formal approach to automatically rank algorithms that should be executed in software with respect to the achieved hardware fault tolerance in duplex designs. The main contributions of this paper are:

- It proposes an approach for quantifying the fault tolerance of algorithms in duplex systems in early design stages.
- It introduces a method that automatically identifies all undetected fault and input combinations that lead to an erroneous output of a 1oo2 system.
- It presents a proof-of-concept of the proposed approach by showing simple exemplary use cases.

This paper is structured as follows. Section 2 introduces basic fault tolerance principles and Section 3 goes on to summarize the related work. Followed by

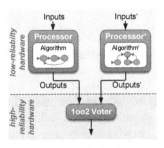

Fig. 1. Multi-processor system realizing a 1oo2 redundant system. Two *low-reliability processors* execute the same or diverse *algorithms* realizing the same functionality. Note, that the unreliability of the redundant components has to be bound. A *reliable 1oo2 voter* compares the results and indicates an error, if they mismatch.

Section 4, which describes the integration of the proposed approach in the development process, presents implementation details and shows how the approach can be used to measure the fault tolerance of algorithms. Then the approach is experimentally investigated in Section 5. Finally, Section 6 concludes the paper.

2   Background

Here, we provide basic knowledge about different types of faults, redundancy techniques and model checking.

2.1   Introduction to Fault Types

For the mitigation of different fault types different fault-tolerance mechanisms are required [10]. With respect to persistence, a fault can be permanent or transient. In contrast to permanent faults that persist for the remainder of the computation, transient faults occur for a short period of time. According to the phase of creation or occurrence, there is a distinction between development faults and random faults. While development faults are introduced either during software or hardware development, random faults denote hardware faults that occur during operation. In this work we focus on permanent and transient random faults.

With the advent of modern nano-scale technology, embedded systems are increasingly confronted with random faults. Especially, multiple bit errors are becoming more likely [16]. This means that multiple cells on one die are affected by a single event such as a particle strike.

2.2   Introduction to Redundancy Techniques

Spatial and temporal redundancy techniques are widely used to design fault tolerant systems [10]. While spatial redundancy means that the calculation is performed on distinct hardware components, temporal redundancy indicates that the same calculation is performed multiple times, one after the other.

Typical spatial redundancy techniques are *M-out-of-N* (*MooN*) architectures, where M channels out of total N channels have to work correctly. In this paper, we focus on spatial redundancy realized with an 1oo2 architecture. This means that there are two redundant channels, which are compared by a voter. When the two outputs do not match, an error is detected. Consequently, the system could go into a safe state to prevent serious hazards. Since the voter is a single point of failure, it has to be highly reliable. To enhance the reliability of the voter it should be primitive, such as a logical *AND* or *OR* built into the actuators. If the voter has to operate with more complex outputs, it has to guarantee a high level of integrity (i.e. by being certified with a high integrity level as described in safety standards). This could be achieved by using highly reliable hardware and performing advanced self checks. A typical realization of a 1oo2 system is a multi-processor system as shown in Fig. 1.

Systems with two redundant channels can detect a violation of the data integrity as long as only one module fails. However, common-mode failures in redundant systems can result in a single failure affecting more than one module at the same time. Examples of sources of common-mode failures are common faults in the production process, the interface, shared resources or mistakes during development. Design diversity can protect redundant systems against common-mode failures. For example, diversity can be achieved with diverse algorithms that perform the same calculation in different ways.

2.3   Introduction to Model Checking

Static verification techniques provide a formal proof for an abstract mathematical model of the system. Model checking has been used for the formal verification of safety-critical systems in the last two decades [18]. In this work we use the well-tested and open source symbolic model checker NuSMV [4]. A model checker operates on two inputs: a Finite State Machine (FSM) model describing system states and transitions between those states and a specification described by formulas in temporal logic. Unfortunately, the applicability of a model checker is limited by the state explosion problem. This implies that a model checker can only handle relatively small examples.

3   Related Work

3.1   Model-Checking Approaches for Fault Tolerance Evaluation

Traditionally, formal verification is used to prove the correct behaviour of a system. However, in order to analyze the reliability, it is necessary to evaluate systems under faulty conditions. Therefore fault injection techniques are used to intentionally introduce faults into a system for the simulation and emulation of errors [13]. Fault injection is applied on hardware-level, software-level or modelling-level. The latter is especially important for fault testing during earlier development stages, before a final device is available.

There are some works describing how to use model checker for fault injection at modelling-level. Most of them focus on the analysis of hardware circuits [1,12]. In contrast to our approach, these works need to change the model checker and only focus on hardware circuits. We propose only extend the model of the algorithm with fault injection. The advantage of this approach is that the well-tested model checker implementation is left unchanged and the fault modelling is more transparent to the user. Similar to our approach fault injection at model-level has been performed in [2,5,7,19]. However, these approaches only consider single-point failures and do not generate multiple counterexamples to get sound statistics of the algorithm-specific fault tolerance.

3.2   Fault Tolerance Analysis of Algorithms for Redundant Systems

Previous research has addressed the issue of reliability analysis of algorithms for redundant systems for specific applications [17] or specific hardware, such as memories [8] and sequential circuits [14]. However, little attention has been paid to the problem of determining the fault tolerance of redundant algorithms at a higher abstraction layer, which is independent of the hardware architecture. The authors of [20] presented a formal approach for analyzing software-based hardware-fault detection methods by using an LLVM-level fault injector. They aimed to rank different algorithms that solve the same problem. However, in contrast to the model-checking approach presented in this paper, their fault-injection strategy was not exhaustive and they focused on final software implementations.

So far, little attention has been paid to the analysis of the inherent fault masking capabilities of algorithms, which are executed redundantly in early design stages. This paper contributes a step towards filling this gap by presenting approaches to the fault tolerance analysis of algorithms for redundancy-based systems based on models that are available prior to the implementation.

4 Fault Tolerance Analysis of Redundant Algorithms with Model Checking

Here, we first present how our approach can be integrated into the development process of resilient systems. Then, we provide details about our fault model, assessment metrics and implementation.

4.1 Fault Tolerance Analysis in Early Design Stages

We propose to integrate the proposed fault tolerance analysis in the development flow as shown in Fig. 2. To guarantee the high quality of the design, model checkers are used in early development phases. Therefore the designed algorithms have to be represented in a model checking language. Additionally, specifications describing the desired functional behaviour as well as safety requirements are formulated in a temporal logic, such as the Computation Tree Logic (CTL). Then a model checker can be used to formally verify that the algorithm fulfils the specifications. This model checking procedure can be integrated in the development flow in a user-friendly way as presented in [3].

We propose a tool called FAnToM (Fault Tolerance Analysis Tool using a Model Checker) for the analysis of the algorithms. Note, that for the analysis of diverse redundancy, multiple algorithm models have to be provided. The tool generates fault tolerance statistics that can be used to quantify the fault tolerance of the algorithm variants. The exhaustive fault tolerance statistics describe all undetected fault combinations. They indicating the input and fault combination that lead to an error as well as the faulty output value. This helps designers to choose from a class of algorithm options for a specific application.

4.2 Advantages for Safety-critical Systems

The IEC 61508 safety standard defines four Safety Integrity Levels (SILs) indicating different probabilities of failures. The highest achievable SIL is limited by

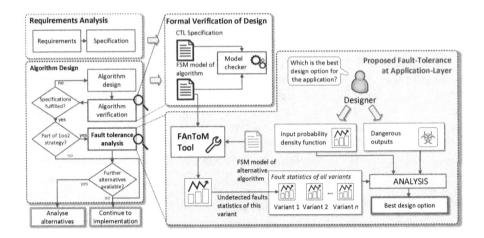

Fig. 2. Illustration of the proposed process for the evaluation of algorithms in early design stages. First, a model checker is used to formally verify the algorithm options. Then, the proposed tool generates fault tolerant statistics. This that can be achieved by using the modelled algorithms in redundant systems. By considering the fault tolerance statistics and application-specific characteristics the best algorithm option is chosen.

the Hardware Fault Tolerance (HFT) and by the Safe Failure Fraction (SFF). An HFT of N defines a minimum number of faults $N+1$ that can cause the system to lose its safety. For example, a duplex 1oo2 system ($N=1$) can fail, if two ($N+1$) failures occur. The SFF is a ratio of failures as shown in (1), where λ_s denotes the number of safe failures, λ_{Dd} defines the number of detected dangerous failures and λ_{Du} covers the number of undetected dangerous failures.

$$\mathrm{SFF} = \frac{\sum \lambda_s + \sum \lambda_{Dd}}{\sum \lambda_s + \sum \lambda_{Dd} + \sum \lambda_{Du}} \qquad (1)$$

Typically hardware redundancy is used to increase the HFT. However, we propose to chose the software algorithms that are executed redundantly in such a way that also the SFF can be increased. The λ_{Du} can be reduced by choosing those algorithm combinations, were the least number of unmasked faults lead to a dangerous output value. This number of undetected dangerous faults U_d is provided by the FAnToM tool.

4.3 Fault Modelling

To further reduce the number of potential hazardous faults spatial redundancy can be used. For example, duplex systems are able to detect single random faults in one channel, since the second channel produces a correct output. However, it may happen that there is a fault in each of the both channels that lead to an undetected erroneous output. This means that the minimal number of faults that cause an erroneous output at application layer is two. Although, also more

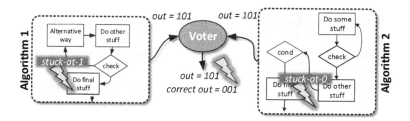

Fig. 3. A dual fault pair can lead to an undetected error in a 1oo2 duplex system. For example, a *stuck-at-0* fault in the first channel and a *stuck-at-1* fault in the second channel could lead to the same faulty output and thus remains undetected by the *voter*.

faults in each channel could be undetected, we focus on dual faults, since they are most likely. Also some safety standards, such as the ISO 26262, prescribe that these dual-point failures are considered. As exemplified in Fig. 3, these failures remain undetected if, and only if, a fault that affects the first variant and a fault in the second variant lead to the exact same, but faulty outputs. Then the voter is not able to detect the faults. The FAnToM tool automatically identifies all these fault combinations.

We model only faults affecting the value of data that is operated. However, we do not consider faults that disrupt the execution flow. The manifestation of these faults at the algorithm level is modelled as bit flips in values of the computational state as follows [20].

- *Permanent faults* are modelled as bit values that always retain the same logical value (*stuck-at-0* and *stuck-at-1*).
- *Transient faults* are modelled as one-time *bit flips* inverting the logical value of a bit.

4.4 Algorithm Modelling

To be interpretable by a model checker, the algorithms have to be modelled as FSMs. Formally, an FSM is defined as a 5-tuple (Q, Σ, T, q_0, F), where Q is a finite set of states, Σ is a finite input alphabet, T is the transition function $T : Q \times \Sigma \to Q$, q_0 is the initial state, and F is the set of final states [9].

We propose to use a development environment for modelling the algorithms such as *mbeddr* [21]. This tool enhances the C programming language with a syntax for state machines and allows to automatically generate both, a NuSMV model and a C implementation, from a common behavioural description written in a domain specific language. This reduces the time needed for modelling the algorithm and the vulnerability to implementation errors.

4.5 Fault Tolerance Metrics of Algorithms for Duplex Systems

To compare the suitability of algorithm variants for duplex systems with regards to their fault tolerance, we propose to consider the metrics as described below.

Number of Undetected Faults. The FAnToM tool provides the number of undetected faults for each fault type. Furthermore, the tool provides detailed statistics indicating the output values that result from the combination of undetected faults and inputs. When providing domain knowledge that indicates, which output values are dangerous for the application, it is possible to evaluate the algorithm variants with respect to undetected dangerous failures as described in Section 4.2.

Dependency Between Fault Tolerance and the Input. Next, the number of undetected faults is considered for each input value, since input highly influences how many faults are masked. Take the boolean expression $A \wedge B$, for example. If both input values are zero, a bit flip in the value of A or B does not influence the correctness of the result. However, if A equals zero and B equals one, then a bit flip in the data variable storing A would lead to a faulty result.

Dual-Fault Coverage Metric. Below, we introduce a fault coverage metric that indicates how many of the modelled dual-fault combinations remain undetected by a voter in a 1oo2 duplex system. Note that this coverage metric does not correspond to the coverage metric defined in safety standards.

The consequences of a fault depends on at which system state it occurs and on the type of fault. Thus, we describe the total number of possible fault occurrences as a sampling space $G = \Sigma \times F$, where Σ is the input space and F is the fault space. The size of the input space $|\Sigma|$ depends on the number of possible input values. When $N_{d_{in}}$ is the bit length of the input data, we assume that $|\Sigma| = 2^{N_{d_{in}}}$.

Furthermore, we assume that the number of possible data fault occurrences in an FSM model of an algorithm depends on the number of data bits N_d the algorithm operates with, and the number of FSM states N_{st}. The number of the various fault type combinations when executing two algorithms on redundant channels is given by the equations shown in Tab. 1. Then the total number of fault type combinations $|F|$ can be expressed as $|F| = |F_{PP}| + |F_{PT}| + |F_{TT}|$.

Table 1. Number of considered fault type combinations

$\lvert F_{PP} \rvert = \underbrace{4}_{\substack{st\text{-}0/st\text{-}0,\ st\text{-}0/st\text{-}1 \\ st\text{-}1/st\text{-}0,\ st\text{-}1/st\text{-}1}} \cdot N_{d1} \cdot N_{d2}$	A permanent fault (*stuck-at-0* or *stuck-at-1*) in each channel.
$\lvert F_{PT} \rvert = \underbrace{2}_{\substack{st\text{-}0/bf \\ st\text{-}1/bf}} \cdot N_{d1} \cdot N_{d2} \cdot (\underbrace{N_{st1}}_{bf\ in\ v1} + \underbrace{N_{st2}}_{bf\ in\ v2})$	A transient bit flip in one channel and a permanent fault in the other channel.
$\lvert F_{TT} \rvert = N_{d1} \cdot N_{d2} \cdot N_{st1} \cdot N_{st2}$	A transient bit flip in each channel.

We define the fault coverage metric for each pair of fault types as

$$C_{\sigma_{(1/2)}} = 1 - \frac{U_{\sigma_{(1/2)}}}{|F_{\sigma_{(1/2)}}| \cdot |\Sigma|}, \qquad (2)$$

where $\sigma_{(1/2)}$ indicates the fault type pair consisting of two permanent faults (PP), one permanent and one transient fault (PT), or two transient faults (TT) and $U_{\sigma_{(1/2)}}$ is the number of undetected fault pairs. The total coverage can be expressed as

$$C_{\text{total}} = 1 - \frac{U_{PP} + U_{PT} + U_{TT}}{|G|}. \qquad (3)$$

4.6   Implementation Details

We first generate a NuSMV model and then use the NuSMV model checker to search for undetected fault pairs as illustrated in Fig. 4.

Automatic Generation of the NuSMV Model. The generated models are written in the NuSMV language [4]. The user provides models of the algorithms that should be analyzed. As shown in Fig. 5, the FAnToM tool automatically generates a NuSMV model by modelling a 1oo2 voting system with the provided FSMs. Then the algorithm models are extended with fault injection. The CTL compares the output of the voter with a fault-free golden model.

Generation of a Duplex System Model. The modules of the algorithm variants are instantiated in the main module as shown in Fig. 7. Each instantiation of an algorithm variant represents a channel in the duplex system. The fault modelling for each of the channels is defined globally. Furthermore, the main module models shared inputs and passes them to each channel. Finally, a signal called `voter_cmp` represents the voter indicating whether the outputs of the two variants match.

Fault Injection Modelling. The random occurrence of faults is modelled by describing the activation of faulty behaviour as input variables (see Fig. 7). In this way, the model checker considers all possible fault combinations. For each channel, the type of the injected fault, the target signal as well as the state when a fault should be injected (for transient faults) are modelled as frozen inputs so that they do not change during the processing of the FSM.

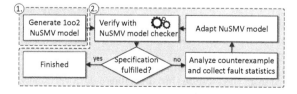

Fig. 4. Procedure of proposed fault tolerance analysis tool using a model checker to collect fault statistics of given algorithms

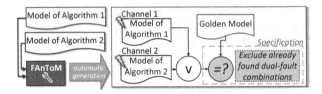

Fig. 5. Generation of a NuSMV model describing a 1oo2 system with fault modelling. The specification uses a fault-free golden model to find incorrect voter outputs.

We model the impact of faults on data by using instances of a module called WORD for representing data signals similarly as proposed in [2]. As shown in Fig. 6, an input parameter of the module indicates, whether a fault should be injected for the instantiated signal. This would be the case, if it corresponds to the globally defined fault injection target signal. The WORD module fetches the remaining fault parameters by referring to the main module.

Specification. Since we observed that when using CTL as specification language the runtimes are faster than when using Linear Temporal Logic (LTL), we use CTL. First of all, if diverse algorithm variants are given, it should be guaranteed that their outputs match for all possible input values. This is can be achieved by checking the first specification given in Fig. 8.

The second specification shown in Fig. 8 is used to find all undetected faults. If both channels have finished their calculations and their outputs match, although the fault-free golden model derives another result, the voter has no chance of detecting the faults. If only dangerous faults should be identified, the specification is extended to describe the dangerous output.

```
-- len length of data variable, fi should a fault be injected?
MODULE WORD(input, len, fi, my_var) --Data word with fault injection
  DEFINE    MAX_BIT_INJ := len - 1;
            fi_type      := my_var.fi_type; --fi-type of variant
  FROZENVAR inj_bit      := 0..MAX_BIT_INJ; --target bit of fi
  DEFINE out:= case
            fi & fi_type = stuck_at_0 : input & !(1 << inj_bit);
            fi & fi_type = stuck_at_1 : input | (1 << inj_bit);
            fi & fi_type = bit_flip & my_var.fi_state = my_var.state :
                                          input xor (1 << inj_bit);
            TRUE : input;   esac;
-- Example how the WORD-module is used
MODULE VARIANT1(in_a, in_b, ..., ch_nr, main_cont)
  DEFINE fi_type    := case ch_nr = 0 : none;
                            ch_nr = 1 : main_cont.fi_type1;
                            ch_nr = 2 : main_cont.fi_type2; esac;
            fi_signal := case
  ...
  VAR  a_   : WORD(in_a, 1, fi_signal=sig_a,  self);
       b_   : WORD(in_b, 2, fi_signal=sig_b,  self);
  ...
  ASSIGN next(out) := case state=state1 : a_.out | b_.out;
  ...
```

Fig. 6. Code snipped from the module that describes a data variable with fault injection and an example of how to use this variable

```
MODULE main
 FROZENVAR
  fi_type1, fi_type2 : {stuck_at_0, stuck_at_1, bit_flip}; --fault mgmt.
  fi_signal1         : {var1_sig1, var1_sig2,…,var1_sign, none};
  fi_signal2         : {var2_sig1, var2_sig2,…,var2_sigm, none};
  fi_state1          : {var1_state1, var1_state2,…,var1_stateN};
  fi_state2          : {var2_state1, var2_state2,…,var2_stateM};
  in_a   : word[length];   --shared inputs
  in_b   : word[length];
  …
 VAR
   ch1: VARIANT1(in_a, in_b,…, 1, self); --alg.variant on ch1
   ch2: VARIANT2(in_a, in_b,…, 2, self); --alg.variant on ch2
   golden1 : VARIANT1(in_a, in_b,…, 0, self); --no fault injection
 DEFINE
   voter_cmp : var1.out = var2.out; --loo2 voter
```

Fig. 7. Code snipped from the main module that instantiates the algorithm variants and describes the fault injection configuration

```
DEFINE
 corr_out := channel1.out_.out = golden.out_.out;
 ready    := channel1.ready & channel2.ready;
 critical := case
 --add already found fault combinations here
 fi_signal=sig_a & fi_type1=stuck_at_0   & channel1.a_.inj_bit=0 &
 fi_signal2=sig_b & fi_type1=bit_flip & fi_state2=s3 &
                                          channel1.b_.inj_bit=1&
 in_a=0ud2_3 & in_b=0ud2_1 & … : FALSE
 -- critical, if both resuts are false, but match
 valid_check & !corr_out : TRUE;
 TRUE : FALSE; esac;
LTLSPEC
 G(ready -> golden1.out=golden2.out) --no FI: results have to match
 G(final_critical = FALSE)
```

Fig. 8. Code snipped from the specification. To get multiple counterexamples, unde-tected fault configurations that have already been found are excluded.

Model Checking and Counterexample Analysis. After checking the generated model, the model checker provides a counterexample that includes a configuration of input values and a fault pair that leads to a failing voter. Unfortunately, the model checker stops the execution after finding one coun-terexample. However, in order to identify all unreliable configurations, multiple counterexamples are desired. To overcome this limitation, the model is edited to exclude configurations that have already been identified (see Fig. 8). As shown in Fig. 4, this procedure is repeated until the specification is fulfilled meaning that all configurations have been found.

5 Experimental Results

Here, we describe simple use cases to demonstrate our approach. We imple-mented the FAnToM tool in Java and executed it on a typical PC featuring a 1.7 GHz Intel Core i5 processor. We applied the tool to support the design of algorithms that should be executed on an industrial Programmable Logic Controller (PLC) for hydro-electrical power plants.

5.1   Example 1: Boolean Expression with Diverse Association

First, we analyzed the following two ways of expressing a boolean calculation that processes 1-bit inputs:

$$\text{Variant } 1 : (A \wedge B) \vee (C \wedge B) \vee (A \wedge C) \vee (B \wedge C) \tag{4}$$

$$\text{Variant } 2 : B \wedge (A \vee C) \vee C \wedge (A \vee B) \tag{5}$$

Tab. 2 summarizes the results of the fault tolerance analysis of the following systems: two duplex systems that execute either the first or the second variant parallel on both redundant channels or a diverse system that executes both algorithm variants.

How the FSMs are modelled is exemplified in Fig. 9. While the FSM of the first variant (4) requires seven states and three temporary variables for storing intermediate values, the second variant (5) requires only seven states and two temporary variables. This leads to different sizes of the sampling space.

Regarding the number of undetected faults, the system executing the second algorithm variant redundantly offers the best solution. This is due to the smallest sampling space indicating that there are the fewest possible states, where a fault can occur. However, the coverage metric indicates that this variant is the least reliable. An increasing sample size leads to a better coverage, although it also implies more undetected faults. This suggests that the coverage should be considered separately from the other metrics.

Furthermore, it is important to keep the final application of the system in mind. For example, consider an application where a safe state is entered whenever the output of the calculation is a *0*. This means that under safety aspects it is only critical if the output assumes the value *1*, although the correct output would be *0*. However, as shown in Tab. 2 for all options more fault combinations U_1 lead to a wrong output of *1* then *0* (U_0). This suggests that the vulnerability to dangerous faults could be decreased by inverting the coding.

Additionally, the tool offers statistics indicating the dependency between the number of undetected faults and the input. Fig. 10 shows that the fault tolerance highly depends on the input value. However, for this example the impact of the input value on the number of undetected faults is similar for all variants.

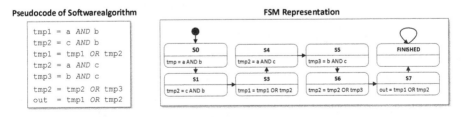

Fig. 9. Pseudocode of and FSM representation of boolean expression as shown in (4)

Table 2. Result statistics of the analyzed examples

Strategy	Size of sampling space					Undetect. fault comb.				Coverage	Outputs	
	$\|\Sigma\|$	$\|F_{PP}\|$	$\|F_{PT}\|$	$\|F_{TT}\|$	$\|G\|$	U_{PP}	U_{PT}	U_{TT}	U_{total}	C_{total}	U_0	U_1
Example 1: Boolean expression with diverse association												
Red. var. 1		144	1008	1764	**23328**	113	352	294	**759**	**96.75%**	117	642
Red. var. 2	8	100	500	625	**9800**	74	184	124	**382**	**96.10%**	108	280
Diverse		120	720	1050	**15120**	91	254	184	**529**	**96.50%**	109	420
Example 2: Disjunctive and conjunctive normal form												
Red. DNF						122	526	581	**1229**	**97.82%**	410	819
Red. CNF	8	144	1728	5184	**56448**	122	526	581	**1229**	**97.82%**	819	410
Diverse						445	494	550	**1156**	**96.10%**	578	578

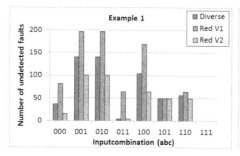 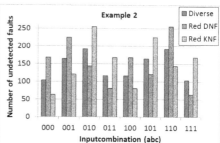

Fig. 10. Number of undetected faults and calculated coverage of redundant and diverse calculations of Example 1 and Example 2

5.2 Example 2: Disjunctive and Conjunctive Normal Form

The next example is a boolean calculation that is expressed in disjunctive normal form (DNF) and in conjunctive normal form (CNF) as shown in (6) and (7).

$$\text{DNF:}(\bar{A}\wedge B\wedge \bar{C})\vee(\bar{A}\wedge B\wedge C)\vee(A\wedge \bar{B}\wedge C)\vee(A\wedge B\wedge C) \tag{6}$$
$$\text{CNF:}(A\vee B\vee C)\wedge(A\vee B\vee \bar{C})\wedge(\bar{A}\vee B\vee C)\wedge(\bar{A}\vee \bar{B}\vee C) \tag{7}$$

The FAnToM tool found the same number of undetected fault pairs for a redundant implementation using the DNF or the CNF algorithm as shown in Tab. 2. Their input dependency characteristics are different as indicated in Fig. 10. Nonetheless, both input dependencies have one thing in common: the reliability of the output strongly depends on the input value. For the worst case the number of undetected fault pairs is four times higher than for the best case. However, the diverse variant that executes the DNF on one channel and the CNF on the other channel reduces the influence of the input value on the reliability. More precisely, for each input value, the number of undetected fault pairs corresponds to the average value of the DNF and CNF version.

Furthermore, Tab. 2 shows that in general the diverse variant is the most resilient regarding faults, since U_{total} is the lowest. However, if it is the case that either an output of *0 or 1* has more hazardous consequences to the application, then the CNF or the DNF variant provide more safe options.

5.3 Scalability

We analysed several examples with the proposed tool to examine the scalability of the approach. As shown in Fig. 11 the runtime depends on the size of the sampling space and the number of identified undetected fault combinations. We observed that for one example time to find one undetected fault combination, thus one counterexample, stays nearly constant. However, due to the state space explosion problem the runtime is growing rapidly with the complexity of the algorithm indicated by the sampling space. Consequently, the approach is not suitable for big amounts of data such as integer or floating point values and should only be applied for very small safety-relevant parts of the system.

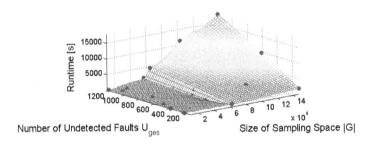

Fig. 11. *Runtime* depending on the *number of undetected faults* and the *sampling space*

6 Conclusion

This paper demonstrates how to automatically identify all undetected dual-point faults of a redundant duplex system by using a model checker. We demonstrated the applicability of the approach with simple examples and showed that the achieved fault tolerance statistics can lead to a better understanding of algorithm-specific fault tolerance characteristics. For example, it has been shown that depending on the algorithms, diversity not always lead to the most hardware fault tolerant system. Nonetheless, diversity enhances the robustness against systematic faults and other common-cause failures. Another conclusion that can be derived is that the number of masked faults highly depends on the input values. Knowing this correlation is particularly helpful for rating algorithms, if the expected distribution of input values is known. Furthermore, it has been exemplified that also the consequences of certain output values should influence the choice of the algorithm option.

Our future work includes the further investigation of high-level reliability evaluation to help conquering the problem of comparing the fault tolerance of algorithms in early design stages also for more complex designs.

References

1. Baarir, S., Braunstein, C., Encrenaz, E., Ilié, J.: Feasibility Analysis for MEU Robustness Quantification by Symbolic Model checking. Formal Methods in System Design (2011)
2. Bozzano, M., Villafiorita, A.: The FSAP/NuSMV-SA safety analysis platform. Journal on Software Tools for Technology Transfer (2007)
3. Campetelli, A., Hölzl, F., Neubeck, P.: User-friendly model checking integration in model-based development. In: CAINE (2011)
4. Cavada, R., Cimatti, A., Jochim, C., Keighren, G., Olivetti, E., Pistore, M., Roveri, M., Tchaltsev, A.: Nusmv 2.4 User Manual. ITCIRST (2005)
5. Ezekiel, J., Lomuscio, A.: Combining fault injection and model checking to verify fault tolerance in multi-agent systems. In: AAMAS (2009)
6. Henkel, J., Bauer, L., Zhang, H.: Multi-layer dependability: From microarchitecture to application level. In: DAC (2014)
7. Höller, A., Krieg, A., Preschern, C., Steger, C., Bock, H., Haid, J., Kreiner, C.: Automatized high-level evaluation of security properties for RTL hardware designs. In: 8th Workshop on Embedded Systems Security (2013)
8. Huang, et al.: A simulator for evaluating redundancy analysis algorithms of repairable embedded memories. In: Workshop on Memory Technology, Design and Testing (2002)
9. Huth, M., Ryan, M.: Logic in Computer Science: Modelling and reasoning about systems. Cambridge University Press (2006)
10. IEC/EN 61508: Functional Safety of Electrical/Electronic/Programmable Electronic Safety-related Systems (1999-2002)
11. ISO 26262: Road vehicles - Functional Safety Standard (2009)
12. Krautz, et al.: Evaluating coverage of error detection logic for soft errors using formal methods. In: DATE (2006)
13. Krieg, et al.: Power and Fault Emulation for Software Verification and System Stability Testing in Safety Critical Environments. IEEE Transactions on Industrial Informatics (2013)
14. Kuznetsova, Y.: Analysis and Evaluation of Sequential Redundancy Identification Algorithms. Ph.D. thesis (2011)
15. Latif-Shabgahi, G., Bass, J.M., Bennett, S.: A taxonomy for software voting algorithms used in safety-critical systems. IEEE Transactions on Reliability (2004)
16. Maniatakos, M., Michael, M.K., Makris, Y.: Investigating the limits of AVF analysis in the presence of multiple bit errors. In: International On-Line Testing Symposium (2013)
17. Peters, A.J., Sindrilaru, E.A., Zigann, P.: Evaluation of software based redundancy algorithms for the EOS storage system at CERN. Journal of Physics: Conference Series (2012)
18. Rafe, V., Rahmani, M., Rashidi, K.: A Survey on Coping with the State Space Explosion Problem in Model Checking. International Research Journal of Applied and Basic Sciences (2013)
19. Seshia, S.A., Li, W., Mitra, S.: Verification-guided soft error resilience. In: DATE (2007)
20. Sharma, V., Haran, A., Rakamaric, Z., Gopalakrishnan, G.: Towards Formal Approaches to System Resilience. In: Pacific Rim International Symposium on Dependable Computing (2013)
21. Voelter, et al.: Mbeddr: Instantiating a Language Workbench in the Embedded Software Domain. Automated Software Engineering (2013)

On Applying FMEA to SOAs:
A Proposal and Open Challenges

Cristiana Areias[1,2], Nuno Antunes[2], and João Carlos Cunha[1]

[1] Instituto Politécnico de Coimbra, ISEC, DEIS, Rua Pedro Nunes, 3030-199 Coimbra, Portugal
{cris,jcunha}@isec.pt
[2] University of Coimbra, Polo II - Pinhal de Marrocos, 3030-329 Coimbra, Portugal
nmsa@dei.uc.pt

Abstract. Service Oriented Architectures (SOAs) are being increasingly used to support business-critical systems, raising natural concerns regarding dependability and security attributes. In critical applications, Verification and Validation (V&V) practices are used during system development to achieve the desired level of quality. However, most V&V techniques suit a structured and documented development lifecycle, and assume that the system does not evolve after deployment, contrarily to what happens with SOA. Runtime V&V practices represent one possible solution for this problem, but they are not possible to implement without the adjustment of traditional V&V techniques.

This paper studies the adaptation of Failure Mode and Effects Analysis (FMEA) to SOA environments. A preliminary technique named FMEA4SOA is proposed and a case study is used to illustrate its usage. This process raises many challenges that must be overcome for the FMEA4SOA to become usable and effective V&V in SOA environments. The paper discusses these challenges while proposing a research roadmap.

Keywords: business-critical, services, SOA, verification, validation, FMEA.

1 Introduction

Service Oriented Architectures (SOAs) are a paradigm for organizing and utilizing distributed functionalities whose main emphasis is on the loose coupling among interacting software agents or components [5]. In practice, a SOA consists of a collection of interacting software elements with well-defined business functionalities that may be combined and reused in different manners to support the information infrastructure of an organization. These elements, known as services, are deployed in a distributed way, and are consumed by other services and applications, frequently over a network. SOAs present particular characteristics as high complexity, extreme dynamicity, and a very large scale of composability. The increasing usage of SOAs in business-critical applications calls for quality assurance approaches that allow continuously asserting their trustworthiness.

Verification and Validation (V&V) is in the foundation of critical applications' development, and has been largely applied in scenarios that involve life and mission

I. Majzik and M. Vieira (Eds.): SERENE 2014, LNCS 8785, pp. 86–100, 2014.
© Springer International Publishing Switzerland 2014

critical embedded systems, including railways, automotive, and space. V&V consists of a quality assurance process for checking if a system meets the specifications and fulfills the intended purpose [15]. Besides the functional behavior, V&V also considers non-functional features such as dependability and security aspects.

The traditional application of V&V consists of the detailed checking of a system prior to its deployment. Moreover, the typical V&V lifecycle assumes a structured and highly documented development process that allows gathering the required quality evidences, and presumes that the system does not evolve after deployment (i.e. the system structure is stable over time). The problem is that this approach does not fit the characteristics of service oriented environments, where a multitude of services is continuously being deployed, interconnected and updated, following software development approaches that favor rapid deployment and frequent updates of services. In fact, the dynamic nature of SOAs, together with the demand from organizations for rapid changes in business requirements, result in an overlapping between the design and usage phases of services.

To overcome these problems, new V&V approaches must be applied at runtime to continuously assure the required quality and thus improve trustworthiness. In [1] it is proposed a framework for Runtime V&V in SOAs that continuously monitors and assesses the services in order to perform verification and validation of the SOA system. However, for the V&V techniques to be usable in the context of this framework, it is also necessary to research ways for their adaptation.

A multitude of techniques and tools for V&V is available in the literature, ranging from software testing to RAMS analysis, including formal methods, simulation or even fault injection [9]. RAMS analysis usually designate processes that that attempt to assess the system according to its properties of Reliability, Availability, Maintainability and Safety and include diverse techniques such as Failure Mode and Effects Analysis (FMEA), its extension to Failure Mode, Effects and Criticality Analysis (FMECA), or Fault Tree Analysis (FTA) among others. In this work, we are particularly interested in Software FMEA [12] that was one of the first systematic techniques for failure analysis [6]. It is based on the review of the components of the system and identification of failure modes, and their causes and effects. This is mostly a qualitative analysis that allows the calculation of a Risk Priority Number (RPN) indicating which failures and corresponding causes should be addressed.

This paper introduces FMEA4SOA, a preliminary approach to apply FMEA in service oriented environments. A new process has been developed considering the specific characteristics of SOA, focusing on the analysis of services instead of system components and also able to deal with the dynamicity of the environment. This approach has three main merits: *1)* it allows a **systematic review** of a SOA environment, achieving a deeper understanding of the most critical services, including their risks and the effects of their failures; *2)* it **prioritizes** the services regarding the needs to apply other V&V techniques; and *3)* every time the system evolves, it helps on determining the services that must be **re-verified and/or re-validated**.

When compared with traditional FMEAs, FMEA4SOA has several advantages, as it was designed to: *1)* fit SOA characteristics, including dynamicity, lack of control over the services and lack of a well-structured development process; *2)* be applicable in runtime; *3)* automate the process, at least partially, to reduce the costs, reduce the time for the analysis and increase the applicability to more services.

A case study was devised to demonstrate the applicability of FME4SOA, serving also as support to discuss its current limitations and highlight some open challenges: lack of the knowledge of the system (that includes third-party services), subjectivity of scales that must be shared across multiple teams but also the difficulty of automatically determining new ranks on the running environment, and the complexity and dynamicity of the system that makes it difficult to determine the impact of controls. Based on these challenges, a research roadmap was defined.

The outline of the paper is as follows. The next section presents relevant background and related work. Section 3 presents our proposal while Section 4 demonstrates its usability with a case study. Section 5 presents challenges and a research roadmap. Section 6 concludes the paper.

2   Background and Related Work

SOAs are increasingly being used in business critical systems and recognized as an accepted approach to make businesses more efficient and agile [14]. SOAs are composed by individual services in order to build dynamic and distributed software systems that perform some business functionality. Services are autonomous and loosely-coupled software components that are delivered through standardized interfaces and message-exchanging protocols providing reusable business functionalities, with clear separation between the interface and the implementation. This allows SOAs to be flexible and dynamic and the best choice for systems integration, including legacy systems [11]. Additionally, its interoperability allows services to invoke others services that belong to external organizations (third-parties) distributed over the Internet in order to perform the intended business functionality.

To assure quality, organizations spend a significant portion of the system development budget in ensuring that software achieves the required levels of dependability and security. In fact, the cost of a failure in a business critical system is usually higher than it is to preventively find and remove defects. Verification and Validation (V&V) is the process for checking if a system meets the specifications and fulfills the intended purpose [15]. While verification checks the conformance to the specifications, trying to identify product faults or errors, which give rise to failures, validation is used to get the necessary evidences to ensure that the system satisfies the intended needs [15], i.e. it is free from failures [2].

Several V&V techniques have been applied during software development, ranging from static to dynamic techniques [15], such as walkthroughs, inspections, traceability analysis and testing [15]. Although testing is probably the most used, in the context of critical systems other more stringent V&V activities are recommended or even required. These activities aim at evaluating the critical parts of the system and directing the efforts of V&V where consequences of failure are the most severe [15]. One of the most used of such activities in the context of safety-critical systems is the Software Failure Mode and Effect Analysis (FMEA) [12].

FMEA is a reliability analysis tool used to forestall failure modes and to mitigate potential risks by studying the effects and possible causes of component failures on a system [13]. It helps to anticipate what, where and how a product, a process or a service might fail, and then assess the relative impact of different failures, in order to identify the parts of the process or the components that need to become more robust in order to mitigate the risk of failure. The FMEA process starts from systematically selecting individual components of the system and identifying their possible modes of failure. It then considers the likely effects of each failure and the probable causes. The output information obtained from a FMEA can be used for troubleshooting activities and to select the most appropriate procedures to mitigate failures. Unfortunately this is a very time consuming process, so it is very expensive to apply to large and complex systems in their entirely.

Notwithstanding the benefits of SOA, its loose coupling and highly dynamic nature poses serious challenges to business-critical systems when it is necessary to apply V&V techniques. In fact, the exact configuration of the environment and the usage of its components can only be seen at runtime [5], meaning that V&V should be applied not only during system development, but also after deployment [1]. The current state of the art on V&V for service-oriented environments focuses mainly in techniques for verifying the correctness of single or composed services across formal methods [10] and testing [3, 5]. Although very useful and effective, these techniques are essentially applied to individual services, based on assumptions that may not hold in SOA environments. Furthermore, SOAs are such a complex environment that it is impracticable (due to time and resource constraints) to apply V&V to all the services and components at runtime.

FMEA offers a way to systematically analyze all the structure of the SOA environment and determine which parts are the most critical in order to prioritize the employment of further V&V. To the best of our knowledge, there is no such application of FMEA to SOAs. In [16] it is presented an example of the application of a FMECA to a service based system, but the runtime requirements of the system were not consider. Our proposal introduces the use of FMEA as a tool to provide an extensive knowledge of the overall environment of the system through the identification of the dependencies and interactions between services, and ranking them according to their relative risks. After this analysis, more V&V efforts can be directed towards the services with higher risk and also to plan effective integration of new services. Finally, the technique provides documentation of failures, which can be tracked over time, helping on identifying appropriate V&V methods to be applied on services or identifying missing requirements.

3   Towards Software FMEAs in SOAs

When performing a FMEA, the developing teams continuously look for answers to questions such as *"What could go wrong?"*, *"How could this failure be prevented?"* or *"What is the likelihood that such failure is detected before affecting other components of the system or its user?"*. Indeed, answering and documenting these questions and then assessing the related risks is the correct way to perform a FMEA.

Different authors present the process in different ways and at various stages of the lifecycle, requiring the teams to adapt the analysis to the characteristics of the system and stage when it is being applied. Nevertheless, there is a consensus on the basic steps of a FMEA. Building on top of this consensus, we designed our proposal for Failure Mode and Effects Analysis for Service Oriented Architectures (FMEA4SOA) to fit the characteristics of a SOA environment. Fig. 1 presents an overview of the steps of the FMEA process that are presented in the next subsections.

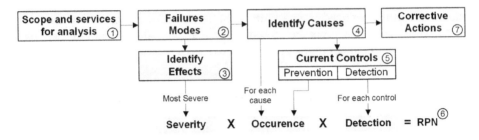

Fig. 1. FMEA4SOA process workflow

3.1 Define the Scope and Items for Analysis

The FMEA process starts **(1)** with the definition of the scope and the boundaries of the system, and the identification of the individual items, components or functions to be analyzed. Since the basic component of a SOA is the service, our approach focuses on the operations of each service that is contained inside the specified boundaries.

This way, the next step of the process consists of characterizing the operations under analysis. For each operation it is necessary to identify the *Operation Name* (name of the operation itself), *Provider* (the identification of the host of the service), the *Service Name* (identifies the service that offers the operation under analysis), the *Description* (portrays the service goals) and the *Type*. The Type refers to the kind of service access control according to the point of view of the provider. It can assume the values *Under Control*, *Partially Under Control* and *Within-Reach* [19].

3.2 Identify Potential Failure Modes

A Failure Mode of a service is a way in which the service deviates from its correct functioning [2]. Following this definition, in this step **(2)** it is necessary to investigate, for each of the previously identified operations, the possible modes of failure.

In the context of SOAs we identified a list of several typical problems that may occur. Table 1 describes service failure modes that should be considered in an FMEA4SOA analysis. It was based on the works presented in [2, 7], and although the list is not exhaustive, it covers most of the functionality, dependability and availability attributes.

Based on this table it is necessary to select, for each operation, the failure modes that apply and that are intended to be analyzed. This selection can be performed manually (before the start of the process or the first time that the service is considered for analysis) or automated based on a set of rules that allow to deduce the failure modes to consider based on the characteristics of the each operation (and respective service).

Table 1. Potential failure modes in services

Failure Modes	Description
Unavailable service or operation	The service is unavailable or the operation invoked does not exist.
Operation execution hangs	The service and operation execution hangs and should be ended by force.
Abnormal termination	The service execution stops abnormally once an unexpected exception is raised by the application.
No error output after time-out	There is no error indicating that an operation cannot be performed after a timeout.
Invalid error code	The error code returned by the service is not correct.
Slow service	The service executes the intended operation but the response is delayed.
Incorrect results	The service provides an incorrect output.
Incoherent results	The service provides incoherent results when it executes non-deterministic actions.
Outdated results	The service returns outdated results according to what was agreed upon in SLA and QoS.

3.3   Identify the Potential Effects and Severity

The next step (**3**) is to determine the effects that each of the previously identified failure modes has regarding the operation itself and the complete system. The severity of these effects should be assessed according to the impact as perceived by the user. Our FMEA4SOA considers the effects of each failure mode and the corresponding level of severity as divided in two different sets:

— *Local Effects:* consequence(s) of a failure mode on the direct consumers, i.e. on the immediate services or resources that are invoking the operation under analysis.
— *End Effects:* consequence(s) of a failure mode on the **end consumer** of the service, i.e. the first level outside the boundaries of the system. It is noteworthy that services may be implemented with fault tolerant mechanisms, meaning that there may be no effects on the end consumer. When the end consumer is directly invoking the service, the local effects are coincident with the end effects.

Due to the complexity and dynamicity of an SOA, it is impracticable to perform this analysis manually. Techniques like fault injection are a possible approach to evaluate the potential effects (local and end) of each failure mode. The injected faults reproduce the failure of the service, in order to evaluate their effects according to their severity as observed by the local and the end consumers.

For the classification of the effects' severity, the use of a scale can be helpful. Such scale should be defined *a priori* by the FMEA team, taking into account the most relevant properties for the analysis. Different FMEA severity scales are used for different domains [6]. However, we have not found any scale matching the characteristics of software services. This way, we propose in Table 2 a severity classification tailored for use in FMEA4SOA.

Although this is a severity classification that focuses on availability and reliability attributes, each organization should adapt it according to its own V&V goals. The rank is listed in ascending order of importance and should be applied taking into account the worst potential consequences of a failure. The automated selection of the rank can be made using a set of rules and values from the monitoring system.

Table 2. Guidelines to determine the severity of the effects

Effect	Severity Description	Rank
None	No effect or the effect will not be perceived by the consumer.	1
Minor	Minor effects on the service operation performance but still working on the SLA threshold. The service operation does not require repair or an acceptable workaround or solution exists. The data were not corrupted.	2
Significant	The performance is highly degraded and the operation may not operate, affecting the consumer with frequent or continuous instabilities. SLA can be seriously compromised so the service operation requires repair.	3
Extreme	The service operation is unavailable or is providing incorrect results with critically impact on business consumers.	4
Hazardous	The failure involves outcomes that affects a bigger part of the SOA environment or even compromise the entire system.	5

3.4   Identify the Possible Causes of Failures

Afterwards, it is necessary to identify the potential causes for each failure mode and assess the likelihood of its occurrence (**4**). System failures can be caused by different reasons, which are designated as faults. In the context of FMEA4SOA we propose the list of causes presented in Table 3.

Table 3. List of Potential Cause of Failures

Class	Cause	Description
Physical	*Network problem*	The network adapters are having trouble to perform as expected or are making the server unreachable.
	Machine reboots	The machine that supports the applications rebooted.
	Application server crash	The application server crashed and needs to be restarted to resume its activity.
	Resource exhaustion	The resources that are needed to perform the action (e.g. memory, storage) were entirely consumed.
	Server overload	The server is receiving more requests than it can handle.
Development	*Incorrect requirements specification*	The functional requirements are not well specified so the service does not perform as expected.
	Incorrect Design	The service/operation was incorrectly designed.
	Codification Error	The service/operation had a function, assignment, interface, timing or algorithm codification error.
	Service description incorrect or missing	The service is well implemented but its description is not clear or is described incorrectly causing a wrong invocation.
	Service requirement changed	The service requirements changed and the interface is inconsistent.
Interactions	*Incorrect SLA*	The SLA that supports the service is incorrect or is outdated due the changes in the service.
	Attacks	Attacks targeting the service implementations, infrastructure or transactions.
	Interoperability problems	The service consumer and service provider use incompatible technologies
	Incorrect permissions	Incorrect settings avoiding the access of the service – due to insufficient or excessive permissions
	3rd parties service failures	The service is composed by 3rd parties services and the interfaces were changed or are unavailable.

The list was gathered from several sources and, inspired by the classification presented in [2], divides the causes of failures in tree main classes: *physical faults*, that include all fault classes that affect hardware; *development faults*, that include fault classes occurring during development; and *interaction faults*, that include all external faults.

For each failure mode, it is necessary to select the possible causes from the table. Then, for each of the possible causes it is necessary to assess the probability of *occurrence*, i.e. how frequent a failure can occur due to such cause, in spite of the current prevention controls in place (next subsection). To facilitate the classification we propose, based in [6], an auxiliary scale of likelihood of occurrence of failures in 5 levels (see Table 4), based on an estimation of the number of incidents that may occur by operation request or, when this measurement not fit the cause of failure, during the system lifetime.

In order to perform this process accurately, historical data should be considered, which requires the use of runtime monitoring to continuously collect updated information. The process may require manual configuration at the beginning, but afterwards it is basically an automated process.

Table 4. Guidelines to estimate and classify the likelihood of the occurrence of causes

Likelihood	Occurrence of Causes *(Incidents per operation requests or Incidents on lifetime)*	Rank
Remote *Failure is unlikely*	Failure eliminated by prevention control or the probability of occurrence is < 1 per 10^6 requests or 1 occurrence in more than 3 years	1
Low *Relative few Failures*	1 in 100000 requests or 1 every year.	2
Moderate *Occasional Failures*	1 in 500 requests or 1 every three months	3
High *Repeated Failures*	1 in 20 requests or 1 every week	4
Very high *Failure is almost inevitable*	> 1 per 10 requests or 1 per day	5

3.5   Identify Current Controls: Prevention and Detection

In order to increase quality and mitigate system failures, some activities or mechanisms are applied when developing or maintaining a critical system. This way, the next step is to identify the current controls (**5**) that are in place to avoid or minimize the impact of the potential failures, and should be considered in the FMEA4SOA activity. There are two classes of controls: *prevention*, which are applied to either eliminate the causes of failures or reduce their frequency, and *detection*, that are used to identify a failure or its cause.

Some activities such as static code analysis and testing are widely used to show evidences of software trustworthiness, while fault tolerant mechanisms are used to prevent software system failures. Other mechanisms such as monitoring systems, heartbeat components and firewalls introduced in the environment are useful in detecting any deviation from normal system operation.

The prevention controls influence the likelihood of the occurrence of causes, as described in the previous subsection. The detection controls, in the other hand, should be ranked according to their ability in detecting the cause, mechanism or weakness of the actual or the potential failure in time for adequate intervention. In Table 5 we present the detection guidelines, adapted from [6], to be used in FMEA4SOA.

Table 5. Guidelines to estimate the likelihood of detection of causes and failures

Likelihood	Description	Rank
Near Certain	The control will almost certainly detect a potential cause/mechanism and subsequent failure mode in time for adequate intervention.	1
Moderately High	Moderate chance of the control to detect a potential cause/mechanism and subsequent failure mode in time for adequate intervention	2
Low	Low chance for the control to detect a potential cause/mechanism and subsequent failure mode in time for adequate intervention.	3
Remote	Remote chance for the control to detect a potential cause/mechanism and subsequent failure mode in time for adequate intervention	4
Near Impossible	Design Control will not or cannot detect a potential cause/mechanism and subsequent failure mode; or there is no control.	5

Although the detection ranking presented is clearly subjective, statistical data can be used to help in this judgment. The severity, occurrence and detectability scales presented should be adapted to the goal of the FMEA4SOA analysis. It is clear that its use depends on the experience and perspective of the analysis team, both in the FMEA development experience and knowledge of the system. However, to develop an autonomously tool to be used at runtime to assist in this hard process, more accurate scales should be created and investigated.

3.6   Assess the Overall Risk

Following, it is necessary to compute (6) the risk associated with each cause of failure. This can be calculated using the three attributes already referred: the *Severity* of the failure effects, the probability of *Occurrence* of their causes and the *Detection* proficiency of the controls used. Each of these components is described on a scale (from 1 to 5 in our proposals, but others could be used), and their product produces a Risk Priority Number (RPN):

$$RPN = Severity \times Occurrence \times Detection$$

The RPN is a critical indicator for each failure mode and corresponding cause; the *higher its value, the greater the risk*. Regarding this computation, different formulas have been proposed in the literature, as it is claimed that the traditional RPN is a poor method, not conveniently representing the real risk [4]. Although this is an important issue, it falls out of the scope of this work, as the presented innovations are not directly affected by the formula itself.

3.7   Identify Corrective Actions and Recalculate RPN

In last step **(7),** every failure mode/cause with RPN over a defined threshold must be subject to corrective actions to reduce the risks. This can be performed through reducing the severity of the failures, reducing the probability of occurrence of their causes, or improving the effectiveness of the detection controls. After the identification and subsequent application of the corrective actions, the process should be repeated and RPN recalculated until the risk is considered acceptable.

Obviously, in the context of a broader Runtime V&V framework, the corrective actions may correspond to the application of other V&V techniques to be applied in the set of services over the threshold.

4   Preliminary Demonstration

In order to demonstrate the proposed FMEA4SOA and to better understand the merits and difficulties in applying the process, we created a simplified SOA system that represents a business process that uses some internal and external resources and services to perform its functionality.

4.1   Description of the SOA Example

Fig. 2 depicts a SOA that represents an infrastructure that includes a composite service able to provide a listing of TV shows, according to some specifics preferences and keywords. The infrastructure consists of a modified subset of the jSeduite SOA [8] able to present different scenarios and functionalities in only one infrastructure. Although this is not a critical environment, it will allow demonstrating the main challenges when applying the FMEA4SOA approach.

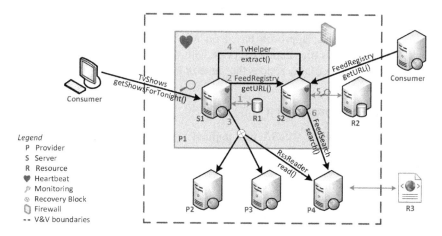

Fig. 2. Simple SOA environment

As observed from Fig. 2, the environment is composed by a small number of services and resources that are distributed among different providers (P). The operations of the services that compose this system are as follows:

— TvShows.*getShowsForToninght()* – a composite operation that provides a list of TV shows for the night. The first step (1) is to search for URLs of TV Feeds in the local database (R1), according to the input keywords. If no information is available, the operation *FeedRegistry.getURL()* is invoked (2) in order to seek out for the desired URLs in services located in other resources (5) and providers (6). The next step (3) is to read, through the *RssReader.read()* service, all information at the URLs previously acquired and then the useful information of these RSS files is transformed (4) through the service *TvHelper.Extract()*, in structured usable data. Finally, a list of the shows for tonight is returned to the consumer.
— FeedRegistry.*getURL()* – a composite operation that provides a list of Feed URLs. If there is no sufficient information in local resources (5) to provide its functionality, the service invokes *FeedSearch.search()* (6), which belongs to other provider, to return URLs that fit some requirements. The *FeedRegistry.getURL()* operation is available to be used internally by consumers under control of the provider and by external consumers.
— TvHelper.*extract()* – extracts the useful information from the RSS file.
— FeedSearch.*search()* – provides a list of URLs of the feeds channels.
— RssReader.*read()* – provides the contents of an RSS from its URL.

Some prevention and detection controls are used in provider P1. A firewall serves as a gatekeeper between provider P1 and the outside world. P1 also contains a monitoring system that is checking if the service TvShows is running within the SLA as well as other monitoring mechanisms such as Intrusion Detection System (IDS) that monitors network or system activities for malicious activities or policy violations. Some heartbeats also exist in services to assure they are still responding. Other relevant information is that static analysis has been applied to services implemented by P1 to improve its quality. Finally, when TvShows.getShowsForTonight() invokes RssReader.Read(),a fault-tolerance approach based on recovery blocks is used: if RssReader.Read() fails, TvShows tries another service with the same functionality available in P3 and, in case of another failure, does the same in P2.

4.2   FMEA4SOA Construction

Our demonstration of FMEA4SOA was applied to the P1 provider that has control over the services and resources inside the gray area in Fig. 2. As described in Section 3, the first step is the identification of the services and operations to be analyzed. The dashed line identifies the boundaries of the system under V&V. This means that the services that reside inside this area are to be analyzed and all systems that are outside this boundary are considered end consumers.

All services hosted in S1 and S2 can be easily assessed as they are under control of P1. This way, all documentation of design and V&V activities already done in these services is available. However, while the *TvHelper* service is under full control of P1, the *FeedRegistry* and *TvShows* is partially under control as they use external services and resources to perform their functionalities. The *FeedSearch* and *RssReader* are within-reach control meaning that, despite being part of the SOA, the provider is only able to invoke and it is not able to access the internals of this service; it just can access its interface. We started by selecting the operation *TvShows. getShowsForTonight* for our analysis, and considered two failures modes: the *Unavailable service/operation* and the *Slow service/operation*. Table 6 presents the spreadsheet used in our FMEA4SOA activity.

The next step is the analysis of the effects of the failure modes. In our cases, both local and end effects are coincident because the only immediate consumer is outside the V&V boundaries. According to the severity guidelines from Table 2, we considered that the end effects impact for a *No Response* in Unavailable service/operation is 4 and for a *Slow Response* in Slow service/operation is 3.

The potential causes for the failure modes under analysis may be quite a few, related with physical problems in the network and the machines, with the development of the services or even with interactions with consumers. In Table 6 we present only some of these potential causes, and classified their occurrences according to hypothetical historical data that might exist in the organization as well as the existence of prevention mechanisms. For example, *Slow Operation* failure mode can be caused by failures in other services (e.g. low performance of the TvHelper), meaning that the probability of occurrence of these third party failures depends on design implementations, the existing prevention mechanisms in the environment and historical data of services performance. Prevention mechanisms such as the recovery blocks have a strong influence on lowering the incidents due to RssReader failures.

Table 6. FMEA4SOA Demonstration – TvShows Service

Provider	Name	Type	Operation	Potential Failure Modes	Effects		SEV	Potential Causes	OCC	Current Controls		DET	RPN
					Local Effects	End Effects				Prevention	Detection		
P1	TVShows	Within Reach	getShowsForTonight	Unavailable service/operation	-	No response	4	Network problem	2		Firewall; IDS	2	16
								Machine Reboots	2		Heartbeat	3	24
								Resource exhaustion	2	Stress Testing		5	40
								Service requirements changed	2	Regression Testing		5	40
								Attacks	3	Robustness Testing	Firewall, IDS	3	36
				Slow service/operation	-	Slow response	3	Network problem	2		Firewall; IDS	2	12
								Machine Reboots	2		Heartbeat;	3	18
								Resource exhaustion	2	Stress Testing		5	30
								Attacks	3	Robustness Testing	Firewall, IDS	3	27
								App. server crash	1		Heartbeat;	5	15
								Server overload	2	Stress Testing		5	30
								Incorrect req. specification	2	Inspections		5	30
								Incorrect design	2	Inspections		5	30
								Incorrect implementation	3	Static code analysis		5	45
								Service requirements changed	2	Regression Testing		5	30
								Incorrect SLA	2		Monitoring system	4	24
								TvHelper failure	3		Monitoring system	4	36
								FeedRegistry failure	4		Monitoring system	4	48
								RssReader failure	2	Recovery Block	Monitoring system	4	24
			...	...	...			...		...			

After the current controls have been specified (either when the mechanisms exist on services or in the environment) the detectability ranks were defined according to historical data. As demonstrated in Table 6, the monitoring system is not efficient in detecting third parties failures. Furthermore, there are many potential causes that have not been addressed for any detection control but influence the risk.

As we can observe by the RPN values presented in the table, the most priority problems are basically four, which present RPN of 40 or above. The one with RPN 48 is due to the use of an external service (*FeedRegistry*) where no fault tolerant mechanisms have been implemented, and the detection controls are weak or inexistent. Another one with RPN 45 is due to the inexistence of detection controls and also to poor prevention controls. The remaining two, with RPN 40, also do not have detection mechanisms, however the history of occurrences is lower.

5   Research Challenges and Roadmap

The FMEA4SOA can be a very useful V&V technique to evaluate the risks of services and operations. Furthermore, all the information collected throughout this process can be very valuable to obtain a deeper knowledge about the system and its environment, and to identify which other V&V techniques can be applied. However, due the characteristics of an SOA, several issues should be overtaken for this technique to be usable in runtime. Overcoming these challenges is what ultimately distinguishes our approach from the traditional FMEAs. We identified the following challenges that can be established as a roadmap for future research:

- **Occurrence, Severity and Detectability:** the definition of the scales to be used for severity, occurrence and detectability and the ranks to be attributed to each case depends on the experience and perspective of the analysis team. Although this is a traditional issue for FMEAs, in this case it assumes special magnitude as parts of the same SOA are assessed by different teams, across organizations, and the data must be shared among them. Also, using these scales in runtime is even harder than during design time.
  - A set of scales may not fit every scenario, thus it is necessary to establish guidelines for each team or organization to define the scale that best fits their scenario also in order to reduce the subjectivity of this process;
  - Different teams/organizations can rank with different values the same conditions, which will influence the overall risk. How to select the adequate values during runtime?
- **Effects of the Failure Modes:** the evolution of the environment originates changes in the environment and the impact of failures can also evolve, requiring the effects analysis to be done at runtime.
  - Fault injection is the obvious solution to assess the impact of failures, by allowing their simulation. However, the running services cannot be stopped to avoid the undesired propagation of failures to other services. Combining fault injection with services virtualization can be a useful approach.
  - For third-party services, where there is no access to the environment, virtualization cannot be applied. However, the effects of a component failure should

propagate through the interconnected components until reaching the V&V boundaries. This way, it is necessary to research for different methods and approaches for analyzing the effects of failures at runtime, according to the access type of the services: full control, partially under control and within-reach.

- **RPN Adapted for SOA:** the traditional risk priority number is ambiguous and is not the best representation for the risk. It is necessary to research new ways for a better representation of the RPN, taking into account the SOA characteristics.
- **Quickly Outdated FMEA Analysis:** since the system structure changes regularly and has no fixed boundaries, the FMEA analysis becomes outdated very quickly. Also, at any moment during the system lifetime, new mechanisms can be inserted to increase the system confidence. FMEA4SOA should be able to adapt to the new requirements at runtime, and provide up-to-date information in a timely way.
- **SOA Complexity:** a service-oriented environment is a complex system, composed of several distributed services where its correctness depends on the correctness of the parts and their interactions. Performing a FMEA at runtime for all the components can take a considerable amount of time, cost and resources. In fact, the structure of this system can have an explosion of combinations and dependencies between services and operations, making this process impossible to execute in all its extension. This way, it is necessary to establish some criteria for selecting the services to analyze.
- **Lack of Knowledge on Services and on the Environment:** the effectiveness of a FMEA process depends on the deep knowledge of the system and its components. However, many services in a SOA environment are used, but not owned. Although historical data of the used services can help, it may be insufficient for a deep analysis. The cooperation between partners in sharing information to perform the FMEA is an approach that should be explored.
- **Dynamic Services Composition:** a SOA system naturally evolves with the dynamically discovery and use of new services, frequently without the knowledge of their quality and associated risks. It is thus necessary to develop risk graphs demonstrating the effects of service failures:
  - when the architecture changes, the evolution of the risk graph will allow to determine which parts of the architecture need to be re-verified and re-validated;
  - in a collaborative world, these graphs will provide a common format for information sharing among partners while limiting the privacy issues.

6   Conclusions

The wide adoption of service-oriented systems in business applications and the need to ensure trustworthiness, calls for the adaptation of traditional V&V techniques to the characteristic of those systems.

In this paper we introduced FMEA4SOA, a failure mode and effects analysis adapted to service-oriented systems. The main idea is to examine potential failure modes, assess their impact and the probable causes in order to anticipate potential problems, their effects and guide to possible solutions. We presented a list of typical failure modes of such environments, potential causes and guidelines to rank the severity of their effects, the probability of occurrences of their causes, and the level of detectability of the existing controls.

This technique was applied to a simple example highlighting some of the open challenges to apply it at runtime. Based on the analysis of these challenges, a research roadmap was established containing the key steps that are necessary to undertake before FMEA4SOA can be applied on a running service-based system.

Acknowledgements. This work has been partially supported by the project DEVASSES (http://www.devasses.eu, PIRSES-GA-2013-612569) and the project CECRIS (http://www. www.cecris-project.eu, FP7-PEOPLE-2012-IAPP), both within the context of the European Union's Seventh Framework Programme.

References

1. Areias, C.: A Framework for Runtime V&V in Business-Critical Service Oriented Architectures. In: 43rd Annual IEEE/IFIP Conference on Dependable Systems and Networks Workshop (DSN-W 2013), Budapest, Hungary, pp. 1–4 (2013)
2. Avižienis, A., et al.: Basic Concepts and Taxonomy of Dependable and Secure Computing. IEEE Trans. Dependable Secure Comput. 1(1), 11–33 (2004)
3. Bertolino, A., De Angelis, G., Frantzen, L., Polini, A.: The PLASTIC Framework and Tools for Testing Service-Oriented Applications. In: De Lucia, A., Ferrucci, F. (eds.) ISSSE 2006-2008. LNCS, vol. 5413, pp. 106–139. Springer, Heidelberg (2009)
4. Bowles, J.B.: An assessment of RPN prioritization in a failure modes effects and criticality analysis. In: Annual Reliability and Maintainability Symposium, pp. 380–386 (2003)
5. Canfora, G., Di Penta, M.: Service-Oriented Architectures Testing: A Survey. In: De Lucia, A., Ferrucci, F. (eds.) ISSSE 2006-2008. LNCS, vol. 5413, pp. 78–105. Springer, Heidelberg (2009)
6. Carlson, C.: Effective FMEAs: Achieving Safe, Reliable, and Economical Products and Processes using Failure Mode and Effects Analysis. Wiley, Hoboken (2012)
7. Chan, K.S.M., Bishop, J., Steyn, J., Baresi, L., Guinea, S.: A Fault Taxonomy for Web Service Composition. In: Di Nitto, E., Ripeanu, M. (eds.) ICSOC 2007 Workshops. LNCS, vol. 4907, pp. 363–375. Springer, Heidelberg (2009)
8. Delerce-Mauris, C., et al.: Plateforme SEDUITE: Une Approche SOA de la Diffusion d'Informations. University of Nice, I3S CNRS, Sophia Antipolis, France (2009)
9. Hsueh, M.-C., et al.: Fault injection techniques and tools. Computer 30(4), 75–82 (1997)
10. Leucker, M., Schallhart, C.: A brief account of runtime verification. J. Log. Algebr. Program. 78(5), 293–303 (2009)
11. Lewis, G.A.: Is SOA Being Pushed Beyond Its Limits? Adv. Comput. Sci. Int. J. 2(1), 17–23 (2013)
12. Reifer, D.J.: Software Failure Modes and Effects Analysis. IEEE Trans. Reliab. R-28(3), 247–249 (1979)
13. Stamatis, D.H.: Failure mode and effect analysis: FMEA from theory to execution. Asq Press (2003)
14. Tesselaar, H.: The future of financial services may be banking on SOA, http://searchsoa.techtarget.com/opinion/ The-future-of-financial-services-may-be-banking-on-SOA
15. Wallace, D.R., et al.: Reference Information for the Software Verification and Validation Process. DIANE Publishing (1996)
16. Zalewski, A.: A FMECA framework for Service Oriented Systems based on Web Services. In: 2nd International Conference on Dependability of Computer Systems, DepCoS-RELCOMEX 2007, pp. 286–293. IEEE (2007)

Verification and Validation of a Pressure Control Unit for Hydraulic Systems*

Pontus Boström[1], Mikko Heikkilä[2], Mikko Huova[2],
Marina Waldén[1], and Matti Linjama[2]

[1] Department of Information Technologies,
Åbo Akademi University, Turku, Finland
{pontus.bostrom,marina.walden}@abo.fi
[2] Department of Intelligent Hydraulics and Automation
Tampere University of Technology, Tampere, Finland
{mikko.heikkila,mikko.huova,matti.linjama}@tut.fi

Abstract. This paper describes the development, verification and model-based validation of a safety-critical pressure relief function for a digital hydraulic system. It demonstrates techniques to handle typical challenges that are encountered when verifying and validating cyber-physical systems with complex dynamical behaviour. The system is developed using model-based design in Simulink. The verification part focuses on verification of functional properties of the controller, where formal automated verification tools are employed. The validation part focuses on validating that the controller has the desired impact on the physical system. In the latter part search-based methods are used to find undesired behaviour in a simulation model of the system. The combination of techniques provides confidence in the resilience of the developed system.

1 Introduction

Development of reliable control software is becoming increasingly important as our dependence on computer controlled machines increases. This paper presents a verification and validation approach for complex cyber-physical systems applied to a case study concerning a safety critical pressure relief function for a digital hydraulic system. A reliable pressure relief function is essential for resilient fluid power systems, as all possible causes of dangerous pressure peaks cannot be eliminated. This is an interesting case study due to the interplay between complex control software and complex system dynamics.

Model-based design has become a widely used approach to develop control software [14,5,7] and it is also used for the digital hydraulic systems here. In this approach, a *simulation model* of the physical system is created in order to be able to simulate the complete system. Such a simulation model is essential for cost effective evaluation of the the designed software. When the software is used

---

* Work funded by the DiHy project in the EFFIMA program coordinated by Fimecc and the EDiHy project (no. 140003) funded by the Academy of Finland.

I. Majzik and M. Vieira (Eds.): SERENE 2014, LNCS 8785, pp. 101–115, 2014.

in the real system, one can already be confident that the controller will work according to requirements. Simulink has been used here as the modelling tool, since it is one of the most advanced tools for this design approach.

Verification and validation of the system in the case study is challenging. The system is a cyber-physical system with a complex non-linear dynamical behaviour (described by differential equations without even analytical solutions), where simulation is the only feasible form of analysis. Verification and validation can be seen as a series of filters to detect various kinds of problems with the design [17]. The verification and validation problem that we tackle can be divided into two subparts:

— Verify that the software is correct with respect to its specification. This includes checking that there are no runtime errors such as division by zero or matrix accesses outside bounds.
— Validate that when the software works according to the specification, it will have the desired effect on the system.

To verify the correctness of the designed software, we use *automatic* formal verification to check that the software components satisfy their specifications. Automatic formal verification of embedded software developed using Simulink has been done before e.g. [14,5,7]. Compared to those case studies, our model contains significant amounts of matrix calculations and real arithmetic implemented as floating-point arithmetic, which provides different verification challenges. We have chosen to evaluate our tool VerSAA and Simulink Design Verifier (SLDV) for verification of functional correctness, since both tools have good support for matrix arithmetic. VerSAA is an automatic static verification tool that supports specifications written as contracts [2,4,20]. The contracts are similar to the ones for reactive components in [12]. SLDV[1] [13] is a static verification tool and model-checker provided by Mathworks as a toolbox of Simulink. Testing is needed to evaluate that the software has the desired effect on the system, since formal verification is unattainable for this purpose with reasonable effort due to system complexity. However, finding test cases were, e.g., high pressure peaks occur in the system can be very difficult. We have used search based techniques [1,21] to automatically find tests that expose problems in a simulation model of the system. Our contribution is twofold: 1) We demonstrate development of a new case study and how we have verified that the software meets its specifications using existing verification tools 2) We demonstrate a new method to generate test cases based on optimisation and constraint solving, to automatically generate tests for system validation.

2   The Pressure Controller

Hydraulic systems are widely used in industrial applications which require high forces and also in mobile machines which demand high power-to-weight ratio.

---

[1] Simulink Design Verifier, http://www.mathworks.se/products/sldesignverifier

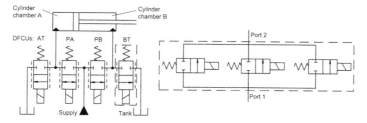

Fig. 1. Distributed digital valve system realised with 4 DFCUs (left). Hydraulic diagram of a three-valve DFCU (right).

A relatively new solution for fluid power systems is digital hydraulics, which offers the same benefits as traditional technology while using simpler components [10,11]. In a digital hydraulic valve system, binary components i.e. on/off-valves are connected in parallel to form digital flow control units (DFCU) as shown in Fig. 1. With a sufficient amount of valves and an intelligent control algorithm, the performance of the system can be better than with traditional proportional or servo valves using simpler mechanical parts.

2.1 Limiting Cylinder Chamber Pressure

In a hydraulic system the maximum pressure has to be limited according to the weakest component of the system in order to prevent system damage. Malfunction presents a risk of serious injury for the people around, break-up for the machine itself and pollution of the environment. A typical hydraulic system has a main pressure relief valve in the supply line to avoid too high pump pressures. Despite the main pressure relief valve, the pressure in a hydraulic cylinder can exceed the rated maximum pressure due to external force acting on the cylinder. Furthermore, rapid deceleration of the piston velocity can generate excessive chamber pressures in case the load inertia is big. Hence, for system resilience a reliable pressure relief function is needed. In this study a pressure relief function is implemented by using an approach relying on chamber pressure measurement and appropriate control of the tank side DFCUs AT and BT (see Fig. 1). This functionality is an extension to an existing model-based control algorithm [8], which neglects sudden changes of the chamber pressure.

2.2 Pressure Relief Functionality

We focus on the pressure relief function for the A-side of the cylinder (see Fig. 1). The pressure controller for the B-side of the cylinder is identical. The idea of the pressure relief function is to gradually open more valves on the tank line AT when the pressure approaches the upper limit p_{max}. This way, the impact of the pressure relief function on other aspects of the system can be minimised. If the pressure p_A in the cylinder chamber exceeds the cracking pressure p_c, the tank side DFCU is opened in order to increase flow Q_{AT} through the DFCU. The

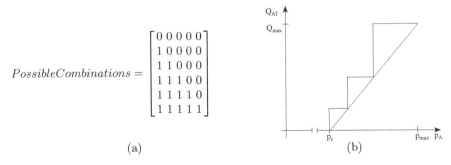

$$PossibleCombinations = \begin{bmatrix} 0\ 0\ 0\ 0\ 0 \\ 1\ 0\ 0\ 0\ 0 \\ 1\ 1\ 0\ 0\ 0 \\ 1\ 1\ 1\ 0\ 0 \\ 1\ 1\ 1\ 1\ 0 \\ 1\ 1\ 1\ 1\ 1 \end{bmatrix}$$

(a)   (b)

Fig. 2. (a) The possible valve combinations opened by the pressure relief function and (b) DFCU command signal as a function of the filtered chamber pressure

more the pressure exceeds the cracking pressure, the larger number of valves is opened on the tank side DFCU.

Here a valve configuration of each DFCU are represented by a 1xn vector containing zeros and ones, where n is the number of on/off valves in the DFCU (here $n = 5$). *Zero* denotes a closed valve, while *one* denotes an open valve. The flow rate for the individual valves used in the algorithm are precomputed and given by the vector $Q_{max} = [2\ 3\ 5\ 10\ 10] \cdot 10^{-4}$. The total flow rate through a valve configuration u is then $Q = u * Q_{max}^T$, where $*$ denotes matrix multiplication. The possible valve combinations opened by the pressure relief functions are given by the rows of the matrix *PossibleCombinations* in Fig. 2(a). The goal of the algorithm is to choose a possible combination that provides the smallest flow rate above the limit Q. The possible combinations are chosen so that when a bigger flow rate is demanded, new valves will only open and no valves will close. The limit Q is defined as a line

$$Q = \frac{p_A - p_c}{p_{max} - p_c}[1\ 1\ 1\ 1\ 1] * Q_{max}^T$$

with zero point at $p_A = p_c$ and $p_A = p_{max}$ requiring opening of all valves, see Fig. 2(b). The algorithm can be summarised as follows:

1. Determine a valve configuration u_{temp} which is the possible valve combination with minimal flow above the limit Q
2. Choose the output u_{out} such that $u_{out} = \mathsf{max}(u_{in} * Q_{max}^T, u_{temp} * Q_{max}^T)$, where u_{in} is the input valve configuration to the pressure controller.

Both the cracking pressure p_c and the maximum pressure p_{max} are user defined parameters; hence this pressure relief function is more flexible than a traditional pressure relief valve. In order to use the chamber pressure measurements, a suitable filtering of the signal is also needed to e.g. reject measurement noise. Here a non-linear filter with hysteresis is used. The nonlinear filtering algorithm includes two phases: Firstly a median value of the three last samples is taken after which a hysteresis function is used. Fig. 3 shows a clarifying example of the hysteresis function. Depending on the application, the dead band of the hysteresis function can be altered through a user parameter. The hysteresis is needed to prevent situations where the system is close to the pressure limit and the pressure relief function would cause excessive opening and closing of valves as the pressure level oscillates around the limit.

2.3   Simulation

In order to test the functionality of the pressure relief function together with the model-based digital valve controller, a simulation model of the mechanics is also realised using MATLAB/Simulink [8]. The system comprises of a digital valve system, two cylinders connected in parallel and a four meter long boom, which is sized to mimic a typical mobile machine boom.

Fig. 4 presents two separate simulation results from a test designed to generate pressure peaks; to the left is a response of the system to an input reference position signal x_{ref} without the pressure relief function, and to the right is the response for the same signal with the pressure relief functionality. The maximum pressure p_{max} is set to 20 MPa and the cracking pressure p_c to 18 MPa. From the simulation results (to the left) it is evident that the model-based controller without the pressure relief function does not react fast enough to the rising chamber pressure p_A resulting in dangerously high pressure. However, the system with the pressure relief function (to the right) reacts to the increase of the pressure level by opening the tank side DFCU sufficiently and it thereby reduces the pressure overshoot. When analysing the position curve x in both cases, one can see that the overall position tracking performance is not optimal, since the reference x_{ref} is intentionally very fast to generate high-pressure transients. However, the pressure controller has only a small additional negative effect.

3   Development of the System

Simulink has been used as the tool for creating and simulating the model of the control software and the system. The language used to create models in Simulink is based on hierarchical data flow diagrams [13] (see e.g. Fig. 5). A Simulink diagram consists of functional blocks connected by signals (wires). The blocks represent transformations of data, while the signals give the flow of data between blocks. Blocks can be parameterised with parameters that are set before

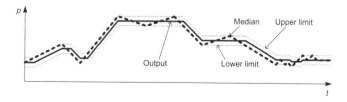

Fig. 3. Hysteresis filtering of the chamber pressure

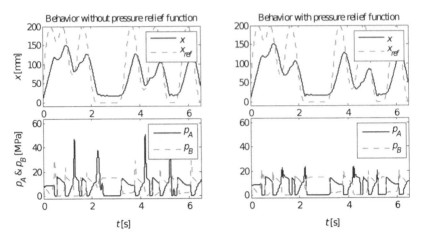

Fig. 4. System behaviour without and with pressure relief functionality. Maximum pressure is set to 20 MPa.

model execution and remain constant during the execution. Blocks can also contain memory. Hence, their behaviour do not only depend on the current values on the inputs, but also on previous input values. The diagrams can be hierarchically structured using the notion of subsystem blocks, which are blocks that themselves contain diagrams. Simulink can model continuous, discrete and hybrid systems. Each block has a timing describing when it is evaluated, which (typically) can be continuous or periodic (discrete) with a given sampling rate. Code can be generated directly from the discrete parts of the model, which eliminates defects introduced by programmers during implementation.

The functionality of the control software is partitioned into subsystems, which in turn are then decomposed into more low-level subsystems. This enables modular verification of the system, one layer of the subsystem hierarchy at the time. We here identify correctness conditions for each subsystem based on the software requirements. These conditions are then checked to hold by formal automated verification as discussed in Section 4. The Simulink subsystem PRC containing the pressure relief function for the A-side of the cylinder is shown in Fig. 5 (a). It implements the filtering algorithm and the pressure relief approach discussed in Section 2.2. The input p_A is the pressure in the A-side of the cylinder. The inputs u_PA_in and u_AT_in are the configurations of open and closed valves for the DFCU PA and DFCU AT, respectively. New configurations of the valves u_PA_out and u_AT_out in the DFCUs PA and AT are then calculated depending on the pressure. We have the following set of correctness conditions:

- $u\_PA\_out = u\_PA\_in$
- If the filtered A-pressure is smaller than p_c, then $u\_AT\_out = uAT\_in$
- If the filtered A-pressure is greater than p_{max}, then $u\_AT\_out = [1\ 1\ 1\ 1\ 1]$ (i.e. all valves open)

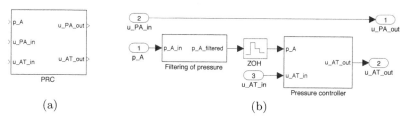

(a)   (b)

Fig. 5. (a) The subsystem containing the pressure relief controller and (b) its contents

- If the filtered A-pressure is between p_c and p_{max}, the flow rate of the output valves is at least the flow rate of the input valves $u\_AT\_in * Q_{max}^T \leq u\_AT\_out * Q_{max}^T$

The subsystem in Fig. 5 (a) is decomposed into one subsystem for filtering and one for the actual pressure control as shown in Fig. 5 (b). The filtering is done on a faster sampling rate than the control. The input pressure is first filtered in the subsystem *Filtering of Pressure* using the chosen filter. The filter (see Fig 6) first computes the median of the three last samples in the subsystem *Median filter*. The resulting median is then fed into a *Backlash*-block [13]. The backlash block provides hysteresis filtering illustrated in Fig. 3. The backlash filter leads to a quite complex input-output behaviour of the *Filtering of pressure* subsystem. However, we know that the output from the backlash block differs at most by half the backlash width $(p_{hyst}/100) * p_{max}$ from the input. Then we can state the desired limits on filtered pressure:

- If $p\_A\_in \geq p_{max} + (p_{hyst}/100) * p_{max}/2$ for three samples then $p\_A\_f \geq p_{max}$
- If $p\_A\_in \leq p_c - (p_{hyst}/100) * p_{max}/2$ for three samples then $p\_A\_f \leq p_c$
- If $p\_A\_in \geq p_c - (p_{hyst}/100) * p_{max}/2$ for three samples then $p\_A\_f \geq p_c$

The backlash width gives the width of the dead band for the hysteresis function.

The filtered pressure signal is then down-sampled to obtain a signal with the same timing as the actuators. In the subsystem *Pressure Controller* the new command signal for DFCU AT is calculated. This subsystem is also implemented as a Simulink diagram. For the pressure controller we have the following properties:

- If p_A is smaller than p_c, then $u\_AT\_out = u\_AT\_in$
- If p_A is greater than p_{max}, then $u\_AT\_out = [1\,1\,1\,1\,1]$ (i.e. all valves open)
- If p_A is between p_c and p_{max}, the flow rate over the output valves is at least the flow rate of the input valves $u\_AT\_in * Q_{max}^T \leq u\_AT\_out * Q_{max}^T$

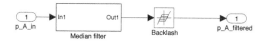

Fig. 6. The content of subsystem *Filtering of pressure*

4 Verification of the Control Software

Formal verification was used to check that the *software* components implement their specification. This gives stronger guarantees than unit tests, since the system is verified for all possible input values over all time. We investigated verification of the system using both our tool VerSAA [4] and Simulink Design Verifier (SLDV) [13]. The Simulink subsystem PRC implementing the pressure relief functionality consists of 69 blocks and contains two sampling rates.

4.1 VerSAA

VerSAA is a contract-based verifier for discrete-time Simulink models that checks that a model annotated with contracts actually satisfies them. Assume-guarantee reasoning is used to stepwise build up correctness arguments for a subsystem by using the contract descriptions of lower level subsystems [4,2,20]. VerSAA is based on using an inductive argument, where given an internal state satisfying an invariant condition (given in the *invariant* clause of the contract) and inputs satisfying the precondition, then the postcondition and the invariant is established again by the execution of the diagram. In addition to checking conformance to contracts, the tool checks absence of integer over and underflow, that matrix accesses are within bounds and that function preconditions are respected, e.g., there is no division by zero. In the verification process, the tool translates the Simulink models to functionally equivalent sequential programs and generate verification conditions using standard weakest-precondition calculations. The resulting verification conditions are submitted to the SMT-solver Z3 [6]. This enables us to automatically prove properties about systems containing e.g. linear and non-linear real and integer arithmetic, arrays and bit-vectors.

The syntax of contracts is shown in Fig 7 (a). There u and y are identifiers, t is a type $\mathsf{matrix}(t_p, n, m)$ where t_p is in the set $\{\mathsf{double}, \mathsf{int32}, \mathsf{int16}, \ldots, \mathsf{boolean}\}$ and n, m are positive integers. For brevity $x : t_p$ can be used to denote a scalar ($\mathsf{matrix}(t_p, 1, 1)$). $C*$ denotes zero or more occurrences of C and Q denotes a predicate. A contract first declares in- and out-ports of the subsystem. These are all given as lists of identifier-type pairs. The behaviour of the subsystem is described by a set of conditions. Here Q^{pre} is a precondition describing valid inputs, Q^{post} is a postcondition constricting the out-ports. Previous values on an input or outport p and can be referred to by the special function $\mathsf{delay}(p, init)$, where $init$ is the initial value of the delay. How the delays relate to the block memories in the diagram of the subsystem is then described by the condition Q^{inv}. Furthermore, the invariant can also give other invariant conditions for the block memories. The expression language used in the contract is essentially a subset of the expression language in Matlab. It is described in more details in [20]. Most arithmetic, relational and logical operators apply element-wise on matrix arguments. One of the arguments can then also be a scalar. Another common type of functions collapse matrices. E.g. the function all collapses a vector into a scalar by applying the *and*-operator between elements. When the function is applied to a matrix it collapses the matrix column-wise into a row-vector.

```
contract :
(inports : u : t)*
(outports : y : t)*
(requires : Q^{pre})*
(ensures : Q^{post})*
(invariant : Q^{inv})*
end
```

```
contract :
inports :
    p_A : double;
    u_AT_in : matrix(double, 1, 5)
outports : u_AT_out : matrix(double, 1, 5)
requires : all(u_AT_in = 0 || u_AT_in = 1)
ensures : all(u_AT_out = 0 || u_AT_out = 1)
ensures : p_A ≥ p_{max} ⇒ all(u_AT_out = 1)
ensures : p_A < p_c ⇒ all(u_AT_out = u_AT_in)
ensures :   (p_A ≥ p_c && p_A < p_{max}) ⇒
    u_AT_in * transpose(Q_{max}) ≤ u_AT_out * transpose(Q_{max})
end
```

(a)   (b)

Fig. 7. (a) The abstract syntax of contracts and (b) the contract that specifies the subsystem *Pressure Controller*

The contract in Fig. 7 (b) directly formalises the correctness conditions for subsystem *Pressure Controller* given earlier. The input p_A is a double scalar and the input valve configuration u_AT_in is a double row vector. The precondition states that all elements in the vector are either 0 or 1. The postconditions then directly encode the correctness conditions.

The contracts for subsystem *Filtering of pressure* and the subsystem *PRC* are given in Fig. 8 (a) and (b). To formalise the correctness conditions for these subsystems, we need to remember old inputs. This is done by using delays delay(p_A_in) and delay(delay(p_A_in)). In the *invariant* sections of the contracts we then describe how the delays relate to block memories in the internal diagrams. To refer to a block memory, VerSAA uses a naming policy similar to the one Simulink uses to textually refer to blocks [4]. E.g. in the contract in Fig. 8 (a), the identifier $Median\_\_filter\$delay1\$X$ refers to the block memory X in block *delay1* in subsystem *Median filter*.

4.2   Simulink Design Verifier

Simulink Design Verifier (SLDV) is a tool for automatic verification of discrete Simulink models, as well as for automatic test generation. To verify the properties in SLDV, the properties are stated using special verification blocks inserted in the diagrams. SLDV is based on k-induction [19]. This is an inductive proof method that instead of looking at a fixed number of time steps, extends the search until either a proof of correctness is found or a counter example is found. Bounded model checking can also used to search for violations. This essentially omits the inductive case from the k-inductive proof. SLDV can handle a large subset of discrete Simulink, including Stateflow.

4.3   Comparision

We formalised the 10 correctness properties in Section 3. Both tools could prove the properties to be valid. Additionally both tools proved absence of runtime

contract :
inports :
p_A_in : double
outports :
p_A_f : double
ensures :
$p\_A\_in \geq p_{max} + \frac{P_{hyst}}{100} * \frac{P_{max}}{2}$ &&
$delay(p\_A\_in, 0) \geq p_{max} + \frac{P_{hyst}}{100} * \frac{P_{max}}{2}$ &&
$delay(delay(p\_A\_in), 0) \geq p_{max} + \frac{P_{hyst}}{100} * \frac{P_{max}}{2}$
$\Rightarrow p\_A\_f \geq p_{max}$
ensures :
$p\_A\_in \leq p_c - \frac{P_{hyst}}{100} * \frac{P_{max}}{2}$ &&
$delay(p\_A\_in) \leq p_c - \frac{P_{hyst}}{100} * \frac{P_{max}}{2}$ &&
$delay(delay(p\_A\_in)) \leq p_c - \frac{P_{hyst}}{100} * \frac{P_{max}}{2}$
$\Rightarrow p\_A\_f \leq p_c$
ensures :
$p\_A\_in \geq p_c + \frac{P_{hyst}}{100} * \frac{P_{max}}{2}$ &&
$delay(p\_A\_in) \geq p_c + \frac{P_{hyst}}{100} * \frac{P_{max}}{2}$ &&
$delay(delay(p\_A\_in)) \geq p_c + \frac{P_{hyst}}{100} * \frac{P_{max}}{2}$
$\Rightarrow p\_A\_f \geq p_c$
invariant :
$delay(p\_A\_in) = Median\_filter\$delay1\$X$ &&
$delay(delay(p\_A\_in)) = Median\_filter\$delay2\$X$
invariant :
$(Backlash\$engaged = -1 ||$
$Backlash\$engaged = 0 ||$
$Backlash\$engaged = 1)$
...

(a)

contract :
inports :
p_A : $double$;
u_AT_in : matrix(double, 1, 5);
u_PA_in : matrix(double, 1, 5)
outports :
u_AT_out : matrix(double, 1, 5);
u_PA_out : matrix(double, 1, 5)
requires :
. . .
ensures :
$p\_A\_in \geq p_{max} + \frac{P_{hyst}}{100} * \frac{P_{max}}{2}$ &&
$delay(p\_A\_in, 0) \geq p_{max} + \frac{P_{hyst}}{100} * \frac{P_{max}}{2}$ &&
$delay(delay(p\_A\_in), 0) \geq p_{max} + \frac{P_{hyst}}{100} * \frac{P_{max}}{2}$
$\Rightarrow all(u\_AT\_out = 1)$
ensures :
$p\_A\_in \leq p_c - \frac{P_{hyst}}{100} * \frac{P_{max}}{2}$ &&
$delay(p\_A\_in) \leq p_c - \frac{P_{hyst}}{100} * \frac{P_{max}}{2}$ &&
$delay(delay(p\_A\_in)) \leq p_c - \frac{P_{hyst}}{100} * \frac{P_{max}}{2}$
$\Rightarrow all(u\_AT\_out = u\_AT\_in)$
ensures :
$p\_A\_in \geq p_c + \frac{P_{hyst}}{100} * \frac{P_{max}}{2}$ &&
$delay(p\_A\_in) \geq p_c + \frac{P_{hyst}}{100} * \frac{P_{max}}{2}$ &&
$delay(delay(p\_A\_in)) \geq p_c + \frac{P_{hyst}}{100} * \frac{P_{max}}{2}$
$\Rightarrow$
$u\_AT\_in * transpose(Q_{max}) \leq$
$u\_AT\_out * transpose(Q_{max})$
...

(b)

Fig. 8. (a) The contract for the subsystem *Filtering of pressure* (b) the contract for the complete pressure relief function, subsystem *PRC*

errors, such as matrix access outside bounds, division by zero, integer over- and underflow. SLDV (Version 2.2, MATLAB R2012a) completed the verification approximately 11 minutes while VerSAA used approximately 30s on a modern laptop. Although the system is fairly small, it illustrates that automatic verification of arithmetic intensive applications that use matrix manipulations is feasible with modern verifiers.

Although large models can be verified in a stepwise manner by inserting appropriate assumptions in SLDV, there is no systematic way to compositionally build correctness arguments as assume-guarantee reasoning with contracts. VerSAA has the potential to scale better than SLDV as it only analyses a fixed number of time steps and it enables modular verification. This is also indicated by the verification times of the tools. However, this comes at a cost of needing to find suitable invariant conditions on the internal state. Thus, SLDV can be easier to use, since we can focus on only those conditions that are of interest.

Conceptually, the calculations in the pressure relief function are carried out using real arithmetic. However, in Simulink the calculations are carried out using floating-point arithmetic according to IEEE 754 standard. Verification involving floating-point computation is hard [15]. VerSAA and SLDV both approximate floating-point arithmetic with real number arithmetic. This approach helps to show that the principles of the system are correct. However, defects relating to when the behaviour of floating-point and real arithmetic differ (rounding and boundedness) will go undetected.

5   Model-Based System Validation

After the software has been verified to satisfy its requirements, we need to show that it actually serves its purpose, i.e., prevents pressure peaks. This cannot be verified formally for two reasons: (1) The system model is an extremely complex hybrid system, where the continuous behaviour is described by non-linear differential equations that do not even have analytical solutions. (2) Even if we manage to prove that the model is correct with much effort, this does not necessarily hold for the real system, since models are always approximations of reality. Therefore, we have opted for using simulation-based testing to validate system correctness. To automate the testing process we have developed a method for automatic search-based test generation approach to automatically find test cases that expose flaws in the system that can be hard to find otherwise.

The idea is to formulate the problem of finding undesirable behaviour as an optimisation problem, where the optimum of the cost function is the undesirable behaviour. Typically the problems are non-convex and no algorithms that are guaranteed to find the optimal solution (the undesirable behaviour) exist. Here we have applied genetic search algorithms, which have been shown to find good solutions to hard optimisation problems in practise. Search-based structural and functional testing of control *software* has been studied extensively before, see e.g. [1,21], and it has been shown to produce good results.

We perform functional *system* testing as we are interested in testing quantitative aspects, i.e., how high can the pressure become in the system. The main problem when testing control systems is that the output does not usually only depend on the input, but also on the internal state. Therefore, it is insufficient to only test instantaneous input-output behaviour [1]. The system needs to be tested over a sufficiently long time [1]. Representing the input of an open system as a function of time in a way suitable for optimisation is a major challenge [1]. By *test* we here mean a simulation of the system during a finite (usually relatively short) time interval. By *test case* we mean a set of functions, one for each input of the system, defined for the time interval of the test.

The system where the pressure relief function is used [8] is an open system with one input signal: the piston reference position x_{ref}. Hence, to create a test case we need to define x_{ref} over a time interval. The reference velocity needs to be realistic, i.e. a signal that can be encountered in the real system. The reference position need to be with the boundaries x_{min} and x_{max}. The frequency content of the signal should also be adequate: As the reference position trajectory will always be low-pass filtered, there is no use in using signals with high frequencies. From these constraints, we have the requirements (1) for all times t in a test.

$$x_{min} \leq x_{ref}(t) \leq x_{max}$$
$$v_{min} \leq \frac{dx_{ref}(t)}{dt} \leq v_{max} \qquad (1)$$
$$a_{min} \leq \frac{d^2 x_{ref}(t)}{dt^2} \leq a_{max}$$

$$x_{min} \leq x_{ref}(T_s i) \leq x_{max}$$
$$v_{min} \leq \frac{\Delta x_{ref}(T_s i)}{T_s} \leq v_{max} \qquad (2)$$
$$a_{min} \leq \frac{\Delta^2 x_{ref}(T_s i)}{T_s^2} \leq a_{max}$$

Since the controller is discrete, we use a discrete approximation (2) of this constraint system. The derivatives are approximated with finite differences, where $\Delta x_{ref}(T_s i) = x_{ref}(T_s i) - x_{ref}(T_s(i-1))$, $\Delta^2 x_{ref}(T_s i) = x_{ref}(T_s(i)) - 2x_{ref}(T_s(i-1)) + x_{ref}(T_s(i-2))$ and T_s is the sampling time. For a vector x_{ref} that represents the input signal for the time interval 0 to nT_s we now have a set of constraints that each of the elements should satisfy. From knowledge about the system we know that high pressures are obtained if the velocity and acceleration of the movement are near the limit of what the system can handle. To create tests with fast movements we have used the following algorithm:

1. Pick k pivot elements where the x_{ref} has the value x_{max}
2. Solve the constraint system for vector x_{ref} so that each element i satisfies the constraints in (2) and so that $\Sigma_i x_{ref}(i)$ is minimised. This is a linear programming problem that maximises the velocity and acceleration in x_{ref} within limits.
3. Simulate the complete system using the generated x_{ref}.

The positions of the pivot elements can be chosen by e.g. a genetic optimisation algorithm to put the pivot elements in optimal positions to maximise the maximum pressure with and without the pressure relief function. To solve the linear programming problem, the linear programming solver from the Optimisation toolbox in MATLAB [13] has been used.

    Results with different limits are shown in Fig. 9 for the maximum pressure p_A in the A-side of the cylinder: 1) is the maximum pressure found without pressure controller, 2) is the result with pressure controller and the same input 3) is the maximum pressure found with pressure controller and 4) is the maximum pressure limit (20MPa). The velocity and acceleration limits in the tests were $x_{min} = 0$, $x_{max} = 0.2$, $v_{min} = -0.11m$, $v_{max} = 0.11m$, $a_{min} = -0.14m$, $a_{max} = 0.14m$, where m is an integer multiplier. The sampling time T_s was 3ms and this resulted in a vector x_{ref} that contained approximately 2000 elements. The linear programming in step 2 above was then typically solved in seconds with the Matlab optimisation toolbox. There are 6 pivots, for which the positions have been optimally chosen by a genetic optimisation algorithm. As can be seen from the figure, at slow movement the system can keep up and no pressure peaks occur. At very fast movements the system acts as a low-pass filter where the fastest movements are ignored resulting in less problems with pressure peaks again. In Fig. 4 the position reference x_{ref} has been generated using this approach (the case where $m = 20$). A pressure of 56MPa, which is significantly higher than the maximum pressure of 20MPa, is attained for the system without pressure relief function. With pressure relief function the pressure level is acceptable (24MPa). The greatest pressure found with the pressure relief function active was an acceptable 25MPa.

    The performance of the pressure relief function depends on the assumption that the valves will open fast enough to reduce pressure. Evaluation on the impact on the speed of the valves was also assessed, i.e. the impact of the sampling time T_s. It was found that this pressure relief scheme is no longer sufficient if the sampling time is twice as long, $T_s = 6ms$. The maximum pressure found with

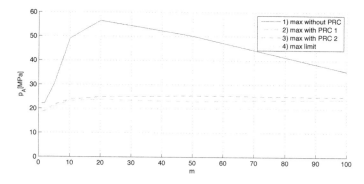

Fig. 9. Maximum pressures in the A-side of the cylinder found by testing using different acceleration and velocity limits

the pressure relief function was then 32MPa. Thus the test generation helped to find the limitations of this pressure relief approach.

We have used search-based functional testing of digital hydraulic systems earlier [3,9]. In the best approach [9], a search algorithm was used to optimise control points of polynomials that in turn were used to construct the input signal. A similar approach to optimise control points of functions is also used in [1]. Our approach has several advantages compared to earlier works for generating the tests needed for the case study. Maximum allowed speed and acceleration will always be used in the movement, which is useful for generating high pressures. Due to this efficient formulation of the optimisation problem, the number of model evaluations needed in the search is significantly reduced compared to [3,9] reducing testing times from days to hours. More generally, compared to [1,3,9] we can efficiently generate input signals that conform to desired constraints for different kinds of systems using variations of this approach. The test generation method presented in the paper is flexible and works well for tests over relatively short time intervals, but will not scale to very long testing times.

6   Conclusions

The paper demonstrates the approach we have used to develop, verify and validate a safety critical pressure relief function in a hydraulics system. A reliable pressure relief function is essential for resilient operation digital hydraulics systems. Automatic formal verification tools were investigated as a complement to unit tests for the *software* parts of the system. Both tested tools, VerSAA and SLDV, verified all desired properties. This case study demonstrates that automated formal verification can be applied to arithmetic intensive systems involving matrix calculations. Automated formal verification of model-based designs has also been successfully in other systems before e.g. [14,5,7].

There also exist verification tools for hybrid systems such as e.g. KeYmaera [18]. However, the size of the complete model is too large (over 4000 blocks) and the continuous time system dynamics is too complicated for the tool. Another approach is to verify the model based on discretisation of the continuous-time model [16], but the complexity of the model is also here an obstacle. As formal verification of all *system* properties is outside the reach of current formal methods in this case study, automated test generation for model-based system validation was investigated. This can be compared to statistical model checking for hybrid systems e.g. [22]. There they statistically estimate a probability for a property to hold by performing simulations and doing statistical analysis on simulation traces. Here we instead aim at searching for one simulation trace that violates the property. Provided that the search algorithm is better at finding optimal values than random search, this gives higher confidence that a property violation does not exist than using statistical model checking as in [22]. Note that, to achieve reliable results in the model-based validation process, an accurate simulation model is essential. Here we have such a model [8]. However, the final validation still needs to be done in the real system. Due to the accurate model, this typically confirms the results obtained from the model. This is discussed in [8].

By combining search-based testing on the simulation model and formal verification we can be confident that the system as a whole functions according to the requirements. Formal verification can prove absence of many low level defects, as well as prove that the control software has certain desirable properties. However, for complex cyber-physical systems we also need to ensure that the software has the desired impact on the system. Here formal verification was unattainable and we used heuristic optimisation methods to search for undesirable behaviour instead. This seems to be a powerful combination that can greatly increase the confidence in the designed system.

Acknowledgements. We would like to thank Kaisa Sere for many valuable discussions on the topics of this paper.

References

1. Baresel, A., Pohlheim, H., Sadeghipour, S.: Structural and functional sequence test of dynamic and state-based software with evolutionary algorithms. In: Cantú-Paz, E., et al. (eds.) GECCO 2003. LNCS, vol. 2724, pp. 2428–2441. Springer, Heidelberg (2003)
2. Boström, P.: Contract-based verification of simulink models. In: Qin, S., Qiu, Z. (eds.) ICFEM 2011. LNCS, vol. 6991, pp. 291–306. Springer, Heidelberg (2011)
3. Boström, P., Björkqvist, J.: Detecting design flaws in control systems using optimisation methods. In: CACSD 2006, pp. 1544–1549. IEEE (2006)
4. Boström, P., Grönblom, R., Huotari, T., Wiik, J.: An approach to contract-based verification of Simulink models. Tech. Rep. 985, Turku Centre for Computer Science, TUCS (2010)
5. Cofer, D.: Model checking: Cleared for take off. In: van de Pol, J., Weber, M. (eds.) SPIN 2010. LNCS, vol. 6349, pp. 76–87. Springer, Heidelberg (2010)
6. de Moura, L., Bjørner, N.: Z3: An efficient SMT solver. In: Ramakrishnan, C.R., Rehof, J. (eds.) TACAS 2008. LNCS, vol. 4963, pp. 337–340. Springer, Heidelberg (2008)

7. Etienne, J.F., Fechter, S., Juppeaux, E.: Using Simulink Design Verifier for proving behavioral properties on a complex safety critical system in the ground transportation domain. In: Aiguier, M., Bretaudeau, F., Krob, D. (eds.) CSDM 2010. Springer (2010)
8. Ketonen, M., Huova, M., Heikkilä, M., Linjama, M., Boström, P., Waldén, M.: Digital hydraulic pressure relief function. In: Plummer, A.R. (ed.) FPMC 2012 (2012)
9. Lillås, K.: Global optimization algorithms in hydraulic controller testing. Master's thesis, Åbo Akademi University (2008)
10. Linjama, M., Koskinen, K.T., Vilenius, M.: Accurate tracking control of water hydraulic cylinder with non-ideal on/off valves. International Journal of Fluid Power 4, 7–16 (2003)
11. Linjama, M., Vilenius, M.: Digital hydraulics - towards perfect valve technology. In: Vilenius, J., Koskinen, K.T. (eds.) SICFP 2007. Tampere University of Technology (2007)
12. Maraninchi, F., Morel, L.: Logical-time contracts for reactive embedded components. In: 30th EUROMICRO Conference on Component-Based Software Engineering Track, ECBSE 2004. IEEE (2004)
13. Mathworks Inc.: Simulink (2014), http://www.mathworks.com/products/simulink
14. Miller, S.P., Anderson, E.A., Wagner, L.G., Wahlen, M.W., Heimdahl, M.P.E.: Formal verification of flight critical software. In: AIAA Guidance, Navigation and Control Conference and Exhibit. AIAA (2005)
15. Monniaux, D.: The pitfalls of verifying floating-point computations. ACM Transactions on Programming Languages and Systems 30(3) (2008)
16. Mosterman, P.J., Zander, J., Hamon, G., Denckla, B.: A computational model of time for stiff hybrid systems applied to control synthesis. Control Engineering Practice 20(1) (2012)
17. Murphy, B., Wakefield, A., Friedman, J.: Best practices for verification, validation, and test in model-based design. Tech. Rep. 2008-01-1469, Mathworks (2008)
18. Platzer, A., Quesel, J.-D.: KeYmaera: A hybrid theorem prover for hybrid systems (System description). In: Armando, A., Baumgartner, P., Dowek, G. (eds.) IJCAR 2008. LNCS (LNAI), vol. 5195, pp. 171–178. Springer, Heidelberg (2008)
19. Sheeran, M., Singh, S., Stålmarck, G.: Checking safety properties using induction and a SAT-solver. In: Hunt Jr., W.A., Johnson, S.D. (eds.) FMCAD 2000. LNCS, vol. 1954, pp. 108–125. Springer, Heidelberg (2000)
20. Wiik, J., Boström, P.: Contract-based verification of MATLAB and simulink matrix-manipulating code. In: Merz, S., Pang, J. (eds.) ICFEM 2014. LNCS, vol. 8829, pp. 396–412. Springer, Heidelberg (2014)
21. Zhan, Y.: A Search-Based Framework for Automatic Test-Set Generation for MATLAB/Simulink Models. Ph.D. thesis, University of York, UK (2006)
22. Zuliani, P., Platzer, A., Clarke, E.M.: Bayesian statistical model checking with application to Stateflow/Simulink verification. Formal Methods in System Design 43 (2013)

Simulation Testing and Model Checking: A Case Study Comparing these Approaches

Richard Lipka[1], Marek Paška[2], and Tomáš Potužák[2]

[1] NTIS
University of West Bohemia, Plzen, Czech Republic
[2] Department of Computer Science and Engineering, Faculty of Applied Sciences
University of West Bohemia, Plzen, Czech Republic
{lipka,paskma,tpotuzak}@kiv.zcu.cz

Abstract. One of the challenging problems in software development is the assuring of the correctness of the created software. During our previous research, we developed a framework for the simulation-based testing of software components *SimCo* that allows us to perform testing of component-based applications or its fragments. The *SimCo* was originally designed to perform the tests according to a given scenario in order to determine extra-functional properties of the components. However, it can be also used to test the correctness of the component behaviour. For this purpose, there are also other ways – the model checking tools, such as Java Pathfinder. We want to compare the strengths and weaknesses of the two approaches as represented by the *SimCo* and the Java Pathfinder. In this paper, the results of the comparison of these two testing methods on a case study using the implementation of the FTP protocol are discussed.

Keywords: software component, simulation testing, model checking, Java Pathfinder, SimCo, defect discovery.

1   Introduction

One of the main concerns of software development is the correctness of the created software. Currently, there are several existing methods for the verification of correctness. The most widespread one is the use of unit tests where separate methods are tested during the development [1]. The test driven development methodology even recommends creating tests first as a form of specification of the created software. However, such specification is hardly understandable by the stakeholders who are not software developers and cannot be applied during the analysis [2]. In most cases, a specification of software exists without any formal connection with the created software. In other words, most software products are not "correct by construction", directly derived from their formal specification.

For this reason, we have created a *SimCo* tool that should allow us to test the behaviour of the software products and compare it with their specifications, specifically with the use cases description. Use cases are widely adopted way for specifying software behaviour, as they can be easily understood even by customers and not only by

I. Majzik and M. Vieira (Eds.): SERENE 2014, LNCS 8785, pp. 116–130, 2014.

developers [3]. The *SimCo* is designed to support creation of the testing scenarios according to the description in the use cases. Ad hoc tests often covers the features that seemed important or, in worse case, easy to test to programmers during the development. Instead, the *SimCo* provides test coverage focused on the expected behaviour of the application. The *SimCo* allows placing software components into the simulated environment, and testing their properties or responses when a service is required. The simulation is used in order to provide all dependencies on the other components and inputs from the rest of the system or from the user.

On the other hand, some software needs much stronger guarantees of the correctness, which can be provided by formal methods such as model checking. Major weakness of these methods (and model checking in particular) is that they scale badly. Model checking is based on traversal of state space, whose size tends to grow exponentially with the size of the examined system.

We have developed a tool set that generates C code and Java byte-code from executable specifications based on the Python programming language. The tool set supports testing based on formal methods. It utilizes the Java Pathfinder, which is an explicit model checker. As this tool set can generate Java byte-code, it can be easily used also for the creating of software components. These software components can be then utilized in the simulation system *SimCo*. Therefore, we can use both testing methods – the model checking to prove some specific properties of a particular component and the simulation testing to ensure that the tested components work properly.

Each of the mentioned testing methods works in a different way. So, we want to compare them and see what types of errors can be discovered by each of them. The experiment is performed as follows. Simple component based application is created. One or more components are checked by the model-checking and then by the simulation. The found errors are investigated. For the comparison of both methods, the errors in the components are created on purpose. So, it is possible to observe, which method is able to detect them.

The remainder of this paper is structured as follows: section 2 describes the *SimCo* simulation testing tool; Section 3 is dealing with our generative framework. The case study is outlined in section 4 and the testing experiment is described in the Section 5, along with discussion of the results. Overview of related work is given in section 6. Section 7 concludes the paper and suggests future work.

2   SimCo - Simulation Based Testing

The *SimCo* is a simulation tool for testing software components in the simulated environment, developed at University of West Bohemia. The *SimCo* is based on the simulation techniques, similar to component simulations such as *Palladio* [4]. Software components play fundamental role in development of large software systems. This paradigm allows decomposing entire system into more manageable entities with well defined interfaces [5]. Traditional software simulation can take advantage of this approach. One can select some set of real components from the system and connect them with simulated components. The *SimCo* allows testing a component application as a whole or only a subset of its components [6].

2.1   *SimCo* Simulation Tool

The *SimCo* tool is implemented in Java language, using *OSGi* component model with the *Blueprint* extension in order to simplify the assembly of component applications. The tool itself is also implemented using *OSGi*, to make it easily modifiable and extendable. Description of its implementation was published in [6].

A discrete event simulation model [7] is used for the testing of the application. It means that the *SimCo* uses a discrete model of time as a sequence of events occurring with arbitrary time intervals. In this case, invocations of methods or returning the values are considered to be events. Between the events, the state of the simulation is not changing. So, the simulator can jump from one to another. The simulation engine stores events in the calendar. Calendar serves as a prioritized queue, which contains all events that should be executed in order of their execution time. When an event is executed, the required method invocation is performed, results are stored in the log, the model time is incremented, and the next event is taken for execution.

It is important that, unlike in the *Palladio* [4], the real components can be used in the simulator directly, without any need to change them. The tested components from the point of view of the simulator are considered to be black boxes. As no instrumentation or modelling of the tested component is needed, we can be sure that the tests are not inducing any new behaviour to the components and they behave the same way as they will in a real application.

The *SimCo* is capable of intercepting all communication between the tested components using transparent proxies. The proxies can be configured only to handle the invocations and returned values or can simulate the communication over a non-reliable medium and simulate for example a packet loss.

One of the main features that we had in mind while designing the *SimCo* was to utilize the tests based on the description of the application behaviour in use cases. Using of scenario-based testing, with scenarios derived from the analytical description, is widely recognized in the literature [8]. Numerous ways of generating the tests from UML were proposed [9], [10], [11], [12]. However, these approaches are using detailed model of the application in UML, including activity diagrams. Our approach to generating the test cases relies only on the text description of the use cases, enriched with annotations, which provide connection between a specific use case and using of specific component services [13].

2.2   Simulated Components

Components in the *OSGi* model provide specific services and require other services from other components. In general, any component can provide and require arbitrary number of services. When we want to test only one component or a part of a component application, we have to provide a valid environment for it. It means that all required services must be available to the component. The *SimCo* tool is helping with this, allowing us to create simulated components. The simulated components are not tested, but are present in the *OSGi* environment in order to provide required dependencies and services. The inner implementation of such component can be very simple. For example, the methods can only return static values or values generated by random number generators instead of performing the real calculations. If it is required, the simulated component can also contain a scenario that prescribes not only the outputs when some service is used, but also other behaviour, such as invocations of other services.

There are several reasons for using the simulated components. The most obvious one is fulfilling the dependencies of the tested component and allow its execution. This is useful during development when not all components are available and simulated components serve as mock objects. The simulated components can be also used in order to simulate the user inputs. For example, the GUI component can be replaced by its simulation that will perform the pre-recorded sequences of actions in the same way as a user would. Another reason is the speedup of the simulation. When a component requires a specific calculation and, for the testing, we just need the result, the calculation can be replaced by returning of a pre-calculated value. For example, when testing the overhead of the component that is responsible for the transfer of data through the network is required, we can replace the process of obtaining of these data by previously prepared files. The last reason is the replacing of a specific hardware. For example, when we want to test the software component responsible for the traffic control, we can do the initial tests only in the simulator, replacing the sensors and actuators (traffic lights in this case) by the simulation.

The simulated components are generated only in a semi-automatic way. So, if more complex behaviour is required, their creation takes significant amount of time. The *SimCo* is able to provide stub of the component according to the published interface and basic probabilistic random values generator for returning simple values. However, if the simulated component should exhibit a complex behaviour, such as using another service in reaction on invocation of its service, this behaviour has to be created manually. Therefore, it is important to choose carefully, which components should be replaced by the simulation.

2.3   Threading Model

Generally, the programs have multiple threads of execution. The *OSGi* component model does not limit the ability of components in this way. The *SimCo* therefore can handle multi-threaded programs. However, the simulation is serialized. Real components are allowed to create multiple threads that interact with other components. If the interaction is bounded to the real components, it is invisible to the simulation framework. On the other hand, every calendar event is strictly executed by one dedicated calendar thread. The calendar thread simply takes the events from the calendar and executes them. If a thread spawned from a real component performs a method call to a simulated component, an event representing the call is inserted into the calendar and the caller thread is blocked. This event is executed by the calendar thread, the targeted simulated component delivers its result, and the event representing the return is inserted into the calendar. When the time comes to the returning event, its execution unblocks the thread of the real component.

It is important to note that the *SimCo* is not designed specifically for simulation of thread interactions; compare with Java threading simulator [14]. However, one can still use the *SimCo* to conduct experiments to test correctness of multi-threaded programs.

3   Framework with Model Checking

Model checking is a well established method of software validation and verification, despite the problems with scaling of this method on large systems. Several approaches for doing this exist, such as traversing of the whole state space of the program [15]. Because of the difficulties with exponential grow of this task, many models are focused on working with the models of the program instead of working with the programs themselves. Finite state automatons can be used in order to model complex programs [16], as well as descriptions of programs in linear temporal logic, which can be then translated into automatons [17]. Automatons might be also derived directly from the source texts of the program, ensuring the compliance of the automaton to the program [18].

Beside the *SimCo* tool, we have developed a framework and also a custom software development process that allows us to generate C code and Java bytecode from an executable specification based on Python programming language. Both C and Java byte-code can be used in production where the C code is intended mainly for embedded devices with constrained computational resources. The executable specification as well as the output codes is generally multi-threaded.

A major advantage of our development approach is that we can take advantage of the tools available for the Java ecosystem. For example, we can use the Java Pathfinder model checker to prove that the code has certain properties. The Java Pathfinder can prove that the code is deadlock-free or that there is no unsafe data access among multiple threads. From the experiments performed on the Java byte-code, we can also reason about the correctness of the C code, because they were generated from the same intermediate code and the threading uses the same locking primitives based on monitors [19].

The generated Java byte-code can be simply turned into a software component (for instance according to the *OSGi* component specification) and used in our component simulation.

3.1   Java Pathfinder

Java Path nder (JPF) [20] is an explicit model checker for Java developed at NASA. Its predecessor Java Pathfinder 1 [15] attempted to translate Java source code to *Promela* language, though it is now retired. The JPF is a special implementation of the Java Virtual Machine (JVM) that has a model-checking facility. The verification is done at the Java byte-code level; JPF does not need access to the source code of the investigated program.

A conventional JVM executes Java bytecode sequentially and the state of the running program is constantly altered during the execution. The JPF, on the other hand, has the ability to store every state of the program and restore it later when needed. This approach allows all reachable states of the program to be examined. The JPF architecture is pluggable; there is a possibility to use various algorithms for the state space traversal. The JPF can also use heuristic methods to determine, which states should be examined first in order to discover an error.

The model-checker can search for deadlocks, check invariants, user-defined assertions (embedded in the code), and Linear Temporal Logic expressed properties. The JPF provides techniques for fighting the state space explosion, such as abstraction and slicing [21].

The JPF also supports non-determinism to be injected into a deterministic program. For instance, the method `Verify.randomBool()` returns either `true` or `false`, and the JPF guarantees that both possibilities will be examined.

4   Case Study

The case study is designed in order to compare bug detection ability of simulation-based testing and model checking. The tested software is a simple file manager. In tests, we focus especially on the component that implements access to the FTP servers.

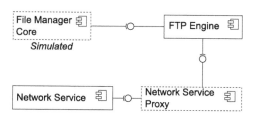

Fig. 1. Component layout used for the experiment

In our experiment, four components are used (see Fig. 1). One of them, *File Manager Core*, is a simulated component, which, in this case, replaces the rest of the file manager application. It performs requests as if the real user was working with the file manager and waits for the results of the FTP transfer. The second component is the *FTP Engine* itself, the real component that we want to test. The third component implements access to the network. This component can be real or simulated depending on the desired experiment. This component is hidden behind proxy component created by the *SimCo* that is there only to capture the communication before it is sent to the network.

The core of the *FTP Engine* component is a state machine, depicted by a diagram in Fig 2. The transitions between the states are associated with some network operations such as sending a command or evaluating the server's response. The transitions named "error" allow cancelling an operation that consists of several transitions. Every state transition can be also viewed as a transaction – it is either fully accomplished or not performed at all. The transaction is accomplished if the associated network inter-action is successfully performed – the command is sent, the response is received and the response is evaluated as a desired one. Particular transitions are relevant only for certain states. When the client application tries to perform an illegal transition, a `StateException` is thrown. Such a situation corresponds with an attempt to vio-late the protocol. For instance, an attempt to change a working directory (CWD) be-fore the login procedure (USER/PASS) is performed.

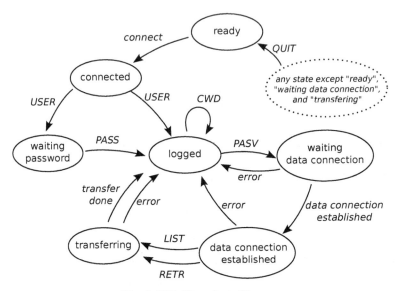

Fig. 2. FTP Client State Diagram

Although, according to the definition in [5], the components should be without ap-parent state, this condition is often ignored in real life applications. In our case, the *FTP engine* component exhibits two states – connected to the server and discon-nected. The state of the protocol is hidden from the user, but using completely state-less FTP connector would be inconvenient. The *FTP engine* is not used directly through the state machine, because it is too low-level. There is a Client class that has a convenient interface and encapsulates the interaction with the state machine. For instance, it handles user's login that consists of one or two state transitions (depend-ing on whether a password is required by the server). On the other hand, this facade does not add additional checks; a user can still generate an incorrect chain of com-mands that is then refused by the state machine.

5   Experiments

We want to compare the explicit model checking conducted by the *Java Path nder* with the simulation tests performed in the *SimCo*. However, we are not going to de-cide, which of this very different method is better in any sense. We intend to figure out what kind of defects is likely/unlikely/impossible to detect by a particular method.

We also do not have human resources to perform two independent sets of experiments by two independent groups of developers. Therefore, we usually perform tests by one approach and if we found a defect, we try to replicate the experiment by the other approach. The usual workflow is to use the model checker earlier in the development stage and the simulation later when the component is ready for integration.

In order to earn a set of guarantees of correctness, we need to construct a set of tests. We need to observe two behaviours:

- The program behaves according to the protocol. That means that, if the server also behaves correctly, there are no malfunctions in the network and the order of commands is valid, then all the commands are successful.
- The program reacts reasonably in the case of server or network malfunction. It means that the communication can be interrupted at any point and the server might even send incorrect response (violate the protocol). In such case, some of the commands may fail, but fail gracefully – without any unexpected exception or unexpected state transition.

5.1   Randomization of Server Responses

This experiment relies on a simulated implementation of the network access component. This implementation does not connect to any network socket; instead, it returns predefined responses as if there was a FTP server connected. This component actually implements a mockup of an FTP server. The server contains a simple hardcoded file system, for example the server can list the root directory and serve several files.

The communication in the FTP command channel consists of commands and replies. Every reply starts with a three-digit code and a human readable message follows. The most significant digit of the code has the meaning defined by the protocol (see Table I).

Table 1. FTP Reply codes

Code	Meaning
1xy	Positive Preliminary reply
2xy	Positive Completion reply
3xy	Positive Intermediate reply
4xy	Transient Negative Completion reply
5xy	Permanent Negative Completion reply

The next step is to prepare a test scenario for the FTP. The test scenario is a script that contains a typical use-case (e.g. to connect, to log in, to obtain the root directory listing, and to obtain a file; see a following test script). This script is executed inside the *File Manager Core* component. The script is correct (contains valid sequence of commands). So, it is always executed successfully under the condition that both the client and the server conform to the protocol.

```
IFSNode node = ftpService.getFSNode
                ("ftp://example.com");
IFSNode[] rootDir = node.getDirectoryListing();
Assert rootDir != null;

IFSNode exampleFileNode = null;
For (IFSNode file : rootDir) {
  System.out.println(file.getName());
        // Download the   content :
  byte[] content = file.getContent();
  assert content != null;
}
```

[Example of testing script – a test script that downloads all files from the root directory]

To check whether our code acts reasonably in a harsh environment, we make the simulated server hostile by randomization of its responses. The response code to every request is random meaning that the server may break the protocol. Because the test scenario is correct, it should never raise an unexpected exception such as `StateException`. It may, however, fail gracefully.

Recall that with the *Java Path nder*, we actually execute all possible runs of the scenarios. This is possible due to the *JPF*'s support for randomization, literally by using `Verify.randInt()` method. One run is defined by a sequence of actual reply codes of every command in the scenario. Among all the runs, there is one that completely succeeds. This means that it is the "happy day scenario" with all reply codes corresponding to client's expectations. However, the vast majority of the runs contain one or more unexpected reply codes. If an unexpected reply code is encountered, the particular scenario's operation (e.g. a directory listing) is considered unsuccessful. The scenario continues with the next operation if the failure is not fatal and ends otherwise. For instance, a login failure is fatal for all the subsequent operations.

If none of the runs ends with an unexpected exception, we have a guarantee that our FTP client behaves reasonably even if the server violates the protocol. Nevertheless, our test ended by an unexpected exception. The bug was found in the Client class of the layer above the state machine. This layer did not react correctly to the fail and did not reset the state of the state machine that stuck in transferring state indefinitely. The exact sequence of events leading to the failure is as follows:

1. Client is in state *logged*.
2. Client sends command "PASV". Server responds as expected by "227 Entering Passive Mode (208.118.235.20.99.38)". Client opens data connection and moves to state *data_connection_established*.
3. Client sends command "RETR filename.txt" and moves state to *transferring*.
4. Server writes the content of filename.txt into the data connection, data channel is closed. However, the server fails to confirm the success and instead sends "500 error, transfer failed".

5. According to the design, the state machine remains in the state *transferring*. The higher layer ignores this error state, the (possibly damaged) content is returned to the user.
6. All subsequent user requests raise `StateException` because they expect the state machine to be in the *logged* state.

After we fixed the defect, the ending of the sequence of events will change:

5. According to the design, the state machine remains in state *transferring*. The higher layer resolves the error by destroying the content of the downloaded file and resets the state machine to the state *logged*.
6. User is acknowledged about the fact that the download failed and can initiate another request.

Now we can try to replicate this bug discovery in the *SimCo* simulator. The component, which implements the fake FTP server, is the same as in the case of the model checking experiment with one notable difference. The randomization of the server's response codes is not done by the *JPF*'s randomization support, but it is implemented simply by the `Random` class from the standard Java Core API.

The test scenario can also remain the same. The only and crucial difference is the way it is executed. In the experiment with the *JPF*, the scenario was executed only once and all possible runs were examined by back-tracking. If we execute the scenario in the *SimCo* simulator, we get just one random run. To get more representative results, we have to run the test scenario multiple times resulting in multiple random runs.

What these two approaches of execution really mean? Let us imagine a tree (an oriented graph) where every node is a state of execution of the scenario. A node with multiple descendants represents a state, in which we have more choices and the simulator pseudo-randomly chooses among them. The root of the tree is the first state of the scenario and the leaves are the terminal states of the scenario. The *JPF* guarantees that the entire tree is traversed whereas one run of the scenario in the *SimCo* simulator pseudo-randomly selects one path from the root to a leaf.

During the simulation runs of the *SimCo*, we were able to replicate the bug. Let us discuss the experiment details on the shortest scenario that is able to discover the bug. In such a scenario, the login is performed and two files are downloaded.

We can measure the state space generated by the scenario by running it in the *JPF* after the bug was fixed. According to report from the *JPF*, it consists of 327 states and the maximal depth of the back-tracking was 10. This depth roughly corresponds with the depth of the tree graph mentioned above. Such a state space can be traversed in about a second (on an ordinary Intel Core i3 processor). If we run the *JPF* experiment with the bug still present, it is halted by exception after 40 states visited.

The *SimCo* simulator discovered the bug after 205 runs of the test scenario on average. The average was computed from 100 measurements that give us even more data – the median was 155 runs and the worst case was 893 runs. The time to execute the 205 runs is about one second. Because we used random number generators in the *SimCo*, it took 77039 runs on average, before the happy day case was achieved, and

368466 runs on average, before the worst case scenario happened. However, the *SimCo* allows to explicitly define the scenario and values used during the run of the test. So, it is possible to prepare the worst case or any other situation manually. Using of random numbers allows us to explore a larger part of the state space of the application.

5.2   Cutting of Server Responses

The second experiment employed a different kind of randomization. Every server response was the expected one (happy day scenario). However, every response was randomly shortened, i.e., zero or more last characters were cut off. In most cases, this behaviour does not harm the communication, because the response code at the beginning of the response gives full information and the following text message is only informative. If the response code is cut off as well, the response is rejected as invalid.

When we run this experiment with the *JPF*, we encountered an unexpected exception, though. There is one situation, in which the response text bears vital information. It is the response to the "PASV" command and it contains an IP address and a port as a sequence of six numbers. An example of the response is "227 Entering Passive Mode (208.118.235.20.99.38)".

If this response is incomplete, the IP address and the port are unreadable, though the response code is still readable and signals a success. The parsing of the IP address fails and returns a `null` object that is then passed for subsequent operations that throws a `NullPointerException` when trying to use the `null` object as a valid one. The fix of this bug is obvious, the "PASV" command is considered correct if the code is positive and the extraction of the IP address and port succeeds.

There were about 1284 states traversed by the *JPF* while running this experiment (measured after the bug was fixed). This is slightly larger number than in the previous experiment. Still, it took only several seconds on the same computer.

The experiment was also replicated in the *SimCo* simulator. The defect was found instantly because random shortening almost inevitably leads to an unreadable response text. The simulated component (*File Manager Core*) can be designed to compare the results provided as return value of the methods with the expected values. So, it is easy to discover functional problems when components are returning unexpected values. This is an important feature of the *SimCo* – as all invocations on the component interfaces are observed, they can be compared with the expected values and the correct behaviour of the component can be checked this way.

5.3   Multi-Threading

The third experiment is not a real bug we found by our testing methods, but rather an artificially injected defect. The state machine that is the heart of the FTP client is a thread-safe one, meaning that only one method is executed at one moment.

The typical use case with multiple threads is as follows. One thread logs in to the server and initializes a download of a file. As a result, it gets a streaming object that represents the file data. At this point, the FTP client is in the transferring state and the only way how to move away from this state is to close the stream. We might need to perform the processing of the stream in the second thread. So, the close operation is also performed by the second thread. Therefore, we need the mutual exclusion of the threads changing the state of the state machine.

The question is whether we are able to discover the hypothetical absence of mutual exclusion. So, we created a test scenario that implements the mentioned use case (i.e. utilizes the streaming object and two threads).

The *JPF* has three ways how to discover a thread-related defect. First, the defect may raise an unexpected exception caused by inconsistent state of inner data. Second, it detects a deadlock. Third, it can detect unsafe data access among multiple thread (i.e. a race condition).

In this experiment, we encountered the unexpected exception as well as unsafe data access error. The enumeration of 2514 states took about 6 seconds. The defect was found in about 3 seconds.

On the other hand, we failed to replicate the experiment results in the *SimCo* simulator. As we mentioned in Section 3, the *SimCo* simulation is using a discrete events whose execution is serialized, all invocations are due to this only pseudo parallel. Therefore, this simple omission of mutual exclusion cannot be detected.

6   Related Work

Despite the fact that both formal verification and testing of software is widespread in contemporary literature, there is only several works dealing with comparison of these approaches. Papers are usually more focused on the verification of presented methods,than on their comparison with other existing methods or tools. More often, comparison of similar methods can be found, for example in [22] four different tools for finite-state machine verification are described. In similar way, [23] evaluates several methods for static deadlock detection.

In [24] a thorough experiment is described, comparing results of two developer teams working on the same project. The paper is focused on more aspects of the software development than just testing; it deals with the whole development process. One team was using Capability Maturity Model level 4, the other was relying on formal specification and code generation method *Specware*. Both teams obtained the same specification of requirements, with two errors seeded into it. The results of both teams were consequently evaluated by third party in order to determine how reliable the created source code is. The formal method team was able to discover both errors in the specification and the produced code, that had a reliability estimation 0.77 (23 failures within 100 test case set). The CMM team did not found the problems in the specification and a reliability estimation of their code was 0.56. Nevertheless, if the errors in the specification were corrected, the reliability estimation would improve to 0.98. In conclusion, authors state that both methods are justified, but none of them led to the complete fulfillment of the user requirements. However, the results are favorable for the formal methods.

Another detailed analysis of formal verification and experimental testing was published in [25]. This paper deals with testing and verification of Martian Rover Software when the *PolySpace C-verifier* is used for the static analysis, the *Java Path-Finder* for the model checking, and the *Java Path Explorer* and the *DBRover* for the runtime analysis. The authors are looking for synergies of different testing techniques. It is demonstrated there that the runtime analysis was useful for the deadlock detection, the runtime testing with a few random generated inputs proves successful, and that the model checking is effective for a systematic analysis, such us covering all inputs up to a specified size. It also shows that the runtime analysis causes fewer false alarms in comparison with the black box testing. Lastly, it is shown that automated tools detect a lot of different defects, without the ability to detect whether they are manifestation of the same error in the source code or to connect them with the exact place of the source code that causes them.

State-driven approach to testing of distributed application is also used in [26], in order to identify and test hard to reach states of a distributed system. The authors claim that artificial workloads or workloads derived from running of performance benchmarks do not provide sufficient covering with tests and demonstrates a formal state-driven method for reaching them.

In [27] a framework for combined static and dynamic analysis of Java programs is presented. It is not a comparison of two approaches to the software testing, but it shows how data obtained from the static analysis can be used in order to improve results of the the runtime analysis. In [28], the model checking with *CBMC* is compared with the static analysis using *Parfait* tool. Model checker in this paper proves to be more effective, with higher true positive error detection, for a cost of a significantly higher time and memory consumption. Also [29] compares the static analysis with the model checking on several case studies (e.g. on implementation of network protocols). The authors demonstrate that the static analysis is working with the entire code of the program while the model checking is verifying only the paths through the code, which are used during the program execution. On the other hand, they also show that the model checking leads to a stronger correctness of the results, as it actually has to execute the code of the checked programs. In discussion, they also give an interesting argument that automatic analytical tools are able to discover a huge amount of bugs, but are not able to determine, which ones are really important and leads to malfunction of the software. Identifying of the important bugs from a large report then requires a manual analysis.

7   Conclusion

In this paper, we examined a simple software system consisting of several software components by two different defect discovery tools. The first tool is a model checker called *Java Path nder*, the second tool is a discrete event component simulator called *SimCo*. The former examines whole state space, the latter traverses through states using pseudorandom number generators.

We prepared three testing scenarios that were conducted by both tools. The first two scenarios discovered a defect in the examined software. The discovery was very quick by both the model checking and the simulation. However, the second test shows a strong side of the simulation-based testing – it allows to utilize the checking of the returned values during runtime. This is something that the model checking cannot provide easily. The third scenario tested an injected bug related to the thread mutual exclusion. The model checker discovered the defect correctly. Due to its nature, the simulator that works with discrete events (and their serialized executions) was unable to detect this defect. For detection of such kind of problems, the model checking is irreplaceable.

According to our findings, it seems that logical defects can be effectively discovered by both methods. Moreover, both methods are rather fast for small systems. The notable exception is the defects caused by an incorrect thread synchronization that cannot be directly discovered by the discrete simulation. On the one hand, the simulation does not necessarily suffer by exponential growth of the state space and therefore may be useful for large systems. The simulation is not designed to be able to search the entire state space; the use of random number generators provides only a limited coverage of the possible program executions. On the other hand, if we have some knowledge of the inner structure of the component, we can prepare test scenarios for the simulation in order to discover specific errors.

Acknowledgements. This work was supported by the European Regional Development Fund (ERDF), project "NTIS – New Technologies for the Information Society", European Centre of Excellence, CZ.1.05/1.1.00/02.0090.

References

1. Runeson, P.: A Survey of Unit Testing Practices. IEEE Software 23(4), 22–29 (2006) ISSN: 0740-7459/06
2. Stephens, M., Rosenberg, D.: Design Driven Testing: Test Smarter, Not Harder. Apress, Berkely (2010) ISBN: 978-1430229438
3. Cockburn, A.: Writing Effective Use Cases. Addison-Wesley, Boston (2000)
4. Becker, S., Koziolek, H., Reussner, R.: Model-Based Performance Prediction with the Palladio Component Model. In: Proceedings of the 6th International Workshop on Software and Performance, pp. 54–66. ACM, New York (2007)
5. Szyperski, C., Gruntz, D., Murer, S.: Component Software – Beyond Object-Oriented Programming. ACM Press, New York (2000)
6. Lipka, R., Potužák, T., Brada, P., Herout, P.: SimCo – Hybrid Simulator for Testing of Component Based Applications. In: van Emde Boas, P., Groen, F.C.A., Italiano, G.F., Nawrocki, J., Sack, H. (eds.) SOFSEM 2013. LNCS, vol. 7741, pp. 420–431. Springer, Heidelberg (2013)
7. Fujimoto, R.M.: Parallel and Distributed Simulation Systems. John Wiley & Sons, New York (2000)
8. Binder, R.: Testing Object-Oriented Systems. Addison-Wesley, Boston (2000)
9. Kim, Y., Honh, H., Cho, S., Bae, D., Cha, S.: Test Cases Generation from UML State Diagrams. IEE Proc. Software 146(4), 187–192 (1999)

10. Offutt, J., Abdurazik, A.: Generating Tests from UML Specifications. In: France, R.B. (ed.) UML 1999. LNCS, vol. 1723, pp. 416–429. Springer, Heidelberg (1999)

11. Riebisch, M., Philippow, I., Götze, M.: UML-Based Statistical Test Case Generation. In: Akşit, M., Mezini, M., Unland, R. (eds.) NODe 2002. LNCS, vol. 2591, pp. 394–411. Springer, Heidelberg (2003)

12. Briand, L., Labiche, Y.: A UML-Based Approach to System Testing. Journal of Software and System Modeling 1(1), 10–42 (2002)

13. Lipka, R., Potuzak, T., Brada, P., Herout, P.: Verification of SimCo – Simulation Tool for Testing of Component-based Application. In: EUROCON 2013, Zagreb, pp. 467–474 (2013)

14. Kačer, J.: Testing Java software for embedded devices using J-Sim and serialization of threads. In: Proc. of Electronic Computers and Informatics, pp. 382–387. VIENALA Press (2004)

15. Havelund, K., Pressburger, T.: Model Checking Java Programs Using Java Pathfinder. International Journal on Software Tools for Technology Transfer 2(4) (2000)

16. Mukund, M.: Finite-state Automata on Infinite Inputs, tutorial talk, Sixth National Seminar on Theoretical Computer Science, Banasthali Vidyapith, Banasthali Rajasthan (1996)

17. Giannakopoulou, D., Lerda, F.: From States to Transitions: Improving translation of LTL formulae to Büchi automata. In: Peled, D.A., Vardi, M.Y. (eds.) FORTE 2002. LNCS, vol. 2529, pp. 308–326. Springer, Heidelberg (2002)

18. Corbett, J., Dwyer, M.B., Hatcliff, J., Laubach, S., Pasareanu, C.S., Zheng, H.: Bandera: Extracting Finite-state Models from Java Source Code. In: Proc. of 22nd International Conference on Software Engineering, Limerick, Poland, pp. 439–448 (2000)

19. Paška, M.: An Approach to Generating C Code with Proven LTL-based Properties. In: Proc. of International Conference on Computer as a Tool EUROCON, pp. 27–29 (2011)

20. Visser, W., Havelund, K., Brat, G., Park, S., Lerda, F.: Model Checking Programs. Automated Software Engineering 10(2), 203–232 (2003)

21. Lerda, F., Visser, W.: Addressing Dynamic Issues of Program Model Checking. In: Dwyer, M.B. (ed.) SPIN 2001. LNCS, vol. 2057, pp. 80–102. Springer, Heidelberg (2001)

22. Avrunin, G.S., Cobert, J.C., Dwyer, M.B., Pasarenau, C.S., Siegel, S.F.: Comparing finite-state verification techniques for concurrent software, Technical report UM-CS-1999-069, Department of Computer Science, Universitz of Massachusetts at Amherst, USA (1999)

23. Corbett, J.C.: Evaluating deadlock detection methods for concurrent software. IEEE Transactions on Software Engineering 22(3), 161–179 (1996)

24. Widmaier, J.C., Smidts, C., Huang, X.: Producing more reliable software: Mature software engineering process vs. state-of-the-art technology. In: Proc. of 22nd International Conference on Software Engineering, Limerick, Ireland, pp. 87–94. ACM Press (2000)

25. Brat, G., Drusinsky, D., Giannakopoulou, D., Goldberg, A., Havelund, K., Lowry, M., Pasareanu, C., Venet, A., Visser, W., Washington, R.: Experimental Evaluation of Verification and Validation Tools on Martian Rover Software. Journal of Formal Methods in System Design 25(2-3), 167–198 (2004)

26. Cotroneo, D., Natella, R., Russo, S., Scippacercola, F.: State-Driven Testing of Distributed Systems. In: Baldoni, R., Nisse, N., van Steen, M. (eds.) OPODIS 2013. LNCS, vol. 8304, pp. 114–128. Springer, Heidelberg (2013)

27. Artho, C., Biere, A.: Combined Static and Dynamic Analysis. Electronic Notes in Theoretical Computer Science 131, 3–14 (2005)

28. Vorobyov, K., Padmanabhan, K.: Comparing model checking and static program analysis: A case study in error detection approaches. In: Proc. of 5th international Wokshop in System Software Verification, Vancouver, Canada, pp. 1–7 (2010)

29. Engler, D., Musuvathi, M.: Static Analysis versus Software Model Checking for Bug Finding. In: Steffen, B., Levi, G. (eds.) VMCAI 2004. LNCS, vol. 2937, pp. 191–210. Springer, Heidelberg (2004)

Advanced Modelling, Simulation and Verification for Future Traffic Regulation Optimisation

Alexei Iliasov[1], Roberto Palacin[2], and Alexander Romanovsky[1]

[1] School of Computing Science, Newcastle University
Newcastle upon Tyne, UK
{alexei.iliasov,alexander.romanovsky}@ncl.ac.uk
[2] NewRail Centre, Newcastle University
Newcastle upon Tyne, UK
roberto.palacin@ncl.ac.uk

Abstract. This paper introduces a new project supported by the UK Technical Strategy Leadership Group (TSLG) to contribute to its vision of Future Traffic Regulation Optimisation (FuTRO). In this project Newcastle University will closely cooperate with Siemens Rail Automation on developing novel modelling, verification and simulation techniques and tools that support and explore in an integrated approach to efficient dynamic improvement of capacity and energy consumption of railway networks and nodes while ensuring whole systems safety. The *SafeCap+* (or *SafeCap for FuTRO*) project builds on the two previous projects (*SafeCap* and *SafeCap Impact*) which have developed a novel modelling environment that helps signalling engineers to design nodes (stations or junctions) in a way that guarantees their safety and allows engineers to explore different design options to select the ones that ensure the improved node capacity.

Keywords: Railway signalling, safety, capacity, energy, ERTMS, ETCS, tool support, verification, traffic management, GPU, formal methods, domain-specific languages, model-based system engineering.

1 Introduction

The UK Future Traffic Regulation Optimisation (FuTRO) programme is a key step to delivering the UK Rail Technical Strategy 2012 (RTS) vision [1]. The ability to regulate trains is in the core of achieving the 4C objectives of this Strategy: reducing carbon by 50%, increasing capacity by 50%, decreasing cost and improving customer satisfaction. The FuTRO programme is very much inline with the traffic management layer of the European Rail Traffic Management System (ERTMS) [2] - an initiative backed by the EU to enhance cross-border interoperability and the procurement of signalling equipment by creating a single Europe-wide standard for train control and command systems.

The RTS Strategy and the FuTRO programme have been endorsed by the UK Technical Strategy Leadership Group (TSLG [3]) representing all stakeholders in the

I. Majzik and M. Vieira (Eds.): SERENE 2014, LNCS 8785, pp. 131–138, 2014.
© Springer International Publishing Switzerland 2014

UK rail industry: from train operators to rolling stock owners, the infrastructure manager, to freight companies, the government, and the regulator.

In our previous EPSRC[1]/RSSB[2] SafeCap project (*Overcoming the railway capacity challenges without undermining rail network safety,* 2011-2013 – [4]) and in its follow-up EPSRC SafeCap Impact project (2013-2014) we developed and evaluated the Eclipse-based SafeCap tooling environment [5] in the industrial settings. This environment supports formal verification of station/junction safety and various ways of simulating train movement to help signalling engineers predict and evaluate railway capacity at the level of individual nodes (stations or junctions) or small networks combining several nodes [6, 7].

Let us consider some of the lessons we learnt while cooperating with the railway industry in the course of these two projects. There is an urgent need to support integrated modelling and verification at different system levels, in particular at these of nodes and of the multi-node and regional networks. It is crucial for the industry to have efficient tool support for scalable simulation and verification (including fully automated safety verification) that can deal with the complexity of large railway systems. To support design of the modern railway systems we need to develop an integrated approach to reasoning about capacity and energy consumption and their interplay. Railway modelling methods and tools need to support dealing with one of the main characteristics of the railway systems, their heterogeneous nature, as these systems always consist of the geographical areas that use different signalling equipment, and the traffic always includes trains of different types that are equipped with different types of on-board systems and follow different driving rules. While modelling and simulating these systems the engineers need to have powerful tool support for efficient dealing with disturbances of different nature. And finally, the importance of ensuring system safety remains the most important principle. This is the paramount concern for the industry as a whole and for all stakeholders involved. Any improvements of and advances in services, supporting technologies and R&D are conditional on safety guarantees.

The new SafeCap+ project, funded by TSLG via the RSSB funding mechanisms, builds on the results of our previous projects and addresses some of the lessons learnt. It will explore the potential of optimising energy consumption and capacity in multi-node systems without undermining their safety, enrich the real time traffic management with capabilities of reasoning about capacity, energy consumptions and safety (e.g. in case of disturbances) and support mixed traffic scenarios, including fixed/moving block signalling and manual/automated driving.

In this paper we introduce the project aims, objectives and outcomes, specifically focusing on the issues directly relevant to the computer science and software engineering. We introduce the context of the project work to be carried out.

The project is fully supported by the railway industry. This creates a productive environment in which the scientific advances will be made only when they are

---

[1] http://www.epsrc.ac.uk/
[2] http://www.rssb.co.uk/

requested by industry, meet the industrial needs and are made to ensure the industrial impact.

2   Project Aim and Objectives

The overall aim of the project is to develop novel modelling techniques and tools that support and explore integrated and efficient dynamic reasoning about capacity and energy consumption of networks and nodes while ensuring whole systems safety.

To fulfil this aim, the following objectives are being addressed:

- to explore the potential, develop the tools and define the framework allowing independent control rules for multiple mixed traffic operation scenarios,
- to develop tools to compute real-time optimum strategies for traffic flow at nodes,
- to identify and understand the energy usage impact on performance of real-time optimum strategies for traffic flow at nodes,
- to define and develop a whole systems modelling approach to integrated optimum capacity, safety and energy strategies at multiple nodes scaling up to a regional network.

3   The Project Advances

The project will make substantial scientific and technological advances in a number of inter-related areas.

3.1   Mixed Traffic Modelling and Verification

The first area of scientific advances is modelling of mixed traffic scenarios. The ways railway is modernised and the high demand for ensuring interoperability of different systems pose the challenge of developing a uniform description and modelling method capable of capturing, on the same semantic ground and in faithful terms, the logic of out-dated, modern and emerging signalling and train operation principles and, at the same time, offering a foundation to experiment with some yet unexplored directions.

To this end the project will develop a unified approach to modelling, analysing and safety verification of systems with fixed/moving block signalling and manual/automated driving. This work will deliver:

- A formal modelling language for uniformly capturing diverse signalling principles and mixing, in a demonstratively safe manner, at the node and/or network-level novel and legacy signalling principles,
- A common approach to modelling of mixed manual/automated driving including spacial regions of fully automated driving overriding manual driving (and vice-versa),
- A safety verification approach based on constraint solving and theorem proving, potentially reducing certification costs for signalling solutions.

The approach will be supported by a number of tools extending the SafeCap modelling environment [5].

We have already started our initial work in this area by developing a modelling notation called Unified Train Driving Policy that captures in a uniform manner and exposes inter-relations of concepts that are often treated separately: track topology and gradients, signalling, fixed speed regime, platform assignment, dynamic re-routing, train schedules and dwelling times, dynamic train headway control, acceleration and braking curves, automated train operation, real-time rescheduling, etc.

3.2   Advisory System

Another area of project advances is real-time optimisation. The aim here is to develop an ultra-fast high-fidelity large-scale railway simulation that can be used in runtime for traffic optimisation. To achieve this aim the project team will work on

- developing the algorithmic foundations for precise, event-based simulation,
- compilation of track topology, train dynamics and signalling rules into highly parallelised code to be executed over a dedicated parallel computing platform,
- utilisation of the readily-available commodity GPU (Graphics Processing Units) to permit the analysis of 10 million and more independent scenarios per second (in our estimation this is required for a medium size network made of five stations).

The areas of the specific interest here are the algorithm parallelisation for GPUs and ensuring the acceptable level of dependability for this GPU-based application. To the best of our knowledge the GPU technology has never been applied in the domain of real-time railway traffic management.

Our initial investigation in this area is focusing on developing a technique for improving capacity and operational stability of busy mainline junctions and stations. The technique, called the SafeCap advisory system, employs a mixture of existing train monitoring and control technologies to introduce an advisory control layer on top of fixed-block signalling [8]. As part of its functionality this real-time control projects the current state of the train configuration along with its set of commands into the future. This allows computing a large number of alternative control scenarios where signalling reconfiguration might be attempted, and the locally optimal control identified. To achieve this control software alters acceleration/ braking curves, sets individual train speed limits, and adjusts dwelling times.

3.3   Modelling Energy

The aim of this strand of work is to identify and understand the energy impact on performance (capacity). To achieve this aim the work will be conducted in the following specific areas:

- Development of a qualitative model to capture train energy expenditure over a track layout,
- Investigation of energy consumption as an optimisation criterion and the ways it can be balanced against performance,
- Application of the energy model to studying the strategies for optimal regenerative braking,
- Producing energy-aware signalling and the automatic train operation technology (ATO).

This work will start with enriching the modelling capabilities supported by the SafeCap tooling environment with reasoning about energy consumption and evaluating the energy consumption for different node layouts and service patterns (using our previous work in [9, 10]).

3.4   Whole System Modelling

The aim is to define and develop a whole systems modelling approach. To achieve this aim the work will be conducted in the following directions:

- Development of a modelling layer to combine railway nodes into local and regional railway networks,
- Design of a provably correct compositional approach to safety verification and capacity assessment,
- Detailed analysis of macro- and microscopic capacity consumption and investigation of causal links of performance bottlenecks.
- Early-stage investigation of connections with other railway operation activities: staff allocation, maintenance, passenger traffic prediction, etc.

These advances will result in extending the SafeCap tooling environment with the new features for modelling node compositions, ensuring their safety and analysing their capacity and performance.

4   Outcomes Planned

The main *outcomes* of the project are as follows
- an integrated open and extendable toolbox providing documentation, user's guides and tutorials,
- algorithms, methods and theories forming a sound foundation for the methods and tools developed,
- a set of medium-scale models/examples demonstrating the usability of the tools,
- an industrial deployment strategy.

In the long term this project will contribute to achieving the long-term FuTRO vision by

- developing capabilities for making optimal real–time (or near real-time) decisions about improving capacity and energy-consumption without undermining network safety,
- providing algorithmic foundations for supporting mixed and diverse types of driving and signalling,
- developing an open tool suite that can be easily integrated with tools developed by various R&D teams in larger FuTRO-level development and real-time environments.

The main advances in software engineering will be in the areas of scalable safety verification, domain-specific modelling, development of the open-source extendable tool support, scalable and dependable GPU-based parallelisation of complex computation in the railway domain, integrated modelling of energy consumption and system capacity, development of formal foundation for reasoning about complex railway systems.

5   Conclusions

The railway domain traditionally brings a lot of challenges to software engineers and computer scientists. The paper introduces the *SafeCap for FuTRO* project and its main outcomes, focusing on the challenges we will be addressing in the area of software engineering of resilient systems. To address them the project, supported by the UK railway industry, brings together a strong team of computer scientists, academics working in railway system research and industrial engineers. The focus on the real industrial needs and on achieving deployment of the methods and tools to be developed is a crucial part of this type of applied research. At the same time as this paper clearly demonstrated there are serious challenges for the computer scientists that need to be addressed to achieve these. These include:

- development of formal theories and supporting tools for modelling, proving safety and analysing capacity of mixed traffic scenarios,
- scalable and dependable GPU-based parallelisation of the simulation engine to allow run-time choice of the scenarios that allow best interplay between capacity and energy consumption,
- scalable safety verification using solvers and provers (and their combinations) to deal with the large network/whole system scenarios,
- development of the open source and extendable Eclipse-based tooling environment ensuring a domain-specific interface that completely hides the use of formal methods.

One of the ambitions of our project is to hide the complexity of using our tools and methods to allow operators, train drivers, signalling engineers and traffic managers to use them without any needs to understand how they are constructed and work. Our tools will speak the domain languages used by the domain experts. We have a very positive experience in hiding the use of formal methods in developing the SafeCap tooling environment [5] – this was achieved by offering a graphical DSL [11] that is used by signalling engineers and mapping it into formal notations used by SAT solvers and model-checkers for verifying safety. The tooling environment is interoperable with the standard data formattings used by our industrial partner and is easily extendable to support any other industrial standards in the railway domain.

The research results will help the industry to achieve both the optimum track and energy infrastructure layout that delivers the requisite timetable, capacity and performance and the optimum signalling of that layout and energy infrastructure to deliver the requisite timetable/capacity/performance. They will support ensuring that different timetable scenarios on those infrastructures deliver requisite service levels and performance, and allow examining the operation of the actual timetable in operation and tweak the train running in real time to deliver optimum performance on the day.

This SafeCap for FuTRO project is in line with the ambitious aims of the European Rail Traffic Management System (ERTMS) Initiative set by the European Commission to ensure interoperability of national railway systems [2]. ERTMS, a major business change programme and a step change in the way we plan, design and operate our railway, requires substantial efforts in advancing our understanding of computer science and software engineering.

Acknowledgments. We are grateful to Ilya Lopatkin for his contribution to the development and evaluation of the SafeCap tooling environment, to Simon Chadwick and Dominic Taylor, our colleagues in Siemens Rail Automation, for their help in this work and to Tony Crabtree for sharing with us his knowledge of the railway domain and for providing very helpful comments on the earlier drafts of this paper.

References

1. The Rail Technical Strategy 2012. The Technical Strategy Leadership Group, UK (2012), http://www.futurerailway.org/RTS/Pages/Intro.aspx
2. European Rail Traffic Management System, http://www.ertms.net
3. Technical Strategy Leadership Group, UK, http://www.rssb.co.uk/groups-and-committees/rssb-board/technical-strategy/technical-strategy-leadership-group
4. The SafeCap project: Overcoming the railway capacity challenges without undermining rail network safety, http://www.safecap.co.uk/
5. The SafeCap Eclipse environment for improving node capacity using formal methods, http://safecap.sourceforge.net/index.shtml
6. Iliasov, A., Lopatkin, I., Romanovsky, A.: The SafeCap Platform for Modelling Railway Safety and Capacity. In: Bitsch, F., Guiochet, J., Kaâniche, M. (eds.) SAFECOMP 2013. LNCS, vol. 8153, pp. 130–137. Springer, Heidelberg (2013)
7. Iliasov, A., Lopatkin, I., Romanovsky, A.: The SafeCap Project on Railway Safety Verification and Capacity Simulation. In: Gorbenko, A., Romanovsky, A., Kharchenko, V. (eds.) SERENE 2013. LNCS, vol. 8166, pp. 125–132. Springer, Heidelberg (2013)

8. Iliasov, A., Lopatkin, I., Mihut, A., Romanovsky, A.: Real-time ATO reconfiguration for operational stability. In: Computers in Railways XIV: Railway Engineering Design and Optimization 135, pp. 163–173. WIT Press (2014)
9. González-Gil, A., Palacin, R., Batty, P., Powell, J.P.: A systems approach to reduce urban rail energy consumption. Energy Conversion and Management 80, 509–524 (2014)
10. Powell, J.P., González-Gil, A., Palacin, R.: Experimental assessment of the energy consumption of urban rail vehicles during stabling hours: influence of ambient temperature. Applied Thermal Engineering 66(1-2), 541–547 (2014)
11. Iliasov, A., Romanovsky, A.: SafeCap domain language for reasoning about safety and capacity. In: Workshop on Dependable Transportation Systems at the Pacific-Rim Dependable Computing Conference (PRDC 2012), Niigata, Japan. IEEE CS (2012)

Using Instrumentation for Quality Assessment of Resilient Software in Embedded Systems

David Lawrence[1], Didier Buchs[1], and Armin Wellig[2]

[1] Université de Genève, Centre Universitaire d'Informatique
Route de Drize 7, 1227 Carouge, Switzerland
[2] Honeywell International Sarl.,
La Pièce 16, 1180 Rolle, Switzerland

Abstract. The obvious growth of complexity in embedded and cyber physical systems requires from developers to be innovative in the way they carry out the verification process. To increase the amount of information available from a system, software instrumentation has been previously used in these domains, therefore solving the problem of observability. In addition, as this kind of systems tends to be increasingly involved in safety critical and dependable applications, ensuring reliability properties must also be considered as a part of the verification process. In this paper, the system observability problem is initially being introduced. Then, as a solution to overcome the previous limitation, instrumentation is being explored. To address the verification concerns of resilient systems, a three components model is designed, the latter explicitly defining degradation and compensation models to capture the resiliency routine. Finally, to conclude the models definition, a handful number of LTL properties are identified and discussed.

Keywords: Instrumentation, Resilience, Modelling, Model Checking, Embedded systems, Cyber physical systems.

1 Introduction

Embedded and cyber physical systems are becoming considerably more ubiquitous in our daily lives as they tend to be involved in a considerable number of applications, ranging from cell phones to car components controllers. Therefore, this omnipresence clearly justifies increased verification needs, especially since a subset of applications is involved in dependable or safety critical environment. Consequently, researches, targeting critical systems notably, must be thoroughly performed to be able to constantly tackle problems hindering the analysis and development of dependable systems. A good starting point to seize this set of problems is to fully understand the meaning of the term *dependability*. Algirdas Avizienis et al. defined in [1] the latter as *the ability to deliver a service that can justifiably be trusted*. In a sub case of dependable systems often called *resilient*, performances degradation is tolerated as long as the system is able to detect it and recover to an acceptable state of it's original behavior. A more recent

I. Majzik and M. Vieira (Eds.): SERENE 2014, LNCS 8785, pp. 139–153, 2014.

definition [2] affirms that a resilient software is a system that keeps track of it's internal state and is able to run close to it's normal behavior notwithstanding disturbances of various sources, either from a natural or malicious nature. For that purpose, instrumentation may provide solutions to overcome the known problems of verification. This well established technique has been used for various purposes in order to improve the observability of a system. In consequence, the instrumentation technique increases the amount of known information about the system to attest both dependability and correctness.

This paper is organized as follow. Section 2 explains the problem of observability and introduces the instrumentation technique. Section 3 explores how to attest the instrumentation relevance using both a specification model and program traces. Section 4 addresses notions of resilience and introduces the resiliency routine. Section 5 conceptually discusses resilient system development and instrumentation usage insights by extending an initial specification to a three components model, involving the system behavior as well as a degradation and a compensation model. In the same section, some key properties of the resulting system are also distinguished. Finally, section 6 identifies and enunciates some possible improvements and future works ideas.

2   Observability

Observation A system corresponds to a blackbox controlled by a finite number of inputs, emitting a finite number of outputs and where the internal state is unknown. Therefore, in some cases, the tester is unsure if the observed outputs are a result of a correct internal state or a falsely fortunate event. To illustrate the

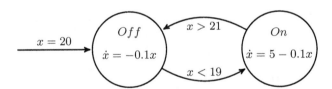

Fig. 1. 1st thermostat

prior explanation, let's consider two simple thermostat systems modelled using *Hybrid Automata*. A hybrid automaton is a formal model often used to represent embedded and cyber physical systems. The latter mixes both discrete events for the transitions and continuous computation on each state. For more details about this formalism, the reader may refer to [8]. Depicted on the figure 1, the first thermostat simply ensures that the room temperature, variable x, mostly stays between two values, respectively 19 and 21 degrees. For that purpose, two states are used, namely *on* and *off*, to either heat up the room or let the temperature decrease naturally. Obviously, this system doesn't need additional internal state variables to run. Illustrated on the figure 2, the second thermostat is slightly more complex. Although it's basic functionality is the same than the first system, this one is equipped with a led which must be lighted up every 5 ticks when the system is in it's *On* state. Here, the timer counter is represented by the internal variable *cnt* and the led is controlled by the event *led*. Based upon this counter and the current system state, the thermostat is going to either light up the led or not. Imagine now that the developer made a mistake concerning the number

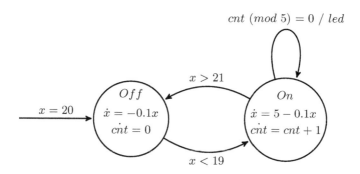

Fig. 2. 2nd thermostat

of ticks required before lighting up the led, defining it to 6 ticks instead of 5 for example. To ensure the complete functionality of such a system, the tester might consider observing the value of the variable *cnt*. Consequently, he is able to confirm that the led is correctly lighted up every 5 ticks by using an extra observation point.

Formally, all system behaviors can be observed through traces of inputs and outputs. Using a specification *spec* given in the form of an automaton, the traces $T(spec)$ are words $\in (\Sigma_{in} \times \Sigma_{out})^*$ where Σ_{in} is the input vocabulary and Σ_{out} the output vocabulary. Therefore, the following simple satisfaction relation can be stated for any program $p \in P$ based on the traces over the specification:

$$p \models spec \Leftrightarrow T(p) = T(spec) \,. \tag{1}$$

In consequence, the system correctness can be assumed by using program traces of reasonable sizes. Moreover, adding additional observation points *obs* requires the following correctness equivalence:

$$obs \text{ is a correct observer for } p \text{ iff } \models spec \Leftrightarrow p + obs \models spec \,. \tag{2}$$

Instrumenting Adding new observation points is a technique called *instrumentation* and can be classified into two main categories [9]. In fact, this techique is utilized in both hardware, with applications of energy usage measurements [3] for example, and software applications, with code coverage measurements [7] or verification techniques such as symbolic execution [4–6].

Relevance Even though instrumentation can be useful, it's relevance could easily be questioned. In fact, the quality of the selected observation points can have an influence on the length of the traces that must be observed to assume the program correctness. In the previous example, the timing correctness of the led activation could be underlined using two distinct observation points. The first one consists of emitting a signal when the modulo of the counter is equal to 0, as depicted on the transition looping on the state *On*. In this case, the traces are rather short. An alternative observation point would consist of the emission of a signal every time the counter is incremented. Therefore, the correctness is assumed after 5 signal occurrences, thus leading to longer traces. As presented previously, instrumentation was discussed and used as a manual process. Consequently, adding observations is more related to a feeling-based method than a formal and clear methodology. At first glance, there is no assurance that the observation points could be of any use. Assuming the inadequacy of the instrumentation, the resulting outputs would be unhelpful to state the system correctness, even though the latter provides additional information about it's execution. Based upon the prior arguments, one might want to answer the following question: is there a way to attest the quality of both instrumentation and implementation?

3   Instrumentation Relevance Assessment

Instrumentation goal The instrumentation process can be seen as a method to capture the same information represented by the specification model. In consequence, one can implicitly understand that additional observation points must be considered if the instrumentation doesn't capture enough information to state the system correctness using only the specification model as referential.

Iterative process Since the instrumentation activity is applied during the development process, adding observations points can be seen as an iterative method, as depicted on the figure 3 where the notation used is as follow: boxes represent artefacts and rounded boxes correspond to processing activities, either manual or automatic. Initially, an implementation with observations points is produced based upon the specification model. Some extra observation points can still be added, even after the end of the development. Using the aforementioned implementation, it is possible to distinguish a set of traces $T(p+obs)$ over the program $p \in P$ with the given observation points $obs \subseteq Obs$. Then, by comparing the specification and the program traces, the relevance of the observation points can be stated. Until now, the process described is entirely sequential. Nevertheless, developers are still able to adjust the instrumentation if needed. This iterative process stops only once the instrumentation is sufficient. In consequence, an order of expressiveness of the observation points can be defined.

To understand this order, one must first define the *Reduce* function. The latter removes redundant or equivalent traces from a set of traces $Traces(p+obs)$ into a subset of traces $Traces(p + obs)' \subseteq Traces(p + obs)$ without violating the following correctness equivalence:

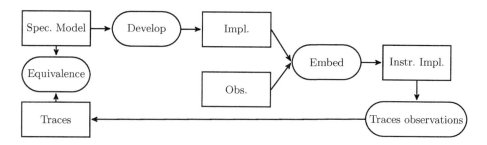

Fig. 3. High level picture of the iterative process

$$\forall p \in P, obs \in Obs, s \in Spec, p \models spec \Leftrightarrow Reduce(T(p + obs)) = T(spec) \,.$$

Reduce is a correct reduction iff (3)

The following non exhaustive methods list provides examples that can be used by this function to reduce the set of traces:

- a trace is a prefix of another trace;
- a trace is a duplicate of another trace;
- reduction hypothesis;
- ...

In her PhD thesis [10], Cécile Péraire described a handful amount of reduction hypotheses, such as uniformity and regularity for example.

Given the set of traces for different observers $obs \subseteq Obs$, the measure of expressiveness of the observers is as follow:

$$\sum_{t \in Reduce(T(p+obs))} |t| \qquad (4)$$

Note that the previously defined notion measure the expressiveness of an instrumented program based on the observers by taking into consideration the number of traces required to be semantically similar to the traces of the specification as well as their lengths. It means that given some observers $\{obs_1, obs_2, ..., obs_n\}$ we are able to totally order them and to exhibit one of the minimum of this set.

To illustrate the relevance of observation points, let's consider the following little piece of software that controls the behavior of the second thermostat example:

```
int Thermostat2 (int* x) {
   // 2nd Thermostat example behavior
   if (x > 21) {
      *x = -0.1 * x;
      cnt  = 0;
      return 0; // LED OFF
```

```
} else if (x < 19) {
    x = 5 - 0.1 * x;
    if (cnt % 5 = 0) {
        return 1;   // LED ON
    }
    cnt  = cnt + 1;
}
}
```

The previous implementation doesn't contain any extra observation points, thus leading to unchanged traces $T(p)$. With respect to the specification, the value of the temperature is obviously a functionality cornerstone of the application. Therefore, it might be interesting to instrument the conditional expressions with the variable x, the latter representing the temperature, to improve the system observability. A sample of the traces observed by the newly instrumented implementation is shown on the figure 4. This sample underlines the fact that new observation points for the temperature, "$x < 19$" for example, are now part of the traces.

$$x = 20 \rightarrow x = 18.1 \rightarrow x < 19 \rightarrow ...$$

Fig. 4. 2nd Thermostat traces sample

4   Resilience

Three components composition To handle resiliency, the system can be seen as a composition of three modules, respectively an initial system, a compensation component and a degradation component. To understand this composition, the resilience process, figure 5, is explained. During this routine, the system initially adopts it's usual behavior as it generally should. Then, due to a disruption, it's execution is being degraded. Consequently, the system detects the performance loss and is able to compensate. Finally, this compensation helps the system to adopt once again a consistent state of it's normal behavior.

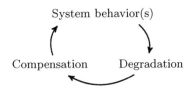

Fig. 5. System resilience process

System goals. A common software doesn't necessarily support any resiliency mechanisms for errors detection and system recovery. Therefore, an initial software must first be extended. In consequence, auxiliary mechanisms, such as feedback signals or state recovery, are implemented. Clearly, the choice of the mechanisms implementation is highly coupled to the errors taken into consideration.

Compensation goals. This component is formed of two distinct subparts, respectively errors detection and state recovery. To cite a concrete example of error detection mechanism, one might mention feedback signals emission, the latter being able to provide enough information to spot a failure and recover accordingly. The feedback content can however differ with respect to the recovery extent. In fact, on the one hand, one might want to store only the last consistent state encountered by the system, whereas on the other hand, runtime data could also be kept for a more precise recovery. The second step of the compensation activity aims to recover the system in an acceptable state. Finally, one might say that the compensation component previously described is closely related to the concept of recovery blocks [11, 12].

Degradation goals. The degradation component is used to be able to inject errors that can negatively affect the system state. The article of Jörg Henkel et. al. [13] non exhaustively enumerated recurring errors caused by a simple bit flip originating either from a hardware or software nature. Amongst the list of errors, system crash has been chosen as part of this study since it is the most obvious software failures distinguished. Therefore, signal noises, radiation or temperature effects are not directly addressed as they are deriving from physical processes, even though a lot of software errors are a consequence of hardware or physical problems [15]

5   Resiliency Model

Goal To be able to attest the quality of a resilient system with instrumentation, one might want first to study a high level model to distinguish required resiliency mechanisms and relevant observations points that must be introduced. For that purpose, this section doesn't directly address the implementation and instrumentation of a resilient system, however it provides insights on these two subjects by designing a model composed of three distinct components. Furthermore, verification techniques such as model checking can be applied to this model to enrich this study. By taking a different approach, the implementation handling the resilience and the instrumentation can be automatically generated from a well defined model. As it was stressed in the article of Markus Voelter et. al [18], code generation in embedded systems helps to overcome common problems introduced by individual developers, thus avoiding unsafe programming.

Modelling formalism Prior examples were modelled using the hybrid automata formalism. Since the study of resilient mechanisms involves only discrete steps, simple finite state automata are sufficient here to clearly specify the modelling of both the system and resiliency mechanisms.

Definition 1 *The finite state automata used in this paper are septuple in the form of* $< \Sigma, S, s_0, F, X, A, AP >$ *where:*

- Σ *is a finite and non-empty set of symbols representing the input and output alphabet;*
- S *is a finite, non-empty set of states;*
- $s_0 \in S$ *is the initial state of the automaton;*
- $F \subseteq S \times \Sigma \times S$, *is the finite set of transitions;*
- X *is a finite and possibly empty set of natural variables;*
- $A \subseteq F \times X \times exp(X)$ *is a finite and possibly empty set of affectation on transitions;*
- AP *is a finite set of atomic propositions;*
- $guard(f), f \in F$ *is a guard condition predicate over the transitions, whose free variables are from X;*
- $\nu : S \rightarrow \mathcal{P}(AP)$ *is a function that returns the atomic propositions for a specific state;*
- $exp(X)$ *is the set of expression on the given types (not detailed here).*

$\square$

To ease the comprehension of the upcoming definitions, the following notation will be used for a transition:

$$(s \rightarrow^e s') \in F, e \in \Sigma, s, s' \in S . \tag{5}$$

Definition 2 *Given two automata FSM_1 and FSM_2:*

$$\begin{aligned} FSM_1 =&< \Sigma_1, S_1, s_0', F_1, X_1, A_1, AP_1 > . \\ FSM_2 =&< \Sigma_2, S_2, s_0'', F_2, X_2, A_2, AP_2 > . \end{aligned} \tag{6}$$

The composition of $FSM_1 \parallel FSM_2$ is an automaton given by:

$$FSM_{compo} =< \Sigma, S, s_0, F, X, A, AP > . \tag{7}$$

where:

$$\begin{aligned} &\Sigma = \Sigma_1 \cup \Sigma_2 . \\ &S = S_1 \times S_2, S_1 \cap S_2 = \emptyset . \\ &s_0 = s_0' \times s_0'' . \\ &X = X_1 \cup X_2 . \\ &AP = AP_1 \cup AP_2, AP_1 \cap AP_2 = \emptyset . \\ &\nu(s_1 \times s_2) = \nu(s_1) \cup \nu(s_2), \forall s_1 \in S_1, \forall s_2 \in S_2, s_1 \times s_2 \in S . \end{aligned} \tag{8}$$

Given the transitions of FSM_1 and FSM_2:

$$(s_1 \to^{\epsilon 1} s_1') \in F_1, s_1, s_1' \in S_1, \epsilon 1 \in \Sigma_1 .$$
$$(s_2 \to^{\epsilon 2} s_2') \in F_2, s_2, s_2' \in S_2, \epsilon 1 \in \Sigma_2 . \tag{9}$$

The new transitions can be defined as follow:

$$if\ \epsilon 1 = \epsilon 2 \Rightarrow (s_1 \times s_2) \to^{\epsilon 1} (s_1' \times s_2') \in F .$$
$$if\ \epsilon 1 \neq \epsilon 2 \Rightarrow \{((s_1 \times s_2) \to^{\epsilon 1} (s_1' \times s_2))\} \cup \{((s_1 \times s_2) \to^{\epsilon 2} (s_1 \times s_2'))\} \in F . \tag{10}$$

The guards over the new transitions are therefore given by:

$$if\ \epsilon 1 = \epsilon 2 \Rightarrow guard((s_1 \times s_2) \to^{\epsilon 1} (s_1' \times s_2')) =$$
$$guard(s_1 \to^{\epsilon 1} s_1') \wedge guard(s_2 \to^{\epsilon 1} s_2'), (s_1 \times s_2) \to^{\epsilon 1} (s_1' \times s_2') \in F .$$
$$if\ \epsilon 1 \neq \epsilon 2 \Rightarrow guard((s_1 \times s_2) \to^{\epsilon 1} (s_1' \times s_2)) =$$
$$guard(s_1 \to^{\epsilon 1} s_1'), (s_1 \times s_2) \to^{\epsilon 1} (s_1' \times s_2) \in F$$
$$\wedge$$
$$guard((s_1 \times s_2) \to^{\epsilon 2} (s_1 \times s_2')) =$$
$$guard(s_2 \to^{\epsilon 2} s_2'), (s_1 \times s_2) \to^{\epsilon 2} (s_1 \times s_2') \in F . \tag{11}$$

Finally, the affectation performed on the transitions are defined as:

$$((s_1 \times s_2) \to^{\epsilon 1}(s_1' \times s_2'), x, t) \in A\ iff\ \epsilon 1 = \epsilon 2\ and$$
$$((s_1 \to^{\epsilon 1} s_1'), x, t) \in A_1 \vee ((s_2 \to^{\epsilon 2} s_2'), x, t) \in A_2, x \in X, t \in exp(X) .$$
$$((s_1 \times s_2) \to^{\epsilon 1}(s_1' \times s_2), x, t) \in A,$$
$$((s_1 \to^{\epsilon 1} s_1'), x, t) \in A_1, x \in X, t \in exp(X) .$$
$$((s_1 \times s_2) \to^{\epsilon 2}(s_1 \times s_2'), x, t) \in A,$$
$$((s_2 \to^{\epsilon 2} s_2'), x, t) \in A_2, x \in X, t \in exp(X) . \tag{12}$$

$\square$

High Level Picture The composition of finite state automata is utilized to represent the three components interaction. In consequence, the complete model is composed of the extended initial system FSM_{spec}'', handling feedback and recovery mechanisms, the compensation model FSM_{comp} and the degradation model FSM_{degr}:

$$FSM_{res} = FSM_{spec}'' \parallel FSM_{comp} \parallel FSM_{degr} . \tag{13}$$

Furthermore, this composition implicitly simulates communications between models by using the alphabet symbols and can be alternatively seen as depicted on the figure 6. In fact, this figure shows the implicit signal exchanges by explicitly representing them. Since only discrete signals are used by the automaton, it was assumed that the alphabet of the initial specification was provided in a discrete form by a continuous environment. For example, the environment would provide to the system the temperature in the form of discrete signals such as "temperature < 19" or "temperature > 21".

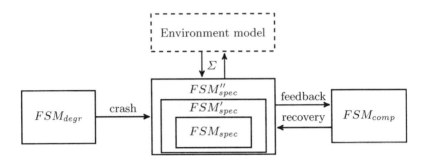

Fig. 6. Communications view

System state identification. A set of atomic propositions AP must first be defined for FSM_{spec} to be able to uniquely identify each system state. This definition is required to express resilient properties related to system recovery. For that purpose, a function σ is defined. σ returns a unique natural number for each state of the specification FSM_{spec}:

$$\sigma : S \to \mathbb{N} .$$
$$\forall s \in S, \forall s' \in S, s \neq s' \,|\sigma(s) \neq \sigma(s') . \tag{14}$$

Then, a function called $ap : \mathbb{N} \to AP$ is defined. This function maps a natural number into an atomic proposition. Consequently, using both σ and ap functions, a unique atomic proposition can be linked to each system state:

$$AP \subseteq \bigcup_{\forall s \in S} ap(\sigma(s)) .$$
$$\nu(s) = ap(\sigma(s)), \forall s \in S \tag{15}$$

Feedback modelling The initial system model FSM_{spec} is extended to FSM'_{spec} in order to introduce the feedback mechanism. Informally, two new states are added. The first one, named $crash^s$, helps to explicitly define a failure system state, whereas the second, named $feedback^s$, defines the state in which error feedback signals are emitted. Obviously, in order to provide a way to reach this new failure state, new transitions are created, linking every existing system states to the $crash^s$ state. Then, an extra transition, linking the crash and the feedback states, is defined to temporarily distinguish the system crash and the feedback signal emission. The extended automaton $FSM'_{spec} =< \Sigma', S', s_0, F', X', AP' >$ can be formally defined as follow:

$$\Sigma' = \Sigma \cup \{crash, feedback\} \,.$$
$$S' = S \cup \{crash^s, feedback^s\} \,.$$
$$F' = F \cup \{crash \rightarrow^{feedback} feedback^s\} \cup \bigcup_{\forall s \in S} \{s \rightarrow^{crash} crash^s\} \,.$$
$$X' = X \cup \{crashed\_state\} \,. \tag{16}$$
$$AP' = AP \cup \{syscrash, sent\_feedback\} \,.$$
$$\nu(crash^s) = syscrash \,.$$
$$\nu(feedback^s) = sent\_feedback \,.$$

As mentioned before, the function σ helps to uniquely identify each state of the system FSM_{spec} and is used to store in the variable $crashed\_state$ the state in which the system failed. The affectation of $crashed\_state$ itself is done on the transitions starting from all system states and ending on the $crash^s$ state:

$$A = \bigcup_{(s \rightarrow^{crash} crash^s) \in F'} (f, crashed\_state, crashed\_state = \sigma(s)), s \in S \,. \tag{17}$$

Given the previous extension, the compensation model is now able to detect a failure using a rudimentary feedback technique, even though the recovery technique still needs to be designed.

Recovery modelling To be able to recover from a failure, another extension of the system model is therefore considered. This extension creates new transitions from the $feedback^s$ state to every existing state of the initial system model. Furthermore, guards are used on these new transitions in order to enable only one possible recovery state. The finite state automaton FSM'_{spec} is extended to $FSM''_{spec} =< \Sigma'', S', s_0, F'', X', A', AP' >$ where:

$$\Sigma'' = \Sigma' \cup \{recovery\} \,.$$
$$F'' = F' \cup \bigcup_{\forall st \in S} \{feedback^s \rightarrow^{recovery} st\} \,.$$
$$\forall f = (feedback^s \rightarrow^{recovery} st) \in F'', st \in S \mid guard(f) = (crashed\_state = \sigma(st)) \,. \tag{18}$$

The guard predicates of these new transitions are using the variable $crashed\_state$, in which is stored the failed state. Moreover, the σ function, that maps a unique index for each state of the initial specification, is used to distinctively identify each running state, as represented on the figure 7. These guards ensure the system recovery to the last consistent state as well as the automaton determinism.

Compensation modelling This model is rather simple. In fact, the compensation component waits until a feedback signal is received from the system. From that moment on, the compensation model sends a recovery signal to the system. This

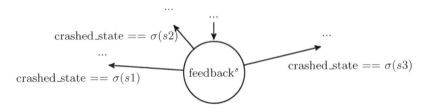

Fig. 7. Guards for state recovery using the stored failed state

model $FSM_{comp} =< \Sigma_{comp}, S_{comp}, s_{0-comp}, F_{comp}, X_{comp}, A_{comp}, AP_{comp} >$ can be formalized as follow:

$$\Sigma_{comp} = \{feedback, recovery\} .$$
$$S_{comp} = \{idle^s, detection^s\} .$$
$$s_{0-comp} = \{idle^s\} .$$
$$F_{comp} = \{(idle^s \rightarrow^{feedback} detection^s), (detection^s \rightarrow^{recovery} idle^s)\} .$$
$$X_{comp} = \emptyset, \ A_{comp} = \emptyset .$$
$$AP_{comp} = \{recvd\_feedback, comp\_idle\} .$$
$$\nu(detection^s) = \{recvd\_feedback\} .$$
$$\nu(idle^s) = \{comp\_idle\} .$$

$$(19)$$

Degradation modelling Similarly to the compensation, the degradation model is also rather simple. In fact, this model is either injecting a system crash or not. The degradation model $FSM_{degr} =< \Sigma_{degr}, S_{degr}, s_{0-degr}, F_{degr}, X_{degr}, A_{degr}, AP_{degr} >$ can be formalized as follow:

$$\Sigma_{degr} = \{crash, return\_to\_normal\} .$$
$$S_{degr} = \{normal^s, inject^s\} .$$
$$s_{0-degr} = \{normal^s\} .$$
$$F_{degr} = \{(normal^s \rightarrow^{crash} inject^s), (inject^s \rightarrow^{return\_to\_normal} normal^s)\} .$$
$$X_{degr} = \emptyset, \ A_{degr} = \emptyset .$$
$$AP_{degr} = \{injected\} .$$
$$\nu(inject^s) = \{injected\} .$$

$$(20)$$

Resiliency properties Part of this study, some resilient system properties can be distinguished. For that purpose, the linear temporal logic formalism is used to express them using the atomic propositions defined on the previous automata. The first few properties are addressing the verification of the mechanisms designed in order to support the system resiliency, whereas the rest are more related to the resiliency routine in general. First, one might want to ensure that a feedback signal is always emitted in the future after a crash:

$$G(syscrash \wedge X(F\,sent\_feedback)) \,. \tag{21}$$

Then, checking for the degradation model correctness is also a desired property. In other words, one might want to verify that the system actually crashes if the degradation model injects an error:

$$G(injected \rightarrow syscrash) \,. \tag{22}$$

Furthermore, the compensation model reactivity might also be checked. In fact, this model must react if a feedback signal is emitted:

$$G((comp\_idle \wedge syscrash) \rightarrow X(sent\_feedback \wedge recvd\_feedback) \,. \tag{23}$$

Finally, verifying the system ability to detect and recover from an error is the most important property to check. More than one LTL formulae are actually required to verify this property since the recover state depends on the last consistent state before the crash. Therefore, the number of LTL formulae needed to check this property is equal to the initial system states cardinality $|S_{spec}|$. For example, if the initial system specification is composed of 3 states with the atomic propositions *1*, *2* and *3*, the following LTL formulae must hold:

$$G(1 \wedge syscrash \rightarrow X((\neg 2 \wedge \neg 3)\,U\,1)) \,.$$
$$G(2 \wedge syscrash \rightarrow X((\neg 1 \wedge \neg 3)\,U\,2)) \,. \tag{24}$$
$$G(3 \wedge syscrash \rightarrow X((\neg 1 \wedge \neg 2)\,U\,3)) \,.$$

6   Future Works

Using instrumentation insights provided by the description of the three components model, the first idea would be to extend a common system to involve resiliency using the discussed mechanisms and relevant observations points. Based upon this system, one might want to study the transformation of enunciated LTL formulae in order to verify these properties using dynamic testing instead of model checking. In fact, without providing any correctness assurance, well chosen test cases can increase the confidence in the system ability in following it's specification and handling crash and recovery cases.

Moreover, since the approach discussed is related to an abstraction of a real world system, one might want to use a model checker on the described components composition to perform model checking. In fact, by applying simple model transformations, model checkers such as *AlPiNA* [17] or *StrataGEM* [16], both developed in the Software Modeling and Verification Group lab, could be used.

Even though time is crucial in a resilient system, this component wasn't considered in this paper. A relevant idea would be to introduce the time component in the defined model in order to be able to express timing properties, yet without reaching the well known problem of state space explosion.

Finally, strong assumptions have been emitted with regards to the available states for recovery. In fact, the approach considered that the system should be recovered to the last consistent state before the system crashed. However, in some cases, one might imagine that not all states are acceptable for recovery. In fact, some states might be safe, whereas others would be considered unsafe. A safety classification of states could therefore provide more precision to correctly handle the recovery process. Moreover, the paper [19] provided interesting intuition to solve this problem by discussing the usage of metadata in order to dynamically adapt the behavior of the resiliency process. Therefore, one might imagine the extension of this idea to dynamically change the state recovery mechanisms, depending on failure rates for example.

7   Conclusion

This paper firstly introduced the usage of instrumentation to adequately assume the system correctness by increasing it's observability. Then, the instrumentation relevance with regards to the observation points has been stated by defining a semantics equality between the traces of the instrumented program and the specification. Afterwards, the resiliency routine was discussed by identifying it's main stages, respectively normal behavior, degradation and compensation. To provide insights on how to instrument a software to address resiliency, an abstract three components model, involving the initial system as well as a compensation and a degradation model, was introduced. Moreover, the degradation model underlines the possibility to explicitly force a system crash. Based upon this study, a handful number of LTL properties for resilient systems were established. Even though this model was mainly aimed for a model checking approach, the usage of more dynamic methods such as testing weren't left out of the scope as a further study of resilient systems. In fact, the instrumentation required in order to verify resiliency properties is now known.

Acknowledgments. This work was funded by Honeywell International Sarl.

References

1. Avizienis, A., Laprie, J.-C., Randell, B., Landwehr, C.E.: Basic concepts and taxonomy of dependable and secure computing. IEEE Trans. Dependable Sec. Comput. 1(1), 11–33 (2004)
2. Rieger, C.G., Gertman, D.I., McQueen, M.A.: Resilient control systems: next generation design research. In: 2nd Conference on Human System Interactions, HSI 2009, pp. 632–636. IEEE (2009)
3. Bouchhima, A., Gerin, P., Pétrot, F.: Automatic instrumentation of embedded software for high level hardware/software co-simulation. In: ASP-DAC, pp. 546–551. IEEE (2009)
4. Sen, K., Marinov, D., Agha, G.: Cute: a concolic unit testing engine for c. In: Wermelinger, M., Gall, H. (eds.) ESEC/SIGSOFT FSE, pp. 263–272. ACM (2005)
5. Kim, M., Kim, Y., Jang, Y.: Industrial application of concolic testing on embedded software: Case studies. In: Antoniol, G., Bertolino, A., Labiche, Y. (eds.) ICST, pp. 390–399. IEEE (2012)

6. Sen, K.: DART: Directed automated random testing. In: Namjoshi, K., Zeller, A., Ziv, A. (eds.) HVC 2009. LNCS, vol. 6405, p. 4. Springer, Heidelberg (2011)
7. Tikir, M.M., Hollingsworth, J.K.: Efficient instrumentation for code coverage testing. ACM SIGSOFT Software Engineering Notes 27(4), 86–96 (2002)
8. Henzinger, T.A.: The theory of hybrid automata. In: Kemal Inan, M., Kurshan, R.P. (eds.) Verification of Digital and Hybrid Systems. NATO ASI Series, vol. 170, pp. 265–292. Springer, Heidelberg (2000)
9. Titzer, B., Palsberg, J.: Nonintrusive precision instrumentation of microcontroller software. In: Paek, Y., Gupta, R. (eds.) LCTES, pp. 59–68. ACM (2005)
10. Péraire, C.: Formal testing of object-oriented software. PhD thesis, ÉCOLE POLYTECHNIQUE FÉDÉRALE DE LAUSANNE (1998)
11. Horning, J.J., Lauer, H.C., Melliar-Smith, P.M., Randell, B.: A program structure for error detection and recovery. In: Gelenbe, E., Kaiser, C. (eds.) Operating Systems. LNCS, vol. 16, pp. 171–187. Springer, Heidelberg (1981)
12. Randell, B.: System structure for software fault tolerance. IEEE Trans. Software Eng. 1(2), 221–232 (1975)
13. Henkel, J., Bauer, L., Becker, J., Bringmann, O., Brinkschulte, U., Chakraborty, S., Engel, M., Ernst, R., Härtig, H., Hedrich, L., Herkersdorf, A., Kapitza, R., Lohmann, D., Marwedel, P., Platzner, M., Rosenstiel, W., Schlichtmann, U., Spinczyk, O., Tahoori, M.B., Teich, J., Wehn, N., Wunderlich, H.-J.: Design and architectures for dependable embedded systems. In: Dick, Madsen (eds.) [14], pp. 69–78
14. Dick, R.P., Madsen, J. (eds.): Proceedings of the 9th International Conference on Hardware/Software Codesign and System Synthesis, CODES+ISSS 2011, part of ESWeek 2011 Seventh Embedded Systems Week, Taipei, Taiwan, October 9-14. ACM (2011)
15. Li, M.-L., Ramachandran, P., Sahoo, S.K., Adve, S.V., Adve, V.S., Zhou, Y.: Understanding the propagation of hard errors to software and implications for resilient system design. In: Eggers, S.J., Larus, J.R. (eds.) ASPLOS, pp. 265–276. ACM (2008)
16. López Bóbeda, E., Colange, M., Buchs, D.: StrataGEM: A generic petri net verification framework. In: Ciardo, G., Kindler, E. (eds.) PETRI NETS 2014. LNCS, vol. 8489, pp. 364–373. Springer, Heidelberg (2014)
17. Buchs, D., Hostettler, S., Marechal, A., Risoldi, M.: AlPiNA: A symbolic model checker. In: Lilius, J., Penczek, W. (eds.) PETRI NETS 2010. LNCS, vol. 6128, pp. 287–296. Springer, Heidelberg (2010)
18. Voelter, M., Ratiu, D., Schätz, B., Kolb, B.: mbeddr: an extensible c-based programming language and ide for embedded systems. In: Leavens, G.T. (ed.) SPLASH, pp. 121–140. ACM (2012)
19. Di Marzo Serugendo, G., Fitzgerald, J.S., Romanovsky, A., Guelfi, N.: A metadata-based architectural model for dynamically resilient systems. In: Cho, Y., Wainwright, R.L., Haddad, H., Shin, S.Y., Koo, Y.W. (eds.) SAC, pp. 566–572. ACM (2007)

Adaptive Domain-Specific Service Monitoring

Arda Ahmet Ünsal[1], Görkem Sazara[1], Barış Aktemur[2], and Hasan Sözer[2]

[1] VESTEK R&D Corporation, Istanbul, Turkey
{arda.unsal,gorkem.sazara}@vestel.com.tr
[2] Ozyegin University, Istanbul, Turkey
{baris.aktemur,hasan.sozer}@ozyegin.edu.tr

Abstract. We propose an adaptive and domain-specific service monitoring approach to detect partner service errors in a cost-effective manner. Hereby, we not only consider generic errors such as *file not found* or *connection timed out*, but also take domain-specific errors into account. The detection of each type of error entails a different monitoring cost in terms of the consumed resources. To reduce costs, we adapt the monitoring frequency for each service and for each type of error based on the measured error rates and a cost model. We introduce an industrial case study from the broadcasting and content-delivery domain for improving the user-perceived reliability of Smart TV systems. We demonstrate the effectiveness of our approach with real data collected to be relevant for a commercial TV portal application. We present empirical results regarding the trade-off between monitoring overhead and error detection accuracy. Our results show that each service is usually subject to various types of errors with different error rates and exploiting this variation can reduce monitoring costs by up to 30% with negligible compromise on the quality of monitoring.

1 Introduction

Service-oriented architecture (SOA) allows composing loosely-coupled services to build software; a typical SOA may utilize several third-party services. However, relying on external services comes with a price; if a service fails or has degraded quality, an error or an unsatisfactory quality can be observed by the users. To remedy this problem, a monitoring approach [24,28,23,27,1] can be utilized to tolerate [16] or avoid/mask [11] detected errors and to measure service quality. These approaches are dedicated to monitoring basic quality factors such as availability, and they detect only common errors such as *file not found* or *connection timed out*. However, there also exist certain types of errors that are specific and highly relevant to particular application domains. For example, services that provide audio/video content over broadband connection might be subject to a variety of content-related errors such as wrong URLs, faulty feeds (e.g. unsupported formats and codecs), or undesired quality (e.g. low resolution). These problems may result in fatal errors, audio/video freezes, long buffering periods, synchronization errors, and poor customer satisfaction. Detecting each type of

I. Majzik and M. Vieira (Eds.): SERENE 2014, LNCS 8785, pp. 154–168, 2014.
© Springer International Publishing Switzerland 2014

error entails a different monitoring cost in terms of the consumed computational resources. For instance, on one hand, a simple ping request is sufficient to check system availability. On the other hand, to detect a codec-related error in a video file, the file should be partially downloaded and the header of the video must be examined. Our work in this paper is built on top of this observation: *different error types have different monitoring costs*. This variation of cost has not been considered by the service-monitoring approaches proposed so far.

We motivate our work based on the architecture and use-case of so-called "Smart TVs". Smart TVs enjoy the existence of broadband connection that has become available to TV systems. Various third-party services are used in Smart TVs, including video content providers, popular social media platforms, and games. In particular, video-audio content is considered to be among the most important services for Smart TVs [17]. In this work, we investigated a Smart TV portal application developed by Vestek[1], a group company of Vestel, which is one of the largest TV manufacturers in Europe. The portal application is being utilized by Vestel as an online television service platform in Turkey. There are more than 200 third-party services in the portal, providing audio/video content, news, weather and finance information, games, social networking, etc. 70% of these services stream video content. The mostly-used applications are also video-streaming applications like Youtube, BBCiPlayer, Netflix, and Turkish national channels. The portal has currently more than 150,000 connected TVs. This number increases by about 7000 every week.

Smart TV market is very competitive; companies strive to provide richer content and more features to their customers by extremely strict deadlines. This pressure magnifies the importance of customer satisfaction. Because the Smart TV portal relies heavily on third-party providers, availability and quality of external services is vital to Smart TV systems. Vestek executes a test application daily to monitor the third-party services. The test application visits the given URLs, checks their availability, downloads and plays a portion of the audio/video content, and reports the findings so that broken links can be fixed, and unsupported content types can be replaced. Some of the content providers frequently change their APIs and migrate/delete their contents without an effective notification mechanism. Therefore, it is common that the test application finds several errors — most typically missing content and video codec errors.

Previously, we provided empirical data that motivated the need for adapting the monitoring for each service based on availability to reduce monitoring costs [12]. However, availability is only one part of the story. It is common to face domain-specific errors such as codec problems that cannot be detected only by availability checks. The detection of such errors is much more demanding in terms of resources; for instance, to check codec validity, a part of the content has to be downloaded and fed into a player that parses the header of the data and plays it. Therefore, extending the monitoring service with the capability to perform domain-specific error checking — in addition to just availability checking — may significantly increase the cost of monitoring. Thus, we propose an

---

[1] http://vestek.com.tr

adaptive strategy based on not only the service availability, but also different types of errors relevant for the service.

Adapting the frequency of monitoring is not a new idea; the novelty in our work is based on the observation that there are certain error types specific to the domain that require separate treatment. We expect cost-reduction benefits from this adaptation to be significant, because although third-party services usually have high availability rates, they have much lower scores when it comes to domain-specific problems. This is because an unsupported codec or a URL change, for instance, are types of errors that occur at the user-side, not at the provider-side. Hence, providers usually fix these problems only when reported by the users. From the customer's point of view [26], however, a codec error is just as disturbing as unavailability because what is observed in both cases is the same: a video playback error.

Contributions: In this work we make the following contributions.

- We propose domain-specific adaptation of the monitoring frequency based on the temporal history and the error rate for a particular partner service *and* error type.
- We formulate a cost model to measure the cost of monitoring. Our cost model is based on the price of paid resources consumed by the monitor in the cloud.
- We present an industrial case study from the broadcasting domain, where the utilization of third party Web services become predominant. We provide a data set collected by using the Amazon Elastic Compute Cloud (EC2) [3] to monitor dozens of services from different locations for more than one month. We evaluate the effectiveness of adaptive domain-specific monitoring on this real-world data, using the cost model we derived. We also share our data set with the research community to enable further analysis.

Our results show that each service is indeed subject to various types of errors with different error rates. We exploit this variation in the broadcasting domain and show that monitoring costs can be reduced by up to 30% by compromising error detection accuracy negligibly.

Here, we focus on the Smart TV domain and take codec-checking as a domain-specific monitoring action. However, the approach we present is not limited to this domain, nor tied particularly to codec-checks. The adaptation approach we propose is applicable to any domain where various error types are experienced, and monitoring of each error type incurs a different cost.

Organization: The remainder of this paper is organized as follows. Section 2 describes our experimental setup. In Section 3 and 4, we describe our approach and present evaluation results, respectively. In Section 5, related previous work is summarized. Finally, in Section 6 we provide our conclusions and discuss future work directions.

2   Experimental Setup and Data Collection

For five weeks, we monitored a set of third-party services used by Vestel's Smart TV portal to collect real-world data regarding errors. We then applied various monitoring approaches to these data as offline processes. We compared the approaches according to the cost savings they offer, and the compromise they make on the quality of monitoring. In this section we explain the experimental setup we used, and provide statistical information.

2.1   Vestel Smart TV Portal

There exist around 80,000 daily connections to the Vestel Smart TV portal from 25,000 different TV's. These connections are related with various types of services, of which about 52% are based on image and video content, 15% are life-style and social networking applications, 9% provide text-based information. Services that are dedicated to sports, music, and games constitute 3%, 3%, and 2% of the whole set of services, respectively. The remaining 16% include miscellaneous services. 75% of all the services are paid, whereas the rest of the services are available for free.

2.2   Data Collection Process

We identified the 6 mostly-used service providers that provide content for free on the Vestel Smart TV portal. Half of these service providers are associated with nation-wide TV channels in Turkey, and they stream video. The other half provide short videos and text-based content.

We developed a data collection application (DCA) to monitor the selected services and to create our data set for offline processing. We ran DCA on three different machines, deployed to Amazon's Elastic Compute Cloud (EC2) [3]. Amazon instances were located in the USA, Ireland, and Japan. We wanted to collect data from geographically far-away locations, because each DCA has its own view of the network. We wanted to see whether the results from different locations are consistent with each other. Each instance on Amazon EC2 ran DCA individually and independent from the others. They queried each service with a period of about 40 minutes. Each DCA had its own database where the results are stored.

For text-based services, DCA checks the availability over HTTP. If the service returns HTTP 200 (OK), the response time is logged into the database. In case of an error, the error stack trace along with the error code is stored. The video services return a page in JSON or XML format where the video links are included. DCA parses the contents, obtains video URLs, and puts these URLs into the list of URLs to be checked. A video service potentially returns a different list of videos each time it is queried (e.g., the video links returned for the category of "cats" are likely to be updated frequently). Hence, the set of videos monitored in each period may have differences when compared to the preceding period.

For each video link, DCA first checks the video's codec type, which is included in the first 1024 Kbytes of the video request response. If no proper codec is found in this header, an error message is logged for the corresponding service. If a proper codec is found, DCA attempts to play the first three seconds of the video[2] using the Windows Media Player API. If the video player successfully plays the video, DCA logs the successful response in the database along with the video duration, file size, resolution and bit rate information. If any problem is encountered during video replay, the error message raised from the player is logged in the database.

2.3   Collected Data Set

The three DCA instances ran on the Amazon EC2 for five weeks. We observed that the data collected from different geographical locations were consistent with each other. This was confirmed by the cosine similarity measures of error rates between data sets collected from each pair of locations: Japan-Ireland (0.99), Japan-USA (0.98) and Ireland-USA (0.97). Therefore, we used the results from one of the DCA instances only. We selected the DCA instance deployed in Ireland since it is the closest geographical location to Turkey. The data we collected are publicly available at http://srl.ozyegin.edu.tr/projects/fathoms/.

The collected data revealed that in total 132,532 requests were made to 51 different services of the selected 6 service providers. Among these requests, 8127 requests were subject to "HTTP 404 not found" error and 9079 requests were subject to a "codec error".

3   Adaptive Domain-Specific Monitoring

The aim of monitoring a third-party service is to detect when it raises errors and notify the client so that the client may omit using the service or may be directed to an alternative service, and hence avoid the error. A monitor that notifies the clients as soon as a service state change occurs is considered to be high quality. To achieve high quality, monitoring should be done very frequently. However, frequent monitoring puts a high load on the monitoring server. To reduce the associated costs, frequency should be kept as low as possible. This raises a trade-off between the quality and cost of monitoring.

To answer the question of how frequent monitoring should be done, we take a domain-specific, adaptive approach. In Section 2.2 we explained how a video codec error checking is different from checking a text-based service. The associated costs also differ significantly as the former requires downloading a piece of the video and playing it. We adapt the frequency of monitoring by taking into account the history of the occurrence of particular errors for a particular service. If a service has been relatively healthy for a certain error check, following the

---

[2] Even if the file header is fine, the content can be inconsistent with the header. Such cases can be revealed by actually playing the video.

temporal locality principle, we decrease the corresponding frequency of monitoring in anticipation that the service will continue to be in good status regarding the same error type. When considering the history of a service, we put more value on the recent past than the older history, and make this adjustable via a parameter.

In the following we first present the model we used to calculate the costs incurred by monitoring, followed by the parameters we used for adaptation.

3.1   Cost Model

The goal of our work is to reduce the cost of monitoring. Text-based services consume very little of the network bandwidth, and require almost no computation. Therefore, their cost is negligible when compared to video-based services. Checking a video service consumes resources in two dimensions: (1) part of the video is downloaded, using the network connection, (2) the downloaded video is played, consuming CPU time. Hence, the cost of a video service check, $\mathcal{C}_{video}$, is

$$\mathcal{C}_{video} = (Size \times \mathcal{C}_{net}) + (Duration \times \mathcal{C}_{cpu})$$

where

$Size$ is the size of the downloaded piece of the video

$\mathcal{C}_{net}$ is the cost of network usage per unit size

$Duration$ is the duration of the video

$\mathcal{C}_{cpu}$ is the cost of using the CPU or GPU per unit time

In our case, the $Duration$ parameter is fixed as 3 seconds (recall that we only play the first 3 seconds of the video). The size of a video is on the average 705 Kbytes for 3 seconds of video content, and the file header is 1024 bytes, adding up to 706 Kbytes in total. The parameters $\mathcal{C}_{net}$ and $\mathcal{C}_{cpu}$ depend on the cloud provider and the allocated instances. For instance, $\mathcal{C}_{cpu}$ is currently around $0.15 per hour, based on the pricing of Amazon [3], Microsoft Azure [19] and Google Cloud [10]. If a service has a charge, it should also be included in the formula; in our case all the services are free, therefore we ignore this issue.

Under these assumptions, the total *cost of monitoring*, denoted as $\mathcal{C}$, is

$$\mathcal{C} = (\# \text{ of videos checked}) \times \mathcal{C}_{video}$$

Hence, $\mathcal{C}$ is directly proportional to the number of video checks performed.

Undetected client-side errors affect customer satisfaction and thus indirectly incur costs (e.g., by influencing the customers' perception of the brand). Because measuring this effect is outside the scope of our study, we do not include customer satisfaction in our cost model; instead, we define the *quality of monitoring*, denoted $\mathcal{Q}$, as

$$\mathcal{Q} = \# \text{ of detected errors}$$

The more number of errors monitoring detects, the better the quality of monitoring is. The quality gets compromised as more errors are left undetected and as such, the error detection accuracy is degraded.

In our evaluation of adaptation, we present the reduction of total cost along with the change in the quality of monitoring.

3.2 Adaptation of Monitoring Frequency

We adapt the frequency of monitoring a service against a particular error type based on the history of occurrence of that error type for that service. To refer to the past, time is divided into enumerated periods (e.g., day 1, day 2, etc.). To keep the discussion straightforward and without loss of generality, we limit ourselves to two types of errors, *availability* and *codec*, with the following counts:

V_i is the total number of video checks during the time period i.

$\mathcal{E}_i^{avail}$ is the number of availability errors during the time period i.

$\mathcal{E}_i^{codec}$ is the number of codec errors during the time period i.

Note that an availability check is a prerequisite to a codec check: if a video is unavailable, no codec validation can be made. So, the codec error rate at time period i, denoted as $\hat{\mathcal{E}}_i^{codec}$, is defined as

$$\hat{\mathcal{E}}_i^{codec} = \frac{\mathcal{E}_i^{codec}}{V_i - \mathcal{E}_i^{avail}}$$

Based on these, the *accumulated error rate (AER)* for codec errors, at the end of the time period n, denoted as AER_n^{codec}, is

$$AER_n^{codec} = \begin{cases} \hat{\mathcal{E}}_0^{codec} & \text{if } n = 0 \\ \alpha \times AER_{n-1}^{codec} + (1 - \alpha) \times \hat{\mathcal{E}}_n^{codec} & \text{if } (n > 0) \end{cases}$$

where α is a coefficient ($0 \leq \alpha \leq 1$) that allows us adjust the weight of the calculated past AER values on calculating the current one. If α is 0, calculation of AER does not depend on the past AER values but is completely determined by the error rate measured in the latest time period. As α gets closer to 1, previously calculated AER values have more influence on the future. Also note that according to this formulation, a relatively older error rate has less influence on the current value than a more recent error rate. This means, the effect of a measured error rate gradually diminishes as time goes by. The value of α must be determined per error type and per application domain. An informed decision can be made based on past experiences by performing what-if analysis to observe the effects of variation of error rate in time.

At the end of each time period, AER is calculated according to the formula above. Then, the monitoring frequency is adjusted based on this AER. The new frequency is used during the next time period. Frequencies are set using a *frequency pattern*. A frequency pattern is a circular bit-value sequence read

Table 1. Adaptation schemes for the monitoring frequency based on accumulated error rates

Scheme	Accumulated error rate cutoff values (%)					
F0	-	-	-	-	0	∞
F1	-	-	-	0	0.001	∞
F2	-	-	0	0.001	0.002	∞
F3	-	0	0.001	0.002	0.003	∞
F4	0	0.001	0.002	0.003	0.004	∞
F5	0.001	0.002	0.003	0.004	0.005	∞
F6	0.01	0.02	0.03	0.04	0.05	∞
F7	0.05	0.1	0.15	0.2	0.25	∞
F8	0.1	0.2	0.3	0.4	0.5	∞
F9	1	2	3	4	5	∞
Frequency pattern	1000	100	10	110	1110	1

from left to right where each bit value denotes whether to skip the corresponding test. For instance, the bit pattern 1110 means that for every four checks, the last codec check shall be skipped, resulting in 25% reduction compared to the original number of codec checks. Availability checks are always performed, regardless of the adopted pattern.

Frequency mappings with regard to AER values are given in Table 1. The table is interpreted as follows. For instance, if frequency scheme F8 is in effect, frequency pattern 1000 is used when AER is less than or equal to 0.1%; pattern 100 is used when AER is larger than 0.1% but less than or equal to 0.2%, and so on. For AER values that are larger than 0.5%, the full frequency pattern is used. Frequency schemes have a varying level of conservatism. On one hand, F0 is very conservative; it uses frequency pattern 1110 (and hence reduces corresponding frequency by 25%) only for extremely reliable services where $AER = 0$. On the other hand, F9 is the most aggressive/optimistic approach; it reduces the frequency of monitoring for any service that has an AER value of 5% or less. In the following section, we evaluate how these frequency schemes compare in terms of cost savings and quality of monitoring.

4   Evaluation

We evaluate the effectiveness of frequency adaptation by simulating an adaptive monitor according to the original data collected during our five-week testing (see Section 2.2). Recall that the data contain responses of services to requests sent in periods of approximately 40 minutes. We call a single 40-minute period a *test batch*. Based on the frequency pattern associated with a service, the simulator may skip monitoring the service in a particular test batch. If the pattern requires the service to be monitored, the simulator reads the response from the collected data instead of sending an HTTP request to the service. This way, our simulator

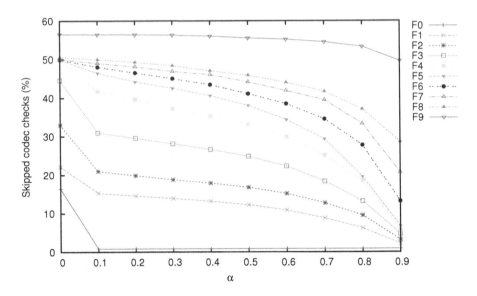

Fig. 1. The change in the ratio of skipped codec checks to the number of checks in the original monitor. Recall that the number of codec checks is directly proportional to the cost of monitoring; hence, this graph illustrates cost savings.

behaves like a second monitor that would have been monitoring requests at exactly the same time as the actual monitor. The only difference is that some subset of the test batches for certain services would have been skipped. Hence, the results of the simulator are perfectly comparable with the actual data.

During the simulation, for each service, we calculate AER^{codec} at the end of each day. The current error rate, $\hat{\mathcal{E}}_i^{codec}$, is calculated over the last three days.

The graph in Figure 1 shows the ratio of skipped codec checks to the number of checks in the original monitor. Recall that the more codec checks we skip, the more we can save on the cost of monitoring; therefore, larger numbers mean more savings. It is not surprising to see that conservative schemes provide less savings (as little as ∼1% skipped checks in F0), whereas significant savings can be obtained when the scheme is more liberal (57% omitted checks in F9). Also notice that savings gradually decrease as we increase α, that is, as we decrease the role of current error rate and put more weight in older history when determining the new frequency pattern.

Figure 2 shows the ratio of undetected codec errors to the number of codec errors in the original monitor. Recall that the fewer errors we miss, the higher the quality of monitoring. Therefore, smaller numbers mean better quality. Not surprisingly, conservative schemes miss fewer errors; at the extreme, F0 misses no errors when the α value is between 0.1 and 0.9. On the other hand, in our most optimistic scheme F9, up to 3.8% of the codec errors go unnoticed. The most interesting observation from this graph is that as the α value increases, undetected error rate gradually decreases for all schemes but F9.

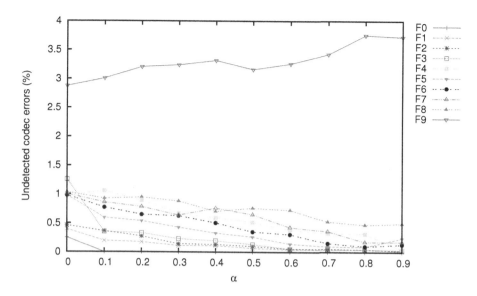

Fig. 2. Ratio of undetected codec errors to the number of codec errors in the original monitor. Recall that the number of undetected codec errors is inversely proportional to the quality of monitoring.

Finally we consider the combination of cost savings and quality. Ideally, one would like to cut costs as much as possible while keeping the quality high. The two are competing factors; to reduce costs, we need to decrease the frequency, which results in worse quality by failing to detect errors. To be able to find an optimum case, we define the following function to give an *effectiveness score*, denoted as $\mathcal{F}$, to a monitoring configuration.

$$\mathcal{F} = (\text{rate of skipped checks}) - \beta \times (\text{rate of undetected errors}) \qquad (1)$$

In this formulation, the effectiveness depends on how much weight, via the β parameter, is given to the undetected errors as opposed to skipped checks. If the calculated score is negative, we conclude that the corresponding configuration is not feasible because the quality of the monitor has been compromised beyond the acceptable limits by failing to detect errors.

Figures 3, 4 and 5 show the effectiveness score of monitoring when β is set to 10, 30, and 50, respectively. As illustrated, more liberal schemes lose ranking as the quality of monitoring is given more weight. In Figure 4, for instance, F9 is not even in the window of positive scores, hence it is not an acceptable choice; in Figure 5, F4 is below the 0-line when $\alpha < 0.3$.

Recall that previously measured error rates are less effective in determining the monitoring frequency when α is closer to 0. In our data set, this results in an increased rate of undetected errors. The penalty for undetected errors is amplified as β increases. Hence, effectiveness score plots become more curvy

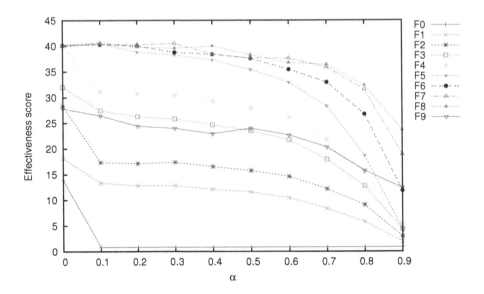

Fig. 3. Effectiveness scores, calculated according to Equation 1 when $\beta = 10$

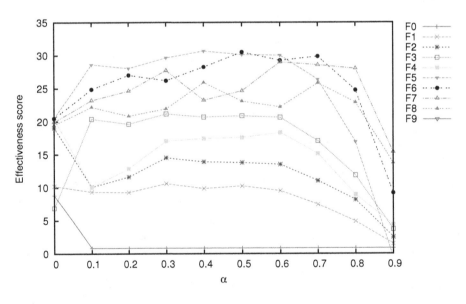

Fig. 4. Effectiveness scores, calculated according to Equation 1 when $\beta = 30$

as β is increased; when $\beta = 50$, F5 scheme for $\alpha = 0.6$ is the most effective configuration. In this case, the cost of monitoring can be reduced by a significant amount of 34% by compromising the error detection accuracy by 0.14%. Even when F1 scheme is adopted for $\alpha = 0.6$, the monitoring cost is reduced by more

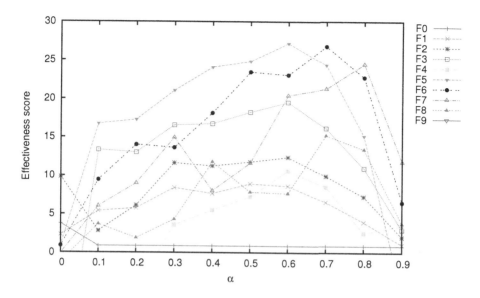

Fig. 5. Effectiveness scores, calculated according to Equation 1 when $\beta = 50$

than 10%, while the ratio of undetected errors is 0.04%. Hence, significant cost savings can be made by compromising the monitoring quality (i.e. error detection accuracy) negligibly.

5   Related Work

There have been many service monitoring approaches [24,28,23,27,1] proposed in the literature to tolerate [28] or avoid/mask [12] detected errors in external services. Techniques and tools have been introduced to automatically generate online monitors based on Service Level Agreement (SLA) specifications [22]. These approaches mainly adopt reactive monitoring. Hence, an adaptation can occur only after observing a failure. Online testing of Web services [18] was introduced for facilitating pro-active adaptation. This approach employs functional testing where test cases are generated and executed based on a functional specification [4]. In general, service monitoring approaches proposed so far rely on such standard specifications (or SLAs) and they consider only common quality attributes such as reliability, throughput and latency. However, standard specifications fall short to express domain-specific errors (e.g., codec-related errors while using a video content delivery service) to detect them and to facilitate runtime adaptation with respect to these error types. We have previously studied adaptive service monitoring for cost-effectiveness [12] but the scope of the study was only a single monitor that considers a single quality attribute (availability) regarding services.

There have been also other approaches that utilize adaptive monitoring; however, the majority of these [2,7,8,13,14] are concerned with the monitoring of hardware resources such as memory, disk, and CPU. Other adaptive approaches [6] mainly focus on general properties of web services such as the availability and response time. There are a few studies, where domain-specific cases are considered. For instance, adaptive monitoring was discussed for dynamic data streams [9]. In this domain, each user has a varying interest in each type of information. The approach exploits this fact and adapts the monitoring mechanism for each user. Another approach for monitoring streaming data [21] was proposed for providing adaptivity based on changes in the content of data. Hereby, they propose an algorithm to detect changes in data. The monitoring frequency is adapted based on the detected changes. A similar approach was proposed for adaptive process monitoring [15] as well.

Domain-specific quality attributes have been taken into account in a recent study [20] for service selection. However, the proposed service selection approach considers service monitoring to be out-of-scope and the selection of services is performed based on monitoring results assumed to be available. A toolset and ontology have been previously proposed [25] to express and monitor custom quality attributes regarding Web services. The toolset enables the specification of custom quality metrics but these metrics are defined in terms of only a standard set of service properties and measurements including, for instance, price, delay, throughput, the number of packets lost and availability. The approach does not support the incorporation of custom domain-specific service properties or errors. Similarly, previously proposed customizable service selection policies [5] rely on reactive monitoring of common service properties such as service cost (price), bandwidth and availability.

6   Conclusion

We introduced a novel domain-specific service monitoring approach. We instantiated our approach for detecting errors specific to the services in the broadcasting and content-delivery domain. We developed a cost model for calculating the monitoring overhead in terms of the consumed resources in the cloud. The monitoring frequency for each type of error is dynamically adapted based on this cost model and the measured error rates. We prepared an extensive data set by monitoring services used in a commercial Smart TV from a monitor deployed in the cloud. We observed more than 30% reduction in monitoring costs without compromising the error detection accuracy significantly.

Our approach can be applied to other application domains as well. In the future, we plan to develop a plug-in architecture to provide a generic framework that can be extended with custom monitor implementations. The execution of these monitors will be managed by the framework based on a configurable cost model.

Acknowledgments. This work is supported by Vestel Electronics and the Turkish Ministry of Science, Industry and Technology (00995.STZ.2011-2). The contents of this paper reflect the ideas and positions of the authors and do not necessarily reflect the ideas or positions of Vestel Electronics and the Turkish Ministry of Science, Industry and Technology.

References

1. Aceto, G., Botta, A., de Donato, W., Pescap, A.: Cloud monitoring: A survey. Computer Networks 57(9), 2093–2115 (2013)
2. Alcaraz Calero, J., Gutierrez Aguado, J.: Monpaas: An adaptive monitoring platform as a service for cloud computing infrastructures and services. IEEE Transactions on Services Computing (to appear, 2014)
3. Amazon.com: Elastic Compute Cloud (EC2), http://aws.amazon.com/ec2 (accessed in, May 2014)
4. Bai, X., Dong, W., Tsai, W.T., Chen, Y.: WSDL-based automatic test case generation for web services testing. In: Proceedings of the IEEE International Workshop on Service-Oriented Systems, pp. 215–220 (2005)
5. Verheecke, B., Cibrán, M.A., Jonckers, V.: Aspect-Oriented Programming for Dynamic Web Service Monitoring and Selection. In (LJ) Zhang, L.-J., Jeckle, M. (eds.) ECOWS 2004. LNCS, vol. 3250, pp. 15–29. Springer, Heidelberg (2004)
6. Clark, K., Warnier, M., Brazier, F.M.T.: Self-adaptive service monitoring. In: Bouchachia, A. (ed.) ICAIS 2011. LNCS, vol. 6943, pp. 119–130. Springer, Heidelberg (2011)
7. Clark, K., Warnier, M., Brazier, F.T.: Self-adaptive service monitoring. In: Bouchachia, A. (ed.) ICAIS 2011. LNCS, vol. 6943, pp. 119–130. Springer, Heidelberg (2011)
8. Deepak Jeswani, R. K., Ghosh, M.N.: Adaptive monitoring: A hybrid approach for monitoring using probing. In: International Conference on High Performance Computing, HiPC (2010)
9. Duc, B.L., Collet, P., Malenfant, J., Rivierre, N.: A QoI-aware Framework for Adaptive Monitoring. In: 2nd International Conference on Adaptive and Self-adaptive Systems and Applications, pp. 133–141. IEEE (2010)
10. Google: Google Cloud, https://cloud.google.com (accessed in, May 2014)
11. Gülcü, K., Sözer, H., Aktemur, B.: FAS: Introducing a service for avoiding faults in composite services. In: Avgeriou, P. (ed.) SERENE 2012. LNCS, vol. 7527, pp. 106–120. Springer, Heidelberg (2012)
12. Gulcu, K., Sozer, H., Aktemur, B., Ercan, A.: Fault masking as a service. Software: Practice and Experience 44(7), 835–854 (2014)
13. Jeswani, D., Natu, M., Ghosh, R.: Adaptive monitoring: A framework to adapt passive monitoring using probing. In: Proceedings of the 8th International Conference and Workshop on Systems Virtualiztion Management, pp. 350–356 (2012)
14. Kwon, S., Choi, J.: An agent-based adaptive monitoring system. In: Shi, Z.-Z., Sadananda, R. (eds.) PRIMA 2006. LNCS (LNAI), vol. 4088, pp. 672–677. Springer, Heidelberg (2006)
15. Li, W., Yue, H., Valle-Cervantes, S., Qin, S.: Recursive PCA for adaptive process monitoring. Journal of Process Control 10(5), 471–486 (2000)
16. Liu, A., Li, Q., Huang, L., Xiao, M.: FACTS: A framework for fault-tolerant composition of transactional web services. IEEE Transactions on Services Computing 3(1), 46–59 (2010)
17. Lo, T.: Trends in the Smart TV industry technical Report (2012), http://www.digitimes.com/news/a20121025RS400.html (accessed in May 2014)

18. Metzger, A., Sammodi, O., Pohl, K., Rzepka, M.: Towards pro-active adaptation with confidence: augmenting service monitoring with online testing. In: Proceedings of the Workshop on Software Engineering for Adaptive and Self-Managing Systems, pp. 20–28 (2010)
19. Microsoft: Windows Azure, `http://www.windowsazure.com`, (accessed in, May 2014)
20. Moser, O., Rosenberg, F., Dustdar, S.: Domain-specific service selection for composite services. IEEE Transactions on Software Engineering 38(4), 828–843 (2012)
21. Puttagunta, V., Kalpakis, K.: Adaptive methods for activity monitoring of streaming data. In: Proceedigns of the 11th International Conference on Machine Learning and Applications, pp. 197–203 (2002)
22. Raimondi, F., Skene, J., Emmerich, W.: Efficient online monitoring of web-service SLAs. In: Proceedings of the 16th ACM SIGSOFT International Symposium on Foundations of Software Engineering, pp. 170–180 (2008)
23. Robinson, W., Purao, S.: Monitoring service systems from a language-action perspective. IEEE Transactions on Services Computing 4(1), 17–30 (2011)
24. Simmonds, J., Yuan, G., Chechik, M., Nejati, S., O'Farrell, B., Litani, E., Waterhouse, J.: Runtime monitoring of web service conversations. IEEE Transactions on Services Computing 2(3), 223–244 (2009)
25. Tian, M., Gramm, A., Ritter, H., Schiller, J., Reichert, M.: Efficient selection and monitoring of qos-aware web services with the ws-qos framework. In: WI 2004 Proceedings of the 2004 IEEE/WIC/ACM International Conference on Web Intelligence, pp. 152–158 (2004)
26. de Visser, I.: Analyzing User Perceived Failure Severity in Consumer Electronics Products. Ph.D. thesis, Eindhoven University of Technology, Eindhoven, The Netherlands (2008)
27. Wei, Y., Blake, M.: An agent-based services framework with adaptive monitoring in cloud environments. In: Proceedings of the 21st International Workshop on Enabling Technologies: Infrastructure for Collaborative Enterprises, Toulouse, France, pp. 4–9 (2012)
28. Zheng, Z., Lyu, M.: An adaptive QoS aware fault tolerance strategy for web services. Journal of Empirical Software Engineering 15(4), 323–345 (2010)

Combined Error Propagation Analysis and Runtime Event Detection in Process-Driven Systems

Gábor Urbanics, László Gönczy, Balázs Urbán,
János Hartwig, and Imre Kocsis

Quanopt Ltd.,
Budapest, Hungary
{urbanics,gonczy,urban.balazs,hartwig.janos,kocsis}@quanopt.com

Abstract. This paper presents an approach and Proof-of-Concept implementation for combined design time error propagation analysis and runtime diagnosis in business process driven systems. We show how error propagation analysis can be made practical in this context with qualitative error propagation notation that is approachable for the domain expert. The method uses models of business processes and their supporting IT infrastructure captured in industry-standard tools. Finite domain constraint solving is used to evaluate system alternatives from a dependability point of view. The systematic generation of event detection rules for runtime diagnosis is also supported. A real life example from the banking domain is used to demonstrate the approach.

Keywords: error propagation analysis, business process analysis, rule based event processing.

1 Introduction

Today, explicitly modelled, directly executed and hierarchically composed business processes serve as the standard tool for implementing complex business-critical processes in many domains, ranging from financial services through logistics to government services. However, state of the art integrated business process design tools and execution environments mainly focus on the *functional* aspects of processes and their executions; design-time analysis and runtime assurance of most *extrafunctional* properties largely remain unaddressed. Arguably, large parts of the classic toolset of design-time dependability evaluation are practically infeasible to apply in this context – either due to their unjustifiable human effort overhead (e.g. classic fault-tree analysis and FMEA) or simply due to the lack of information (e.g. "component" failure rates for stochastic analysis).

At the same time, there *is* a growing need for dependability analysis in this domain with a distinct emphasis on *qualitative* evaluation. IT systems are becoming more and more complex while serving an increasing number of critical applications. Service-oriented design and virtualization at different levels of

I. Majzik and M. Vieira (Eds.): SERENE 2014, LNCS 8785, pp. 169–183, 2014.

abstraction result in systems where dependencies between components and services used by operational processes are punishingly inefficient to follow manually. When failures happen during process execution, diagnosis and recovery have to be performed in a timely manner even for the less critical processes. For the truly business critical ones, design time evaluation has to determine which faults are to be tolerated by all means – and how.

Our contribution addresses this definite need for *qualitative error propagation analysis* for business processes with a method and its prototype implementation. At design time, explicit process and infrastructure models are used for error propagation evaluation – with the widespread adoption of model-based Business Process Management (BPM) and Configuration Management Databases (CMDBs) it is increasingly realistic to assume the simultaneous presence of these in industrial settings. We use an adapted version of the Fault Propagation and Transformation Calculus (FPTC) [19] for describing component error propagation, even offering templates for common component types (e.g. infrastructure elements and dependability mechanisms). FPTC-style qualitative error propagation modelling is crucial for capturing expert knowledge w.r.t. the specific propagation behaviour of process steps and infrastructure elements.

With the lightweight adaptation of the error propagation semantics and "solution" concept of FPTC for business process execution, we use finite domain constraint satisfaction problem (CSP) solving for analysis. This way, we can support root cause as well as sensitivity analysis (and their mixture) for dependability design evaluation. Also, the optimization constraints present in modern CSP solvers open up the road towards automatically searching for dependability measures resulting in qualitatively optimal setups in the above sense. This approach is also by design modular and hierarchically composable.

The same models are used as a basis for *runtime process monitoring synthesis*. We automatically generate the inference logic of event processing rules that perform runtime system diagnosis by identifying system-level dependability state from process execution and infrastructure events. This not only serves for the root cause diagnosis of service failures; runtime tracking the "remaining possible solutions" of the diagnostic problem can provide early warning capabilities as well as validate the error propagation assumption used at design time.

The paper is organized as follows. Sec. 2 discusses related work with an emphasis on business process analysis in the state-of-the-art industrial process design tools. Sec. 3 introduces our framework architecture and main concepts. Sec. 4 presents the error propagation modelling and constraint solving based evaluation approach, Sec. 5 presents the results on a case study while Sec. 6 concludes the paper with discussing further research directions.

2   Tool-integrated Process Analysis: State-of-the-Art

Current business process management systems (BPMSs) provide a wide range of features of varying capability [20, 12, 8, 16, 2, 18, 15] in order to support the entire lifecycle of a process-centric business, including business process discovery, design and implementation, Business Activity Monitoring (BAM) and process analytics.

Even entry-level products provide the building blocks for implementing BAM, where usually low-level process metrics are collected by the execution engine during runtime and derived Key Performance Indicators (KPI) are visualized in customized dashboards. They enable business users to track the running processes in a *(near)real-time manner* and to *pin-point bottlenecks* in the process, such as an overloaded resource. Despite visual aids or a widely used "drill-down" approach, such methods are inherently reactive and ad-hoc as opposed to a proactive and exhaustive analysis. Collecting and observing the execution of the processes also allow for *historical trend analysis*, which is supported by more advanced products. As a natural extension, sophisticated tools employ *predictive analytic* techniques, too.

Many vendors offer design-time *process simulation* [4, 15, 16, 18] features combined with well-known analysis techniques, such as what-if, root cause or quantitative analysis but they are mostly focused on business-relevant properties (e.g. resource utilization, or expected frequency of a given execution path in the process). Only a handful of sophisticated enterprise tools promise process optimization (from a business point of view), even fewer provide any completeness checking (e.g. on the business rules that are incorporated by many BPMSs). Even recent literature (e.g., [17, 7]) concentrates more on process level events as means for root-cause analysis without considering a model of the underlying physical infrastructure.

In general, current BPMSs either completely lack or provide only a limited means of truly exhaustive system analysis, which is especially true for extra-functional attributes of dependability. The latter aspect gains even more importance with cloud deployments getting increasingly common.

3 Process Diagnosis and Analysis Framework

The framework presented in this paper (Fig. 1) provides event processing and diagnostic methods that enable process analysts to perform both runtime and design time analysis focusing on the dependability of the system. *Design time (or static) analysis* refers to any kind of evaluation of the system model taken place without the need of executing the process, while *online (or runtime) analysis* is performed during the execution of the process instances.

There are two major inputs to the framework: i) a generalized process model (see Sec. 4.1) that can be imported from process descriptions of existing BPMSs, and ii) the captured execution of process instances in forms of runtime events generated by the execution engine, e.g. start and end of an activity, change of process variables or termination of the process. In the current prototype, Bonita[4], a widely used open source BPMS, was used both for editing the input process models, and as execution platform for the online analysis. Having converted the Bonita-specific input model into a generalized process description, it is then extended with a) resource level references, which link activities to

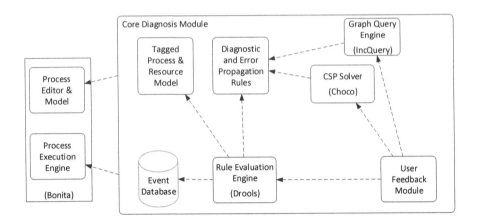

Fig. 1. Architecture of the diagnosis & analysis framework

physical and logical components of the infrastructure, and b) a fault/error/failure model with qualitative error propagation characteristics of the resource-level components and the process-level activities. Process-level, active recovery measures, e.g. explicit Error Handlers in the process, and resource level recovery mechanisms, such as hot-standby components, can also be described using the aforementioned extensions.

The cornerstone of the framework is a set of rules that form the basis for both the online and the design time analysis and consists of two major types of rules.

Error-propagation rules describe how the faults defined in the fault model can be activated, and how errors are propagated to other elements of the system. Propagation of errors can occur through dependencies among the components of the infrastructure and through the process execution paths (see also Sec. 4). The constraints described by these rules are converted to a constraint satisfaction problem (CSP) on the fault configuration of the resource components and token-passing error propagation paths of the process level. This problem is then solved by Choco[11], a general CSP solver, in a *backward-chaining* fashion yielding answers to questions like "Under what fault conditions is it possible in the described process (and resource) model that the output of the process becomes faulty?" The solutions of these problems provide an exhaustive analysis of the model space as defined by the fault model and error propagation rules. It is also an intrinsic part of this analysis step to confine the resulting model space by additional constraints that a) either correspond to general system-independent analysis goals (e.g. requiring exactly one fault activation in the model) or b) restrict the possible outcome of the CSP solution by e.g. binding fault modes of certain components in the input model. In contrast to tools widely used in the industry, the framework is able to *incorporate process and resource level, as well as, dependability* attributes into the analysis in an exhaustive manner, thus extending its applicability beyond simple simulations or ad-hoc analysis.

Online event processing rules are deployed to a Rule Evaluation Engine that receives detailed events captured during the execution of the process instances, and evaluates the rules in a *forward-chaining* fashion. These rules consist of a left-hand side (LHS) which describe a pattern that is sought for, and a right-hand side (RHS) specifying actions to be taken when the LHS is satisfied. A widespread business rule engine, the Drools project and its language are used for this purpose. This way the online event processing logic is decoupled from the actual evaluation and can easily be edited by non-technical process experts, while the option remains to perform formal checks on the rules. In the LHS a wide range of runtime attributes – e.g. process variables, timestamps of activities or actors – can be included in complex condition formulae.

Each time the LHS is satisfied, a number of actions can be taken: *i)* a notification about the match can be recorded or *ii)* an update of a rule-specific process metric can be triggered.

Furthermore, the proposed modelling approach serves as a basis for performing coverage checks and synthesis of the runtime event processing rules. Aided by domain experts, the process and resource model can be extended with tags, e.g. a process activity can be marked as "suspicious" or a resource component as "susceptible" to fail. Based on this enrichment, the skeleton and the initial content of the event processing rules can be generated specifically to the tag and the type of the model element. Moreover, by synthesizing the set of rules, their coverage can be formally checked, even if the related rule is modified by a diagnostic expert. In the prototype, rudimentary checks (e.g. overlapping rule conditions, coverage of model elements) were implemented using EMF-IncQuery[1], an open source declarative graph query engine. The natural next step will be to make use of the results of the Error Propagation Analysis by automatically suggesting tags for the model elements.

Finally, the architecture also includes an User Feedback Module with two major goals: *i)* w.r.t design time analysis, the process and resource models are presented graphically to the user where various CSP solutions can also be inspected, and *ii)* it is also the primary user interface giving an overview of the results from the online diagnostic analysis including filtered list of events matched, or plots and tables summarizing calculated metrics.

3.1   Motivational Example

The framework's diagnostic and analytic capabilities are demonstrated in an example describing the process of depositing cash in a bank. Fig. 2 depicts the process in three layers: the process layer shows activities initiated by the cashier, the layer in the middle contains logical components and services executing the non-human tasks, and the bottom layer is comprised of the physical components in the infrastructure required by the middle layer. Arrows in the figure capture the dependencies among the components (of all layers) and the possible process execution paths.

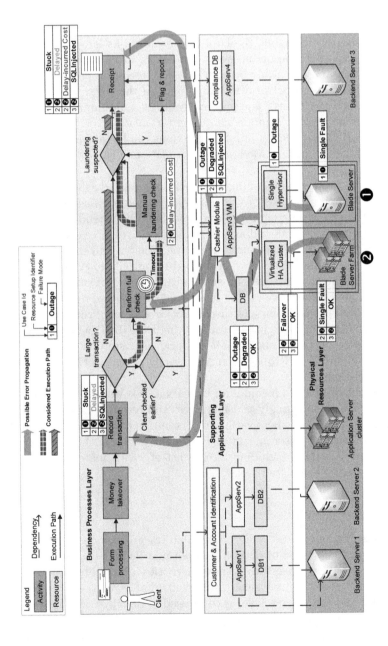

Fig. 2. Motivational example. The symbols ❶ and ❷ refer to two different resource configurations. At once only either of them is considered, as depending on the resource configuration the effect on the components in the upper layers and on the process is different, even if the root cause, i.e. a single fault, is the same. The small tables next to the components and activities correspond to the syndrome configurations where the same symbols are used to refer to the given resource configuration.

Each row with the same identifier in the table-like labels belongs to one composite configuration comprised of the failure modes of all components and activities. (Note that this figure is for the compact representation of the overall system model.)

The process is a motivating example with the following analysis goals in mind:

- Find all possible combinations of fault activations that affect the process in a way that result in an incorrect (process) output. The analysis is constrained by binding selected resources, the "Customer & Account Identification" and the "Compliance DB" components, to correct behaviour.
- Identify the process-level effects of using resource configurations differing in fault tolerant capabilities (infrastructure configurations ❶ and ❷). Even if direct effects of a service degradation are known, it is not trivial to determine their exact overall effects at the process level. By using Error Propagation Analysis, this aspect can be brought under scrutiny.
- Find non-trivial, data-dependent error propagation alternatives where process level errors can manifest as resource level failures, such as a non-prevented SQL injection deleting database tables. In the cash deposit process, the "Record transaction"→"Cashier Module"→"Receipt" propagation is such an alternative.

The analysis is performed on two versions of the same model which differ only in that the "Blade Server" and "Single Hypervisor" components are replaced by a "Blade Server Farm" and "Virtualized HA Cluster", respectively. In terms of dependability the HA cluster is assumed to provide better fault tolerant capabilities and can hide a single fault in the server farm by means of a seamless failover.

4   Modelling Approach

Besides proprietary metamodels, a number of de-facto standards exist and are widely utilized in the industry for describing business processes and resource models *separately*. In the presented framework custom metamodels have been defined that are able to jointly describe both the execution aspects of the business processes and the physical and logical resources of the infrastructure underneath the process. (See the metamodel on Fig. 3 for the main concepts.) Standard modeling languages as e.g. the Business Process Model and Notation (BPMN) or the Common Information Model (CIM) can be easily transformed into this language.

Furthermore, qualitative characteristics of faults/errors/failures – that is, fault-/error/failure "libraries" and the description of error propagation behaviour – can be attached to both levels as decorating models. In terms of the model, annotations can be used to define a diagnostic/sensitivity analysis problem and to "back-annotate" the results of analyses.

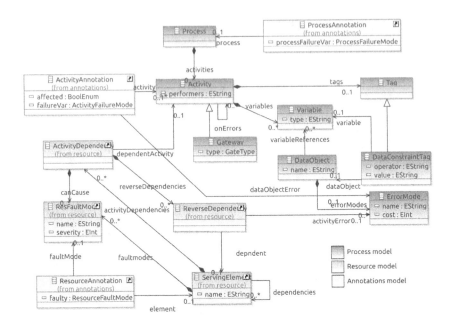

Fig. 3. Main elements of generalized process meta-model

4.1   Process and Resource Modelling

A generalized process meta-model (see Fig. 3) is employed in our framework
that is based on BPMN[10] and XPDL[6], both of which are de-facto standards
in the field. One distinguishing feature of the generalized process language is its
ability to describe the resource-level dependencies of the process elements, thus
establishing the connection between the two layers.

The resource meta-model describes a dependency graph between the so called
Serving Elements which represent the smallest modelled units from the point
of view of error propagation. They typically correspond to physical or logical
components of the infrastructure underlying the business process.

Furthermore, the language also allows for assigning annotations to activities
and resources which later can be used in the analysis, e.g. for specifying constraints.

4.2   Error Propagation Analysis for Instance Executions

Generally, the fundamental concept in the behavioural semantics of business
process models is the *execution* of a single *process instance*. Input data (and/or
control) is provided to the underlying business process execution engine that in
turn orchestrates the execution of activities and manages the passing of data and
control between them, up to the (normal or abnormal) termination of the process
instance execution. Usually multiple *instances* of the process may be executed

in parallel in response to multiple activation requests, but these influence each other only indirectly via data and control sources that are external w.r.t. the process model. (Databases that are updated and read by process instances are an eminent example.)

As a consequence, in the context of business process model execution most natural notions of service failure can be expressed in terms of properties of *single executions*. Informally: why the execution of "single transaction" was, or how can it be, erroneous. Conceptually, this constitutes a middle ground between classic approaches for structural error propagation analysis – such as fault trees – and the mathematically precise, abstraction driven modelling and analysis of error propagation in dynamic systems [14, 13]. On the one hand, the not only data, but also *error* driven differences in possible execution paths can not be easily "abstracted away" to a simple static representation. On the other hand, we do not want to reason on generic, unbounded input-output data and control streams - just the response of the system to a single "stimulus".

This does not mean that there may be no need to investigate the input-output error sequences of a business process execution unit in its *systemic* context; rather, we argue that this is a different problem, that can be actually supported by establishing the possible error propagation characteristics of single executions. The modelling constructs that we use to enable error propagation analysis will reflect these characteristics.

4.3   Qualitative Fault/Error/Failure Modelling

We aim at supporting *qualitative* error propagation analysis; "qualitative" in the sense that the notions used to describe faults, errors and failures are neither simple boolean predicates (as is usual for e.g. fault tree based analysis) nor are numerically precise deviations in the time and data domains. Rather, they are the elements of small, *qualitative* sets of labels that can be applied to describe the fault/error/failure state of such system elements on which this can be meaningfully defined.

For instance, a now classic approach for the qualitative dependability modelling of (component) service failures is presented in [3]. There, generic, detectability oriented qualitative categories are set up to characterize service failures. These are *Correctly-valued*, *Subtle Incorrect* (i.e. hard or impossible to detect based on current knowledge of the system), *Coarse incorrect* and *Omission* in the value domain and *Correctly-timed*, *Early*, *Late* and *Infinitely Late* in the time domain. Although these are failure categories, note that they can be used directly as (external) fault categories under the usual composition logic of error propagation (output service failures become external faults on inputs). Also, they can be used as component error modes in a phenomenological style. For instance, an activity being in a "late" error mode can have the error propagation semantics that all its executions will produce "late" tokens on its output(s). Later works extend on this generic – that is, system and business context independent – failure dictionary. E.g. [9] uses an additional (w.r.t. the simple network-of-components abstraction) work-unit notion to introduce other common failure aspects such as "incompletion".

In our prototype, *data object types*, *activities* and *resources* can be assigned *error, failure and fault mode dictionaries*, respectively, expressing the (pairwise disjoint) error/(output) failure/fault state they can be in at any given moment in a single process instance execution. While our approach does support existing dictionaries, users can refine and adapt these to their needs. That being said, as we gather experience in domain-specific process error propagation modelling, it seems more and more apparent that not only value domain failure types ("subtle" and "coarse"), but also provision failure types ("omission" and "commission") are indispensable. As for business processes executing the right branch selectively is extremely important, one can not realistically omit modelling omission – no output provided when it should be – and commission – output provided when not expected – as output failures modes of activities. Omission in our setting can be modelled as a special, "empty" data object with omission error mode; this way, the effects of a missing output token can be propagated in the process network.

4.4   Describing Error Propagation

Describing the qualitative error propagation characteristics of components is routinely handled as establishing a relation (in the mathematical sense) between input fault categories, internal fault categories and (output) failure categories. Such a relation captures the combinations that are deemed possible; e.g. the error propagation relation of a fail-silent component will not allow (coarse) data errors as failures on the outputs, only omissions. There are even languages that allow the practitioner to specify a propagation relation at a higher level than enumerating the tuples; potentially in a reusable manner for generic behaviours and dependability mechanisms. The description languages incorporated in the *Generalized Failure Logic* (GFL) [21] and the *Fault Propagation and Transformation Calculus* (FPTC) [19] are important examples.

We have adopted a slightly modified version of the FPTC language for our current implementation. In FPTC, the ways a component can "transform" incoming failures (i.e. external faults) into outgoing ones is expressed with input-output tuple pairs, where the cardinality of the left hand side corresponds to the number of "true" component inputs plus activity failure mode and that of the right side to the number of outputs. For instance, the rule in Listing 1 can specify what happens to an activity when a) its input is subtly incorrect and b) the physical infrastructure it uses pushes it into a temporary outage failure mode: the data object passing through is still subtly incorrect and additionally it is also delayed.

(SUBTLEINC, TEMPOUTAGE) → (SUBTLEINC_AND_DELAYED)

Listing 1. Sample transformation rule

There are a number of things to note here. First, there *is* important domain knowledge embedded in this statement; namely, the "input error checking" capability of the activity is at least not perfect and that the execution environment is robust in the sense that temporary processing element outages do not lead to the process execution getting stuck – only delayed. Second, the specification does not have to cover all input combinations; a default behaviour can be chosen for these cases on a component by component basis (not allowed combination; propagation of the "worst" input fault; propagation of "normal" behaviour). For a full description of the language, see [19].

FPTC has some drawbacks; in its original form, guard predicates over the input-output variables (even without quantification on the input and output "ports") are missing. However, this would be necessary to be able to express behaviours such as e.g. Triple Modular Redundancy succinctly.

Table 1 shows example transformation rules for the "Record transaction" activity from the cash deposit case study (see also in Fig. 2). For example, the first row describes that if the activity's failure mode is `Slow`, it sets the failure mode of the token passing through the activity to `transaction.Delay` independently of its input.

Table 1. Example transformation rules for the "Record transaction" activity

Activity Input	Activity Failure Mode	Output Token Failure Mode
<any>	Slow	transaction.Delay
<any>	Stuck	transaction.Delay
OK	SQL-Injected	transaction.Corrupted

On a technical level, fault, error and failure dictionaries and error propagation rule sets are defined separately from the process and system model.

FPTC clauses are grouped into named *propagation behaviours*; in the process and system model, activities and resources are annotated with these types. Resource behaviours are different from activity behaviours in the sense that they do not specify data token passing; rather, their DAG (rooted in the "most low level" resources) expresses the state of the execution platform by propagating special "platform state descriptor" data tokens. The sink of these are special inputs of activities; FPTC clauses define how these inputs are reflected into activity failure modes. Before weaving together the model and the behaviours for analysis, simple checks (as e.g. input-output cardinality conformance) are performed to verify the correctness of the behaviour-marking.

4.5 Propagation Rule Semantics and Analysis

[19] defines a *token-passing network* semantics for FPTC clause sets (augmented with static system topology). Under this interpretation, transformation rules are defined on (connected) components; a solution of the error propagation problem consists of the edge-wise maximal sets of failure/fault tokens that can appear on each edge. For this notion of solution, a simple fixpoint algorithm is offered that stabilizes on the maximal tokensets. Naturally, this not only allows for non-determinism in error propagation (although non-determinism may lead

to pessimistic overabstraction), but also topologies with cycles (loops) can be handled efficiently.

We solve the same fixpoint-problem by transforming the behaviour-typed system model and behaviours into a Constraint Satisfaction Problem (CSP) that is subsequently solved by the Choco solver. Each edge of the system is mapped into a set of boolean CSP variables representing whether each there allowed data object error mode can appear on the edge or not. Resource fault modes and activity failure modes become CSP variables, too. FPTC clauses are rewritten to finite domain implication constraints on these variables, defining which input needs which output to be present and vice versa (modulo fault and failure modes). Additional constraints can be injected into the problem formulation very easily by additional model annotations binding the activity output data error modes and the resource fault modes to specific values (either for diagnostic reasoning or sensitivity analysis). Based on these constraints, the maximal propagation fixpoint can be computed by additionally minimizing the weight of the edge-bitvectors.

One of the main reasons for using CSP solving instead of direct fixpoint-computation is utilizing the expressive power of the tools available today. The rich set of available constraints will enable us to use a whole range of more complex failure transformation declaration constructs than what is available in FPTC (e.g. quantification); instead of bearing the burden of incorporating these into a fixpoint algorithm, simple rewriting to CSP declarations will suffice.

5   Error Propagation Analysis by Example

As discussed at the motivational example (Sec. 3.1), the executed analysis had three goals.

SPOF Analysis. Consider an initial resource configuration designated by ❶ in Fig. 2. A SPOF is identified assuming an annotation of the model where *a)* both the "Customer & Account Identification" and "Compliance DB" modules are working correctly and *b)* only one single fault is allowed. The "Blade Server" has no fault tolerant capabilities, thus the error caused by a Single Fault propagates to the upper layers (brown thick arrows). As a result, resources en route to (and including) the "Cashier Module" become faulty with "Outage" (see rows with Id 1 in the failure mode labels). At process level, the "Outage" manifests at three activities as "Stuck" failure mode (see e.g. "Record transaction" as all of them require a fully functioning "Cashier Module" (only two of three activities marked in the figure for presentation purposes). The example is simplified in that the failure mode of the activities are always equal to the data token's. As a consequence, the output of the whole process is marked as "Stuck", too.

Process-level Effects of Resource Faults. A more fault tolerant infrastructure is represented by ❷ in Fig. 2 where the single hypervisor is replaced by an HA cluster. Using the same constraints as before, a single fault in the "Blade Server Farm" does not cause outage of the "Cashier Module". Instead, on account of the failover, the service is "Degraded" and thus the dependent activities take more time, which is modelled by the presence of the "Delayed" failure mode (see e.g. row No. 2 at "Record transaction"). The single fault leads to multiple failure modes on the process output due to the many process execution paths, even if the resource state underneath is the same. The execution path highlighted in green (filled with diagonal lines), for instance, leads to a "Delayed" process output. On the other hand, in another execution path (blue checked pattern) the by-design automatic activity "Perform full check" can time out owing to the introduced delay. As an active recovery mechanism, this error is handled by a costly manual error handler (see "Manual laundering check") updating the data token's, and thus the output's, failure mode to "Delay-incurred cost".

Propagating Process Errors to the Resource Layer. The third important use case, where error propagation analysis was used, is the propagation of process level errors via the underlying resources. A typical example for this is an activity vulnerable to SQL injections represented by the configuration with Id 3. In the example, the activity "Record transaction" is prone to such error and all resources the activity depends on are considered possible propagation targets. If a resource is sensitive to such failure, e.g. the "Cashier Module" in the example, the resource's fault mode is updated in the analysis (see "SQLInjected" fault mode), and consequently, the error can be propagated to dependent activities. In this case the "Receipt" activity (and simultaneously the output) is also affected.

6   Conclusions

The presented approach merges two complementing methods for enhancing system dependability: i) Error Propagation Analysis to systematically determine weak points in design time and ii) rule-based runtime diagnostics to detect suspicious situations based on design time findings and to refine the initial fault model according to runtime operational experience. While in the paper we concentrated on presenting our own metamodels, it is important to note that the framework is able to work on industrial de facto standard models like BPMN as input and is already integrated with a freely available BPMN tool ([4]).

Runtime diagnostic rule synthesis based on analysis results is one of our next goals. The framework we developed supports this by the definition of categories (tags) for system elements and attaching the analysis results to system description (e.g., a certain step in the process is depending on unreliable infrastructure element). In this case, if there is no possibility for system re-design (e.g., replace the infrastructure element or include additional fault handling mechanism at the process level) we still can support fault detection by including event processing rules concentrating on the result of this particular process step. This needs additional research on connection of non-interpreted fault models with event description at a monitorable level and will always need a human expert for the mapping of abstract concepts to domain interpretation (e.g. thresholds).

Error propagation validation and refinement can be performed by the analysis of runtime events; the fault models and other assumptions behind the analysis can be refined and improved on the basis of runtime monitoring. This can be supported in multiple ways; first in design time the completeness and consistency of both error propagation and event processing rules can be checked to validate the rulebase. This can reveal wrong assumption on fault modes and modelling flaws as well. (E.g., two solutions provided by constraint solving label an element in two contradictory ways and both are considered during processing rule generation). Our framework already has an initial support of rulebase completeness/consistency check where the semantics of system elements are defined by tags attached and we follow a pattern-based evaluation approach of rule conditions. On the other hand, when applying processing rules on runtime events conflicting situations can be detected and also post mortem analysis can detect situations which were not covered by the error propagation model. The framework has an early support for this at the model level but there is clearly more to be done on mechanisms and algorithms behind. Further improvements will be the explicit support of fault tolerant patterns at the high level model description and the systematic evaluation of existing fault taxonomies (e.g. [5]).

References

1. Bergmann, G., Horváth, Á., Ráth, I., Varró, D., Balogh, A., Balogh, Z., Ökrös, A.: Incremental Evaluation of Model Queries over EMF Models. In: Petriu, D.C., Rouquette, N., Haugen, Ø. (eds.) MODELS 2010, Part I. LNCS, vol. 6394, pp. 76–90. Springer, Heidelberg (2010)
2. BOC-Group. ADONIS BPM Suite,
   http://www.boc-group.com/products/adonis/product-details/
3. Bondavalli, A., Simoncini, L.: Failure Classification with Respect to Detection. In: Proc.. Second IEEE Workshop on Future Trends of Distributed Computing Systems, pp. 47–53. IEEE Comp. Soc. Press (1990)
4. BonitaSoft. Bonita BPM – The Open Source Business Process Management suite,
   http://www.bonitasoft.com/
5. May Chan, K.S., Bishop, J., Steyn, J., Baresi, L., Guinea, S.: A Fault Taxonomy for Web Service Composition. In: Di Nitto, E., Ripeanu, M. (eds.) ICSOC 2007 Workshops. LNCS, vol. 4907, pp. 363–375. Springer, Heidelberg (2009)
6. The Workflow Management Coalition. XML Process Definition Language (XPDL) (2012), http://www.xpdl.org/standards/xpdl-2.2/XPDL
   %202.2%20(2012-08-30).pdf
7. Conforti, R., de Leoni, M., La Rosa, M., van der Aalst, W.M.P.: Supporting Risk-Informed Decisions during Business Process Execution. In: Salinesi, C., Norrie, M.C., Pastor, Ó. (eds.) CAiSE 2013. LNCS, vol. 7908, pp. 116–132. Springer, Heidelberg (2013)
8. Craggs, S.: Comparing BPM from Pegasystems, IBM and TIBCO. Lustratus Research (2011)
9. Gallina, B., Punnekkat, S.: FI4FA: A Formalism for Incompletion, Inconsistency, Interference and Impermanence Failures' Analysis. In: 2011 37th EUROMICRO Conference on Software Engineering and Advanced Applications, pp. 493–500 (August 2011)
10. Object Management Group. Business Process Model and Notation (BPMN) version 2.0 (2011), http://www.omg.org/spec/BPMN/2.0/

11. Jussien, N., Rochart, G., Lorca, X.: The CHOCO constraint programming solver. In: CPAIOR 2008 Workshop on Open-Source Software for Integer and Contraint Programming, OSSICP 2008 (2008)
12. zur Muehlen, M., Shapiro, R.: Business Process Analytics. In: Handbook on Business Process Management 2. Springer (2010)
13. Pataricza, A.: Model-based Dependability Analysis. DSc Thesis. Hungarian Academy of Sciences (2006)
14. Pataricza, A.: Systematic Generation of Dependability Cases from Functional Models. In: Formal Methods for Automation and Safety in Railway and Automotive Systems (FORMS/FORMAT), pp. 9–10 (2007)
15. ProcessMaker. Process Maker Workflow Management Software, http://www.processmaker.com/product-overview
16. SAP. Business Process Management and Integration Solutions, http://www.sap.com/pc/tech/business-process-management/software/
17. Suriadi, S., Ouyang, C., van der Aalst, W.M.P., ter Hofstede, A.H.M.: Root Cause Analysis with Enriched Process Logs. In: La Rosa, M., Soffer, P. (eds.) BPM 2012 Workshops. LNBIP, vol. 132, pp. 174–186. Springer, Heidelberg (2013)
18. TIBCO. TIBCO Business Studio, http://developer.tibco.com/business_studio/default.jsp
19. Wallace, M.: Modular Architectural Representation and Analysis of Fault Propagation and Transformation. Electronic Notes in Theoretical Computer Science 141(3), 53–71 (2005) ISSN: 15710661
20. Ward-Dutton, N.: What Drives BPM Technology Requirements? MWD Advisors (2013), http://www.mwdadvisors.com/library/detail.php?id=441
21. Wolforth, I., et al.: Capture and Reuse of Composable Failure Patterns. Int.l Journal of Critical Computer-Based Systems 1(1/2/3), 128 (2010) ISSN: 1757-8779

Author Index